An Introductory History of British Broadcasting

In *An Introductory History of British Broadcasting* Andrew Crisell provides a concise and accessible history of British radio and television. This book considers the nature and evolution of broadcasting, the growth of broadcasting institutions and the relation of broadcasting to a wider political and social context.

Beginning with the genesis of radio at the turn of the century, Crisell discusses key moments in media history, from the first wireless broadcast in 1920, to issues which affect the media today. The topics covered include:

- the evolution of the BBC from private company to public institution
- notions of public service broadcasting and the cultural values of the BBC
- broadcasting in wartime and the golden age of radio
- the rise of television and the birth of ITV
- the changing role of radio in a television age
- BBC 2, Channel 4 and the development of minority television
- the rise of cable and satellite TV
- the convergence of broadcasting and other media

As well as discussing individual programmes and programme genres, the author offers insights into phenomena which are closely bound up with broadcasting such as advertising, pop music, sport, questions of artistic judgement, high and popular culture, patterns of leisure and employment.

An Introductory History of British Broadcasting analyses the current state of broadcasting in Britain and argues that the era of traditional broadcasting is coming to an end. Looking to the future, Crisell discusses recent developments in satellite, cable, information technology and telecommunications. He considers the debates which surround the future of the BBC, audience interactivity, digitization and globalization, access, ownership and control.

Andrew Crisell lectures in Media and Communications at the University of Sunderland. He is the author of *Understanding Radio*.

An Introductory History of British Broadcasting

Andrew Crisell

To my dear old pal,
Mickey
(also known as
Professor Mike O'Mahony)
from
his old mate
Andy
(also known as a
plonker — + in this
case, by coincidence,
the author: Andrew
Crisell)
With every good wish
September 1st, 2000

ROUTLEDGE

London and New York

First published 1997
by Routledge
11 New Fetter Lane, London EC4P 4EE

Simultaneously published in the USA and
Canada by Routledge
29 West 35th Street, New York, NY 10001

Typeset in Perpetua by Keystroke, Jacaranda
Lodge, Wolverhampton
Printed and bound in Great Britain by T.J.
International Ltd, Padstow, Cornwall

British Library Cataloguing in Publication Data
A catalogue record for this book is available
from the British Library

Library of Congress Cataloging in Publication Data
Crisell, Andrew.
An introductory history of British broadcasting
/ Andrew Crisell.
Includes bibliographical references and index.
1. Broadcasting—Great Britain—History.
I. Title.
HE8689.9.G7C75   1997
384.54'0941—dc21   97–9354

ISBN 0–415–12802–1 (hbk)
      0–415–12803–x (pbk)

Contents

Contents

Contents

To Maggie, Ellie, Hattie, Peter and the Captain,
and in memory of my father, Arthur Edmund Crisell,
and my grandfather, William Morgan

Acknowledgements

I MUST FIRST DECLARE my warm gratitude to Rebecca Barden, my editor at Routledge, whose support for the idea of a single-volume yet fairly comprehensive history of British broadcasting has never wavered during the vicissitudes of its composition.

For many years before I thought of this book, as well as while writing it, I benefited greatly from discussions with Ken Stephinson of Stephinson Television, who combines experience of virtually every aspect of television production and a long record of distinguished programmes for both the BBC and ITV with a larger, philosophical view of broadcasting. I owe a similar debt to Marjorie Lofthouse, also of Stephinson Television, as well as being an experienced radio and TV broadcaster in her own right, she directed me to certain sources of information about the BBC. Another who was able to tell me much about the Corporation was Jane Bywaters, who has spent many fruitful years there as a researcher in the field of television arts programming.

For similar enlightenment about ITV I must express my warm thanks to David Thomasson of Yorkshire/Tyne Tees Television. A former student of mine, Anita Sharma, who is now a research assistant at the Open University, kindly briefed me about ITV's educational programming and aspects of the 1990 Broadcasting Act.

I am most grateful to two media consultants, Robert Palmer and Toby Syfret, who were generous with their time, first-hand knowledge and the printed materials at their disposal. Both directly and indirectly, they furnished me with much information about the recent history of independent, satellite and cable broadcasting and thus helped me to gain some perspective on the present state of the media.

I owe a double debt to my brother-in-law, Tony Humphreys. Through his work in information technology at the Post Office, he kept me as abreast of the latest developments in interactive television as my limited understanding would allow; and second, via telephone tutorials and with a patience verging on the saintly, he helped me to get to grips with a new computer and new software. Another redoubtable assistant was my daughter, Harriet, whose informatic skills are, thanks to the mystery of the genes, everything that her father's are not.

My employer, the University of Sunderland, readily granted me half a semester's leave during which I managed to write what was for me the hardest part of the book. My penultimate debt is to the students on the 'History of the Mass Media' syllabus – first, and quite simply, by making it clear to me that an introductory history of broadcasting needed to be written, and second by forcing me during our seminars to think long and hard about the main themes and issues that should shape it. Despite all these forms of assistance, I alone am responsible for any mistakes or omissions which the reader may detect.

My last and largest debt is to my wife and two daughters, whose stoicism in living with 'an author' was rewarded only by the fact that his abstracted silences during meals allowed them to talk animatedly to one another without risk of clumsy male interruptions.

Introduction

M ANY STUDIES OF broadcasting are characterized by searching analyses of media institutions, their cultural contexts, their ownership and social structure, their programming policies, and their relations with the state and with dominant ideologies; but the heart of the matter – the nature of the broadcasting process and the way in which audiences experience it – often seems to be missing. Relatively little note is taken of the actual character of radio and television, whose power to determine listenable and watchable content precedes anything that can be imposed by the institutions that provide them or the governments that seek to influence them.

This history takes the nature of broadcasting and the situation of the audience as its main focus, weaving a crowded chronology of events, facts, personalities and trends around a simple account of its technological evolution. Part I considers how broadcasting is distinguishable from the other modes of mass communication in being live and, for the most part, domestically or even individually received. Part II explores how in due course broadcasting began to be modified by a growth of audience activity, and Part III traces its gradual convergence, even integration, with other media, thus affording a convenient point to conclude our history. With television sets no longer used only for the reception of broadcasting but for home shopping, teletext, video and a variety of other things, we can blow the dust from a journalistic cliché and claim that we are, indeed, reaching 'the end of an era'.

However I hope I need hardly add that in tracing the rise of an 'active' audience during the later part of the history, I am using this word in the literal, naive sense of 'able to modify broadcast output in ways additional to merely switching it on or off'. I am not implying that before the arrival of remote controllers, teletext and VCRs, the audience was inactive in the sense of being passive, supine or intellectually inert.

As part of my aim to illuminate the essential character of broadcasting, the reader will note the preoccupation with its various *genres*, both those which radio and television have borrowed or adapted from other media and those they seem to have originated. This has largely determined which programmes I have chosen to discuss, though choice is always an idiosyncratic matter: the reader will certainly question some I have included and others that I have omitted deliberately, accidentally or from sheer ignorance. I have also mentioned programmes and series which do not illuminate the medium particularly but which were extremely popular and successful in their time, reason enough for inclusion in a broadcasting history of any kind.

But of course a history of broadcasting cannot simply be a chronology of programmes. The paradox which seems to explain why so many studies of the media ultimately focus on media *contexts* rather than on the media themselves is that broadcasting is in itself a mere process, little more than an abstraction; yet the conduct of it is so complex, costly and (in one way or another) so significant, that it is inevitably a highly social and political matter, too – and any history of broadcasting which did not reflect this could not even claim to be 'introductory'.

Great care has therefore been taken to set the process of broadcasting within its social and political contexts. Indeed as the history approaches the present, an analysis of these almost entirely supersedes the discussion of individual programmes. This is partly because now that both radio and television are old media many of their original or distinctive programmes were made many years ago, and those that are more recent will in any case be known to the reader; but mainly because these broad contexts and their impact on media institutions seem to give a better perspective on broadcasting's growing convergence with other forms of communication.

My concern with development and perspective also implies, intentionally, that this history should not primarily be treated as a reference book to be dipped into in the way that its more scholarly sources can be. It is a continuous narrative, a matter of themes and of logical or causal connections rather than a mere chronological succession, and should be read as such. This is why I have condensed those aspects of broadcasting which seemed amenable to it into one or two summary sections – often at their first or early occurrence in the history – rather than returning to them in a fitful and piecemeal way which would have denied the reader a coherent overview of them.

This approach is particularly obvious in the case of the BBC's external services, which, since domestic broadcasting is the main subject of the book, are given only a single synoptic account in Chapter 2. One or two other subjects are similarly condensed: educational broadcasting, television advertising, the effects of TV on audiences, government policy on broadcasting. Television and politics also occupy separate if extended sections, but the reader will swiftly grasp that in one guise or another politics suffuse the entire history.

With the nature and experience of broadcasting firmly at the centre of our picture, certain other topics get little if any mention: labour relations within the broadcasting industry, programming budgets, media publications, the finer details of commercial media ownership. Though fascinating in themselves, it would be hard in a history as cursory as this to show what direct effects these things have had on content or the audience. Yet wherever possible, sources are provided for those who wish to pursue them.

In sum, this book aims to create in the reader a composite impression of British broadcasting as a single though luxuriant growth, ramifying and flourishing from relatively modest roots. Yet so inseparable is it from the society that it reflects, results from and partly shapes that (to change the metaphor) it often prompts us as we follow its route to peep into, and sometimes take a few steps down, side-alleys with tempting vistas – subjects whose relations with broadcasting would each make a book in themselves, and in most cases already have: advertising, rock and pop music, sport, debates about artistic value and its relation to highbrow and popular culture, media effects and influences, questions of authority, expertise and the public's 'right to know', patterns of leisure and employment.

Two points about style. I have been blithely inconsistent, though I hope not confusingly so, in my use of the word 'medium', sometimes applying it to radio and television individually but often, and less accurately, describing broadcasting in general as 'a medium' in order to stress what radio and TV have in common and how they differ from other media such as print, cinema or photography. I believe that the contexts make clear which meaning of the term is intended.

The second point relates to the vexed question of 'gendered language'. Since an important theme of this book is the frequent individuality of broadcasting consumption, it is not always helpful to refer collectively to 'the audience', 'the viewers' and so on. Since I do not wish to weary the reader with dualisms such as 'him/her' and 'he/she', and since there are as yet no singular epicene pronouns which will satisfy the gender politicians, I have quite arbitrarily referred to the viewer, listener, broadcaster or whatever, as 'he' at some points and 'she' at others. I therefore assure the reader that when she/he encounters these feminine/masculine pronouns she/he may take it that where one gender is used the other is also implied.

Part I

The phenomenon
of broadcasting

It seems a good time to write a history of British radio and television because we can now see broadcasting as a distinct phase in the development of communications technology. Broadcasting followed upon print, the first mass medium, but is itself, after a relatively brief reign of some seventy-five years, being caught up in newer technologies that will bring about a convergence, even a blurring, of mass and private media. Before offering an account of these seventy-five years we therefore need to isolate the distinctive characteristics and functions of broadcasting by locating it within the broader history of mass communication. Inevitably this broad historical sketch will be simple and crude, containing no room for specifics, subtleties and exceptions, but if it gives the reader a general and roughly accurate perspective it will have justified itself.

We might begin with a simple definition of mass communication: the sending of messages to a multitude of receivers. Its original mode was *live* in the sense that the receivers were in the presence of the sender – that is, within hearing and/or sight of him – and in a space which, in needing to be large enough to accommodate both parties, was most likely *public*. In these circumstances mass communication was inevitably a kind of *performance*, so we might term this public space a *theatre* even though it could accommodate almost any kind of message – political speeches, philosophical disquisitions, educational lectures, storytellings or factual accounts, spectator sports and circuses, as well as the more conventionally theatrical kinds of performance such as drama and light entertainment. Indeed it is probable that not only drama but poetry, that other great literary genre, was originally performed in this space. Before the advent of printing, literacy was very rare, and poetry's inherent acoustic features of rhythm and rhyme suggest that it was intended to be recited to numbers of listeners rather than silently read to oneself.

The first automated mode of mass communication was *print*, which was first utilized in Britain in 1475. The cultural, intellectual and political consequences of printing were enormous – truly incalculable – but it was made possible only by a pre-existing and even more momentous technology: writing. For several thousand years writing had provided a way of fixing speech, of taking human utterance out of its natural, constantly dissolving element, *time*, and putting it into *space*, where it could remain permanently accessible. What print did was to turn writing into a mass medium by allowing an indefinite number of copies of an 'utterance' to be made. In so doing it also, of course, introduced a gap in space and time between the senders and the receivers of these utterances or messages: that public, live medium which we have loosely termed 'theatre' was superseded by a private, 'lifeless' one, print, whose receivers could withdraw into their own separate environments. A paradox thus arose which applied not only to print but to most subsequent modes of mass communication, and which terms like 'mass' and '*broad*casting' belie: for while these modes have enormously *increased* the size of the audience they have also 'atomized' it – reduced it to small groups or isolated individuals who read or listen or watch in their own private spaces.

From about 1839 print technology was complemented by *photography*, which could offer fixed images of reality; but what the next two mass media technologies did was to provide fixed messages or 'recordings' in which one or both of the two most important live or time-based elements of the communication act, sound and moving vision, would be re-created. We might usefully term the first of these 'phonography', which from the 1890s produced recordings of different kinds of sound, notably speech and music, and which over the years has variously taken the form of wax cylinders, graphite platters, vinyl records, several kinds of audio tape including cassettes, and compact discs. Phonography was always a *private* mass medium in the sense that sound reproduction equipment and the recordings themselves were purchased and 'consumed' by families, households or single individuals.

Cinematography, which developed from about 1895, was another quasi-live medium since through its 'moving text' of pictures and (from 1927) sound, it could simulate the conditions of the earliest mode of mass communication. Not surprisingly, the kind of material that seemed most suited to it and likeliest to appeal to its audience was conventional drama, and in focusing upon drama, 'film', as it came to be known, created a corpus of work – of definitive, 'best possible' performances which differed from those of the conventional theatre in being infinitely reproducible. However, like its predecessor, film was a *public* medium in the sense that its audiences gathered in theatres – 'cinemas', as they were called. Although individual cinema audiences were no larger than theatrical audiences, film was much more of a mass medium than theatre because the number of cinemas in which it was possible to show copies of a single film far exceeded the number of theatres to which it was possible to tour a single dramatic performance.

However, broadcasting was the first genuinely *live* mass medium since 'theatre' because it was instantaneous: it did not offer fixed messages in the form of printed texts and photographs or recordings of sounds or moving images. From 1922 radio transmitted live sound to a private, domestic audience, and from 1936 television provided the same kind of audience with live sound and live moving pictures.

The different characteristics of all these modes of mass communication – modes which are often simply termed 'mass media' – might usefully be summarized in the table on the following page.

As we might expect, different media develop their own kinds of message which we will term *genres*, and the relationships within and between media and genres are often tangled. Print was the medium which fostered the third of our great literary genres, the novel, as well as news and current affairs. News is clearly not

	Live	Recorded	Public	Private
		Fixed text / Moving text (Writing; | (Soundtrack; Pictures) | Film)		*(Domestic /* *Individual)*
Theatre	•		•	
Print/ Photography		•		•
Phonography		•		•
Cinematography		•	•	
Broadcasting (Radio/TV)	•			•

a genre in the sense that the novel or poetry is, since these are *formal* categories whereas the term 'news' refers to *content*. In poetry, drama and the novel the nature of the content is immaterial: what is significant is the shape or structure it assumes. In news the nature of the content – its newness and sometimes also its usefulness – takes absolute priority over formal considerations. Nevertheless its miscellaneous, amorphous nature means that the news can no more be defined in terms of a particular *kind* of content than poetry or fiction can, so for the sake of convenience we might refer to it, too, as a 'genre'.

To say that print fostered news and the novel is not of course to deny that they were very much the product of such contemporary social and cultural factors as the growth of capitalism, the political ascendancy of the middle class, the rise of literacy, and changes in the patterns of work and leisure: it is merely to say that print provided the technical preconditions for such factors to operate, as other media have in their turn. Since photographs in themselves are limited or ambiguous in meaning, photography became a mass medium as an ancillary to the print genres, enhancing the content of newspapers, books and magazines.

Though certain genres have remained peculiar to certain media, it is clear that many can be taken over by other media with varying amounts of adaptation and variable degrees of success. In the case of recorded music which is broadcast on the radio, so little adaptation is involved that we can talk of one medium, phonography, being subsumed by another, sound broadcasting. On the other hand, the amount of adaptation may be so great that we might almost speak of a new genre being created. It is clear, for instance, that the cinema feature film has its origins in theatrical drama; but the difference which the physical flexibility, recording and editing techniques of the newer medium have made to acting methods and to the location and changes of scene is such that the two no longer seem closely related.

A genre may migrate to a new medium and become so at home there as to be no longer identified with the old one. Poetry moved from theatre to print, and though poetry readings are occasionally staged it is clear that the move has generally been for the better. Its acoustic elements of rhythm and rhyme can still be appreciated by the private reader even though she may internalize them, and its transformation into a fixed, visible text which she can mull over means that the genre is probably capable of a much greater sophistication of structure and meaning than it was in an oral medium.

For similar reasons, the novel remains largely confined to the print medium in which it was born. It is obvious that the medium of television can subsume that of print (as in the case of teletext, for instance): nevertheless, for the time-based characteristics of radio, cinema and television the novel is invariably turned into *drama* (though straight, abridged readings are sometimes heard on the radio). Only print is equal to the fact that the novel is quite as much concerned with the workings of the inner consciousness as with the sensory world of actions and events.

News has been a cosmopolitan genre. It has always flourished in its native medium, print, which affords the scope and depth that it needs. Photography added a useful visual dimension to the newspapers, but cinema brought the vivid illustration of sound and moving pictures. Later, television could match this illustrative power, and in addition offer the absolute up-to-dateness of a live medium, and cinema capitulated with the demise of Pathé News in 1969.

The rise and fall of cinema as a news medium is reflected in the fortunes of its word 'newsreel'. Though offering live sound, radio news, which evolved at much the same time, could not match cinema's visual power. The BBC therefore sought to borrow this power by titling one of its programmes 'Radio Newsreel', but once television news had established itself during the 1950s the word 'newsreel' implied something not up-to-date but merely recorded, and thus declined in status.

We might also note in passing that because it can subsume the medium of print, television can borrow something of the stability and continuous accessibility of newspaper news as well as offering its own kind of news, for it gives us not only live bulletins but the fixed summaries of teletext.

Drama is another much-travelled genre. Although it has always remained in the theatre its dialogue and stage business were soon transposed to print, and several centuries later it was adapted for cinema, radio and television. Drama in the latter medium may take the form either of theatrical adaptation or feature film, and the genre is a good illustration of the fact that the historical development of the mass media has not been a simple matter of continuous improvement, but that what is in one respect an advantage is in another a limitation. Theatrical drama was hit by the cinema, cinema was hit by broadcasting, and broadcasting will certainly be hit by 'multimedia': but because each of them has irreplaceable characteristics or functions, all of the older media survive, albeit in reduced circumstances. Cinema and television incorporate the visual, auditory, temporal elements of theatrical drama in a way that a printed script cannot; but handy, portable print can 'stabilize' it and permit an overview of its structures and themes in a way that is beyond the other media. These qualities mean that it is print, above all, which has facilitated the enormous expansion of scholarship and intellectual inquiry that has taken place over the last five centuries. The domesticity of radio and television is in general a great asset, but a visit to the cinema is a public, communal experience which can be much more pleasurable than an evening at home – and in addition to this pleasure, the theatre affords a genuinely live performance that the cinema cannot.

Yet however contingent they might be, the advantages of broadcasting were clearly considerable because they embraced so many of those of the other mass media. First, radio and then television domesticated various live or live-seeming genres which hitherto could be experienced only in public. Any kind of instantaneous performance that had been received in a collective, 'theatrical' space – talks, plays, narratives, debates, spectacles and light entertainment – could now be received at home. Likewise, television could domesticate the cinema film – an important achievement since film's earlier attempt to re-create the liveness of theatrical performance had resulted, almost incidentally, in a body of dramatic productions which were both optimal or definitive in themselves and capable of being shown many times over.

Second, broadcasting was able to make live – to 'animate' – those genres that were already private because they were native to print, notably news. Radio and television conveyed the sound and sight of public events to audiences in an environment where they had previously been used only to written descriptions and fixed images of them. To spectator sport, which is both theatrical entertainment and 'news', broadcasting did a double favour, domesticating it as a spectacle and animating it as news.

As we would expect, it is older people who are more aware of the changes broadcasting has wrought, for they remember the original media from which its genres have been taken and still tend to conceive of them in those terms. For older people especially, radio and, above all, television have brought the cinema, theatre, sports stadium or, in the case of news, the world itself, into our living rooms – a perception which focuses upon the peculiarly invasive, irresistible quality of the medium and reminds us that the question of its effects and influences on the audience is not the less important for being complex and elusive.

Thus broadcasting makes private experience out of what was formerly public or, as in the case of news, which was always private, immeasurably enriches it; and we can see this achievement as part of a tendency towards that individualism of consumption or ownership which is one of the great themes of modern civilization. What broadcasting did for one kind of communication the motor car did for another, transforming travel from something public and collective into a private, atomistic activity, and the consequences of this general tendency have been so diverse and far-reaching as to be almost incalculable. The car has largely determined where and how people live, their modes of work and leisure, and within this context broadcasting, as part of a process which begins with print and continues with video and information technology, has had an enormous impact on the kinds of information and entertainment that can be disseminated; on notions of intellectual property and copyright; on the problem of artistic standards and judgement; and on the issue of audience influences and effects.

Yet of course certain of these matters are determined not simply by the inherent nature of broadcasting, which forms the motif of this brief history, but by the particular way in which it was adopted and developed in Britain. We must therefore look closely at the philosophical and cultural forces that have shaped it in this country, at how it has been organized and funded, and at the consequences in terms of its content and, as far as we are able, its impact on generations of listeners and viewers.

Sources/further reading

Some of the vast intellectual and cultural consequences of the development of the technology of writing are succinctly indicated in Ong (1982), while the analogous consequences of the development of print technology are explored in McLuhan (1962).

For the genesis of media technologies and the tendency to domestic or private consumption which they created – also for the relationships between media and genre – see Armes (1988). The classic definition of literary genre based on the relationships between the communicator and the audience is in Frye (1971), and the relation between the development of print technology and the rise of the novel is explored in Watt (1963). For essays which provide a composite view of media power in the twentieth century see Curran, Smith and Wingate (1987).

Finally, a history of broadcasting, like any other specialized history, needs to be set within its broader context. For a general yet marvellously detailed chronicle of the twentieth century see Mercer (1988); and for a magisterial overview of the movements which have shaped it, together with some percipient remarks on the role that broadcasting has played, see Hobsbawm (1994).

The birth of radio

Chapter 1

The birth of radio

The development of radio technology

It was the great Australian operatic soprano, Dame Nellie Melba, who first demonstrated the power of radio broadcasting. On 15 June 1920, in the prosaic setting of the Marconi wireless works near Chelmsford and under the sponsorship of the *Daily Mail*, she gave a special concert in English, French and Italian. Her voice was heard throughout Europe and in parts of North America, and almost sixty years of trials and experiments were at an end.

In order to understand radio technology a little better we need to distinguish it from certain other technologies which were thrown up by the same long process of experiment and discovery. The first of these was *telegraphy*, the transmission of electronic impulses over distances. These impulses could be arranged into a code by the sender and then translated into words by the receiver, and the most commonly used code was that which was named after its American inventor Samuel Morse.

Telephony is the transmission of sounds, particularly spoken words, over distances. *Wireless* telegraphy or telephony is transmission not by means of wire or cable but through the atmosphere.

The final distinction we need to be aware of is between *point-to-point* transmissions, which take place between a sender and a single receiver, such as those which normally occur on the telephone, and *broadcast* transmissions, which take place between a sender and an indefinite number of receivers. Broadcast transmissions are usually offered to anyone who has the equipment to catch them.

Radio technology could thus be described as *broadcast wireless telephony*, and this helps to explain why despite being wreathed in wires the early radio receiver was known as a 'wireless', a paradox which was often celebrated by writers and cartoonists. One length connected the receiver to the aerial, another ran to the earth, and one or more went to the headphones; but *no* wire spanned the considerable distance between the station transmitter and the listener's aerial.

As we might expect, these communication technologies have a common ancestry but a number of progenitors, most of whom were at work in different parts of the world. In 1864 James Clerk Maxwell, a professor of experimental physics at Cambridge, expounded his theory of the existence of electromagnetic waves. During the 1880s the American Thomas Edison showed that an electric current could jump through space, and the German Heinrich Hertz showed that you could catch the waves with a receiver and reflect them with a metal sheet. In 1894 the Englishman Sir Oliver Lodge used wireless waves to send messages in Morse Code, thus inventing wireless telegraphy, and three years later he showed how a receiver could 'tune' to a particular transmitting station.

However the Italian, Guglielmo Marconi, is justly regarded as 'the father of radio' because it was he who brought together so many of these discoveries and inventions. A man of endless energy, Marconi was adept not only at developing his own research and combining it with that of others but at exploiting the *business* potential of telecommunications. At the turn of the century he came to England and patented his own system of telegraphy, formed the first company for the manufacture of wireless apparatus (the Wireless Telegraph and Signal Company), saw his system adopted for ship-to-shore Morse communication, and in 1901 received a prearranged Morse code signal (the letter 'S') which was sent from the far side of the Atlantic.

A year later the American R. A. Fessenden used wireless waves to carry the human voice over the distance of a mile, thus inventing wireless telephony, and in the same decade work by J. A. Fleming in England and Lee de Forest in the United States led to better amplification and to wireless transmissions over greater distances. By 1910 ship-to-shore messages were common and air-to-ground radio contact had also been achieved.

Thanks largely to the experiments of Fessenden and de Forest the Americans began to take the lead in wireless telephony, and by 1915 the American Telephone and Telegraph Company was able to send speech signals a distance of 3,500 miles from Arlington, Virginia, to Paris, and later 5,000 miles to Honolulu.

At a political level the ability of wireless telephony to *broadcast* was noticed only rarely and then in largely negative terms. In Britain, as elsewhere, it was prized as a means of *point-to-point* communication with considerable strategic and military possibilities – a preoccupation not altogether surprising in a world about to be engulfed in the Great War. If its messages could be picked up not just by designated individuals but by all and sundry this showed not the potential of telephony but its crudity, its technical limitations: the growing numbers of private wireless enthusiasts were at best a nuisance and at worst a threat to national security.

It was doubtless from similar fears about national security, fears which new technologies so often arouse, that the British government had in any case always kept telegraphy and telephony under its control. The Telegraphy Act of 1869 gave the Post Office the exclusive right to transmit telegrams within the United Kingdom – and the Post Office was a government department, its head, the Postmaster General, a government minister. A further Act of 1904 gave the Postmaster General control of wireless telegraphy, and when *wireless telephony* developed he regarded that, too, as subject to his control. This explains why the Post Office operated Britain's telephone system for so many years as well as carrying the mail, and accounts for its status as the first licensing body for broadcasting.

Nevertheless there were some, especially in America, who foresaw radio's possibilities as a broadcasting medium. David Sarnoff, a young employee of the American Marconi Company, was among the most prescient (even though Marconi himself was not), for in 1916 he pointed out that if telephony were used to broadcast regular entertainment and information this would act as a colossal stimulus to the sale of radio receivers:

> I have in mind a plan of development which would make radio a 'household utility' in the same sense as the piano or phonograph. . . .
>
> The receiver can be designed in the form of a simple 'Radio Music Box' and arranged for several different wavelengths, which would be changeable with the throwing of a single switch or pressing of a single button. . . .
>
> The box can be placed in the parlor or living room, the switch set accordingly and the transmitted music received. . . .
>
> This proposition would be especially interesting to farmers and others living in outlying districts removed from cities. By the purchase of a 'Radio Music Box' they could enjoy concerts, lectures, music, recitals etc., which may be going on in the nearest city within their radius.
>
> (Armes 1988: 107)

The seductiveness of this vision perhaps explains why wireless broadcasting got off to a slightly earlier start in the United States than in Britain.

The establishment of a public broadcasting service

With the end of the Great War in 1918 it became harder for the British government to resist on military grounds the wireless manufacturers' plea to be allowed to promote the sales of their receivers by transmitting some kind of regular service – especially as the plea was echoed by those private enthusiasts who had already built their own receivers and were keen to have something to listen to. In 1920 the Post Office therefore gave the Marconi Company permission to make broadcasts from its transmitter at Writtle near Chelmsford, but it was instructed to avoid encroaching on the secret point-to-point transmissions of the armed forces. As Raymond Williams points out, the situation was always:

> complicated by the fact that the political authorities were thinking primarily of radio telephony while the manufacturers were looking forward to broadcasting . . . . When the Marconi company began broadcasting in 1920, there were complaints that this use for entertainment of what was primarily a commercial and transport-control medium was frivolous and dangerous, and there was even a temporary ban, under pressure from radio-telephonic interests and the Armed Forces.

> (1974: 32)

In spite of the achievement of Dame Nellie Melba, it was not until 1922 that the Post Office acknowledged a distinction between wireless technology which addressed designated individuals and that which addressed all and sundry. In the same year the Marconi Company began regular broadcasts from Writtle and opened a London station, known by its call-sign '2LO'. Another London station, 2WP, was opened by Western Electric, which also started 5IT in Birmingham, while Metropolitan Vickers began broadcasting from Manchester as 2ZY.

However, the Post Office did not license any of these on a permanent basis, for it was unwilling to deny other companies future access to what was a limited number of frequencies. On the other hand, it was equally loath to follow the early lead of America, where insufficient restriction had resulted in a kind of aerial anarchy: too many stations crowded the waveband, some on pirated frequencies and some using stronger signals to drown out their rivals.

Its solution was to invite the leading British wireless *manufacturers* (six large companies and several small ones) to form a broadcasting syndicate. The service they collectively provided would stimulate the sales of the receivers they made, which the government would protect from foreign competition. As a result of this scheme the manufacturers created the *British Broadcasting Company* to which the Post Office granted a *de facto* though never a *de jure* monopoly, and which began transmissions on 14 November 1922. The manufacturers guaranteed the company's solvency, and its funds came from three sources: the original stock, the royalties on the wireless sets which the manufacturers sold, and a share of the revenue from the broadcast receiving licences which the Post Office collected from the listening public on the company's behalf.

The person who was appointed general manager was a 34-year-old engineer named John Reith, an austere Scot of Calvinist upbringing. When he applied for the post he scarcely knew what broadcasting was, yet through energy and force of personality he shaped it according to a moral vision whose traces are discernible even today. Reith soon came to the conclusion that broadcasting was a precious national resource – too precious to be used merely to deliver audiences to wireless manufacturers (or to any other commercial interest) by the easiest, hence most frivolous, forms of content. For the nation, only the best was good enough – and while there have always been many who have attacked Reith's notion of 'the best' as starchy, tendentious and patronizing, there are many more who have been grateful that because his values have coloured all sections of it, British broadcasting has not followed the paths taken by other countries.

This ambition to deliver what Reith perceived as the best was closely bound up with certain other principles, all of which made up his idea of 'public service' broadcasting. First, although established in order to stimulate sales for the wireless manufacturers, the British Broadcasting Company was not driven solely by the need to make a profit. Indeed the government had approved the licence system precisely in order to cushion the company against this need. Second, through the *variety* as well as the excellence of its programmes the company set out to serve everyone in the community who was prepared to listen. And third, in operating as a kind of disinterested monopoly the company would forestall any attempt by sectional interests to exert an undue influence on the public.

The first programmes

In the early years broadcasts ran for only a few hours each day: typically, they might not begin until the afternoon and would conclude well before midnight; but they were varied. There was music in abundance – much of it classical, but orchestral dance music, even though rather sedate by later standards, was often heard too.

Radio talks were also frequent and covered a range of topics. While some were light and humorous, many were serious and instructive, embracing such subjects as literature, film and drama. In 1924 Reith affirmed his belief in broadcasting's potential to teach and train by approving the creation of a Central Education Advisory Committee to give guidance on schools programmes. These began in the same year, as did talks in the sphere of adult education. A year earlier he had approved an advisory committee to offer similar guidance on religious broadcasts.

Programmes for the young date from the very beginning of radio: *Children's Hour* originated in Birmingham in 1922. Entertainment for older listeners included live relays of song and comedy from the music halls, with a commentator on hand to describe inaudible acts such as jugglers and dancers. The first straight drama to be heard on radio was an adapted scene from Shakespeare's *Julius Caesar*, but the first to be written especially for the medium was *A Comedy of Danger* (1924) by the novelist Richard Hughes.

In devising a play which could not be presented in a conventional theatre (it was set in a coal-mine where the lights have failed) Hughes perhaps showed an excessive concern for radio's limitation. On the other hand some drama producers ignored it to the extent of requiring their actors to broadcast in theatrical costume! This was presumably intended to help them enter into the spirit of the play despite the absence of spectators, but like the outside broadcasts from music halls it really shows that some years would pass before broadcasters could conceive of radio as a dramatic venue in itself rather than as the mere blind witness of events which were taking place on a stage.

The company also covered sport, but its early relays of the major events in horse-racing, rugby, soccer and golf, among others, were not wholly successful; indeed its first attempt at an outside broadcast was not sporting at all but operatic – a 1923 performance of *The Magic Flute* from Covent Garden.

Though varied and popular this programming diet suffered from one serious deficiency. All too aware that in its coverage of current affairs radio would prove itself much more fleet than Fleet Street, the Newspaper Proprietors' Association put pressure on the government to forbid any news broadcasts until 7 pm. Even then, the company was obliged to take its news from the main agencies such as Reuters – and this was supplied in the form of bulletins which had evidently been drafted with newspaper readers in mind rather than radio listeners. The restriction on the supply of the news was not finally thrown off until 1938, and in the early years of broadcasting the Post Office also banned all political commentary and controversy and most political speeches.

The company's first programmes were transmitted not only from London (initially Magnet House and then Savoy Hill) but from a series of main regional stations such as Manchester, Birmingham, Newcastle and Glasgow, and from a number of smaller relay stations. Thanks to the relative compactness of Britain and the enormous popularity of the new medium, enough transmitters had been built by 1925 to reach about 80 per cent of the population. The company soon introduced a networking system which would enable the regional stations to take simultaneous broadcasts of important London programmes such as talks or concerts, but any of the regional stations could also supply the network.

At first the output of the regional stations fairly closely reflected the localities they served, while the relay stations were largely sustained by London; but from 1925 Reith developed a centralized programming policy which within five years resulted in the elimination of genuinely local radio. By 1930 London was transmitting a service called the National Programme (until the 1970s the term 'programme' was used to mean 'network' as well as an individual broadcast that could be heard on a network – a usage that sometimes confuses the modern student). But an alternative Regional Programme was broadcast from centres serving the Midlands, North, South, West and Scotland, with Wales and Northern Ireland added later. Part of its programming was also supplied by London and part originated from the large and in most cases ill-defined areas the Programme was intended to serve.

Radio listeners and wireless receivers

The country took to sound broadcasting with boundless enthusiasm: during the mid-1920s houses in towns and cities began to sprout aerials like a strange new vegetation. In 1923 the Post Office issued 80,000 licences, but in 1924 these jumped to one million, a figure which doubled over the next three years. By 1939 nine million wireless receivers were under licence. However, because there were anomalies and loopholes in the licensing system, these figures represent only a fraction of the total listenership. At first there were three separate categories of licence, for ordinary listeners, experimenters and constructors. Though the company was entitled to royalties on ready-made wireless sets, many listeners bought and assembled their own from simple kits on which no royalties were payable, and then qualified for the much cheaper, experimental licence. Many more simply avoided paying any licence fee at all. It has therefore been estimated that in the early years of broadcasting there were five times as many unlicensed as licensed sets in use. The actual audiences were huge. After 1928 no programmes were heard by fewer than a million listeners and some attracted 15 million.

In 1923 the Postmaster General appointed a committee under Major General Sir Frederick Sykes to review the company's finances. Impressed even at this early stage by the quality of its programmes the committee declared that broadcasting was 'of great national importance as a medium for the performance of a valuable public service' and rejected advertising as a possible source of revenue on the ground that it would lower standards. Instead it recommended a single licence fee of 10 shillings, three-quarters of which should go to the company. However this proportion would be subject to a sliding scale as the number of licences increased, and royalty payments on wireless receivers should cease.

What were these receivers like? The very first were 'crystal sets', so called because they were based on the discovery that if certain kinds of crystal were touched in the right place with a fine wire known as a cat's whisker they could 'detect' radio waves and transform them into electric currents. The technology was unreliable, to say the least: because the signal would often fade and drift, the listener would spend much time tickling it back with the cat's whisker. But in the sense that listening was via headphones and thus a solitary activity the crystal set ironically prefigured that most sophisticated receiver of the 1980s, the personal stereo. It was easily assembled from kits or bought from the company ready-made and with two pairs of headphones for between £2 and £4.

However, the crystal set was soon followed by the valve wireless, whose much improved reception by way of a loudspeaker transformed listening into a group activity. The first valve sets cost £17 10s 0d in 1923, but mass production reduced the price to little more than £5 within two years, and by the 1930s they had virtually replaced crystal sets. Valve wirelesses also marked the transition from radio receivers as unsightly pieces of apparatus, the playthings of enthusiasts and eccentrics which had to be hidden in cupboards when not in use, to aesthetic objects – pieces of furniture in their own right. The first step in this process was to design receivers so that they could be passed off as something else – sewing boxes or cocktail cabinets. But as broadcasting grew in confidence and wove itself more closely into the fabric of domestic life their designs began to proclaim wireless sets for what they were.

These changes reflected something of a shift in the appeal of wireless from males to females. The earliest sets were largely a male preserve: it was mostly boys and men who rose to the technical challenge of building them and who, because the headphones severely limited the numbers of listeners, made up a large part of the first audience. But the development of loudspeaker sets enabled women to listen, too – and women, often housebound for much of the day, rapidly became a very important section of the wireless audience. Since they also assumed the main responsibility for 'making the home look nice' this would have acted as a powerful spur to manufacturers to design aesthetically pleasing sets.

During the 1930s wirelesses could be bought for between £5 and £6 but this was still quite expensive for the less well-to-do. Many found an alternative in the relay exchange, a central receiver which was cabled to individual homes in return for a modest weekly rent and was therefore also known by the quaintly paradoxical term 'wired wireless'. Running costs could be shared among as many subscribers as could be connected to the exchange, but this meant that the system was viable only in densely populated areas. Furthermore, relay exchanges were opposed by the Post Office, the wireless manufacturers and the BBC. The Post Office disliked them because although their subscribers each paid a licence fee in the normal way, it was obliged to give the relay operators another licence to pass messages over wires – something on which it otherwise enjoyed a statutory monopoly. The manufacturers disliked them because they enabled people to hire a mere loudspeaker instead of buying a full wireless set; and the BBC disliked them because they threatened its monopoly by carrying foreign stations as well as its own programmes.

The first of the relay exchanges opened in 1925: in 1929 there were thirty-four, and this number increased tenfold over the next six years. By 1939 they had attracted just over a million subscribers, and there was a further and rapid increase during the Second World War. But the arrival in 1944 of the widely affordable 'utility' set marked a turning-point, and thereafter the popularity of wired wireless began a slow decline.

The Crawford Committee and the General Strike

For the financial ills of the British Broadcasting Company the Sykes Committee had found a palliative rather than a cure. Anomalies in the licensing system persisted, and in any case the Post Office was unwilling as a public body to collect fees on behalf of a private company, even though the proportion it retained more than covered its costs. For this and other reasons the wireless manufacturers were growing eager to abandon their offspring. Their need to compete ever more keenly with one another in order to sell wireless sets had cut their profits, and in a nearly saturated market there were few prospective buyers to be tempted by the company's programmes, however excellent these might be. In 1925 the government therefore set up a new committee under the Earl of Crawford to consider the future development of British broadcasting.

Despite the company's difficulties Reith maintained his belief in broadcasting as a public service, and one which the public itself, rather than advertisers, should pay for. The government took the similar view that it was a public utility, the logic of which was that as the agent of the public the government ought to take broadcasting into its own hands. But Reith thought broadcasting much too serious a matter to be controlled by politicians, whom he was inclined to despise, and the proposal which he put to the Crawford Committee was for the company to become a public institution which would be free from commercial pressures by continuing to be funded by the licence fee, yet also free from government interference.

The Crawford Committee enshrined this proposal in its recommendations, but before the government could decide on them a national crisis arose which would put the BBC to a severe test – and if it failed this test the government would almost certainly reject the committee's recommendations.

For some years labour relations within various major industries had been worsening. The Great War had been followed by economic problems which some employers, notably the mine owners, sought to mitigate by imposing wage cuts on the workforce. The trade unions reacted by calling a general strike, which lasted from the 3rd to the 12th of May 1926 and paralysed the country's essential services. Since most of the press was affected the restrictions on the BBC's news coverage were temporarily lifted: it was allowed – indeed needed – to report the strike; and therein lay its dilemma. If it were seen to favour the strikers the government was empowered to turn it into a mouthpiece and even commandeer it altogether, something one of its members, Winston Churchill, was already keen to do. If on the other hand the company were perceived as being simply pro-government it could be closed down by the strikers or lose credit with the many who supported them. Unless it was seen as neutral by people of all opinions it would be unable to realize its aim to be an institution above politics and commanding universal trust.

The company broadcast news of the strike in five daily bulletins – at 10 am and 1, 4, 7 and 9.30 pm. At the end of the crisis it had succeeded in walking the tightrope: though it sometimes lost balance it never quite fell off. Absolute even-handedness was impossible because the government perceived the strike not simply as an industrial dispute but as a political and constitutional threat, and outlawed it. Consequently the company could only pre-empt interference in its news reportage by broadly reflecting the government's position and suppressing information which favoured the strikers or would encourage the strike to spread. It gave the unions' point of view but little else. It explained what was happening and what the citizen could do, but not why the strike came about. The company was twice humiliated by the government, first when its attempt to bring a union leader to the microphone was vetoed, and second when it was bullied into refusing to broadcast a peace formula devised by the Archbishop of Canterbury.

Nevertheless it achieved much. The tone in which it reported the strike was cheerful and conciliatory throughout. Furthermore its perspective on events was never wholly identified with the government's. At the beginning of the strike there was a general assumption that the BBC would simply be a conduit for the views of its political overseers: by the end millions had come to depend on the accuracy of its information, many strikers among them.

Thus, however little it availed the disputants, the General Strike was good for both the BBC and broadcasting. It enhanced the status of the former and eased that transition from private company to public institution which Reith and Crawford desired. And the strike was good for broadcasting because it enabled even those who disapproved of the BBC as a biased news *source* to appreciate radio's power as a rapid news *medium*, despite the fact that more than ten years would pass before that power could be fully exercised. In one's own home one could not only read about the events of yesterday but be told about the events of the hour: as Asa Briggs (1961) points out, broadcasting had become a major force in the nation's life, it could no longer be dismissed as a novelty for amateurs and enthusiasts. By the end of 1926 the government had accepted the recommendations of the Crawford Committee and John Reith had received a knighthood.

Sources/further reading

There are many useful accounts of early wireless technology, of which Williams (1974) focuses on its political and social contexts and Barnouw (1966; 1977) and

Armes (1988) deal mainly with its institutional developments. Gorham (1952), Paulu (1956; 1961; 1981) and Smith (1976) all offer concise descriptions of the beginnings of broadcasting in Britain.

Golding (1974) includes a good chapter on the early history and development of the British media, while Briggs (1961) – the first of a classic five-volume history of broadcasting, much of which is condensed in Briggs (1985) – contains an account of the foundation and life-span of the British Broadcasting Company.

For Reith's own account of his early years at the Company, including the problems posed by the General Strike, see Reith (1949) and also Stuart (1975), which contains many of Reith's diary entries for this period. His broadcasting philosophy is set out in Reith (1924), a useful summary of which is in McDonnell (1991). The standard biography of Reith, which includes an account of this period, is Boyle (1972).

Smith (1974) contains extracts from key texts relating to early broadcasting history, and there are a number of helpful general accounts of this first era of broadcasting. Briggs (1981) combines 'scrapbook' material with a lively narrative; Curran and Seaton (1991) are concerned to set early broadcasting firmly within its political context; Pegg (1983) focuses on the social dimension; Scannell and Cardiff (1982; 1991) deal with the early development of the BBC as a public service broadcasting institution; Parker (1977) concentrates on early programmes and personalities rather than on institutions; and Black (1972a) offers his own reminiscences as a listener.

Of narrower scope but equal interest, Gielgud's study of radio drama (1957) includes an account of its first years and migration from the theatre to the studio, while Moores (1988) discusses the early design of wireless sets and the change in the behaviour and profile of the listenership which it reflected.

Chapter 2

The BBC: from private company to national institution

The BBC: from private company to national institution

Regional, national, global

On 1 January 1927 the British Broadcasting Company became the *British Broadcasting Corporation*, a publicly funded yet quasi-autonomous organization whose constitution and statutory obligations have remained largely unchanged for seventy years. It was established by Royal Charter, with a board of governors and a director-general, Sir John Reith, who was answerable to it. Although the Charter determines the Corporation's structure, its activities are regulated by a Licence and Agreement which is conferred by the government. It was, and is, obliged to inform, to educate and to entertain; to report the proceedings of Parliament; to provide a political balance; and in a national emergency to broadcast government messages. It may neither editorialize nor carry advertising. Its income is guaranteed from broadcast receiving licences and it strives to maintain a position of editorial independence.

However, it has never been entirely free from state pressure. Its licence to broadcast has always been granted for fixed periods, never in perpetuity; the state appoints its board of governors; and the state, not the BBC, determines the cost of the receiving licences, part of which it may withhold. Hence it is fair to say that throughout its history the BBC's relations with governments of all political hues have been delicate and occasionally strained.

Soon after its foundation the Corporation underwent a period of rapid expansion. In 1932 it moved its headquarters from Savoy Hill to the purpose-built Broadcasting House in Portland Place, an act which symbolized its coming-of-age as a national institution, and by this time both of its domestic networks, the National Programme and the Regional Programme, were accessible to most of its listeners. The National Programme originated mainly from London while the Regional Programme drew its material mostly from the regional centres but was also fed by a London sustaining service.

One network was not markedly different from the other: both broadcast *mixed programming*, which was at the heart of Reith's public service philosophy. Every day each network offered a variety of programmes – drama, sport, light and classical music, news, religion, talks, interviews and discussions, light entertainment. This meant that as many tastes as possible could be satisfied, and from time to time sections of the audience were explicitly targeted – children, women, business people, farmers, gardeners and so on.

But it was not simply that each individual should seek and find her own interest and then switch off: the hope was that she would be enriched by exposure to the *full range* of the programming. Consequently, except in the case of news bulletins, regular or 'fixed point' scheduling – the practice of offering the same or similar programmes at the same times every day – was deliberately avoided. The high-minded intention was continually to renew the listener's alertness to the medium, not only to make her listen instead of merely hear but to 'surprise' her into an interest in a subject she had previously not known about or disliked, and at all times to give her 'something a little better than she thought she wanted'.

Essential to this varied diet was the maintenance of the BBC's monopoly, for if a competitor were allowed, the fight for audiences would reduce programming simply to that which was known to be preferred by the largest number: minority-interest programmes, intellectually demanding programmes, even new kinds of programming which might *turn out* to be popular, would all be sacrificed.

As well as providing two domestic networks the BBC inaugurated its *Empire Service* in 1932. This was the first of a series of external services, of whose history we here offer only the barest sketch before returning to domestic broadcasting, our main theme in this book. The Empire Service catered mostly to colonials of British origin, it did not set out to serve all the ethnic elements of the Empire; but by 1935 the BBC knew that an empire service of any sort was no longer enough. To counter the radio propaganda of Hitler's Germany and Mussolini's Italy the Corporation would have to make overseas broadcasts in languages other than English, and these were started under the threat of war in 1938. In the following year the Empire Service became a part of the *Overseas and European Services*, which not only broadcast but gave invaluable help to the government by monitoring foreign stations. This was acknowledged in the fact that whereas until the war the cost of external broadcasting was met from the licence fee, it was funded thereafter by a parliamentary grant paid through the Foreign Office. Until recently the government determined the languages in which the BBC broadcast and the length of its transmissions, but the Corporation has always kept editorial control.

In 1948, these services were renamed the *BBC External Services* and thenceforward reflected the vagaries of government policy and the national economy. In the 1950s they contracted, in the 1960s they expanded, and after the 1973 oil crisis they suffered cuts. By 1995 the *BBC World Service*, as they have been collectively known since 1965, was broadcasting in English and forty other languages to a confirmed weekly audience of 130 million, plus uncounted millions in places such as China, Burma and Iran. Its English language broadcasts alone are heard by over 100 million listeners. They run for twenty-four hours a day and consist half of news and half of mixed programming such as music, sport and drama. The World Service also offers a transcription facility of recordings and scripts for use by stations in other countries.

In 1991 the BBC hastened to exploit the arrival of TV as the major mass medium throughout the globe by launching *World Service Television*, an operation which the Foreign Office decided not to pay for. The Corporation therefore took the momentous but little noticed decision to seek commercial funding for it, and now both the government-financed World Service Radio and the commercially funded World Service Television have become part of a holding company called *BBC Worldwide*. To reach a global TV audience the Corporation must expand within satellite broadcasting, a pond with room for only a few big fish, and it is therefore looking for partners such as the New York based News International Network. In 1995 and in conjunction with the Pearson Group, BBC Worldwide launched two satellite services to Europe, *BBC World* and *BBC Prime*. It will soon begin a twenty-four hour world news service on American cable TV, followed shortly by an entertainment channel there. What all this portends is a convergence of internal and external broadcasting – a situation in which major media institutions like the BBC will no longer make radical distinctions between their domestic and international strategies.

Growing pains

The expansion of its output during the early 1930s meant that as an institution the BBC had to undergo a fairly large and rapid growth. When it went to air in 1922 it had a staff of thirty-one; by 1927, when it became a Corporation, the staff numbered 773; and by 1938, the year of Reith's departure, there were nearly 5,000. This growth required organizational changes, and in an effort to maintain the corporate ethos Reith favoured a policy of unified control rather than devolved responsibility. At the same time he drew a distinction between a centralized administration, which he favoured, and a uniformity or conformism of output, which he sought to avoid.

For this reason he made an attempt during the early 1930s to separate administrative from creative staff: while the administrators developed a cost-effective, smoothly running organization, the producers and broadcasters could get on with the business of making programmes. In practice, however, the line between the administrative and the creative was often blurred and the concerns of the former usually seemed to prevail over those of the latter. It has therefore been said that before the Corporation moved from Savoy Hill all was 'intimacy and harmony' whereas after, all was 'bureaucracy and conflict'.

The Regional Programme neatly encapsulates the way in which administrative and technical considerations could override editorial, creative and even audience needs, sometimes producing successes but of a rather limited kind. As Maurice Gorham points out, the Regional Programme destroyed the local basis of early broadcasting, which had drawn on local talent and catered to local needs. The new 'regions' were based not on any cultural or even geographical identity but on technical coverage and administrative convenience, and were to that extent arbitrary. The Black Country was thrown together with the Cotswolds, industrial Manchester with the agricultural North Riding, urbane Bristol with bucolic Cornwall. The result was that the distinctiveness of each region was not immediately and authentically expressed but only gradually and somewhat artificially achieved: the West Region pioneered agricultural programmes, the Midlands industrial documentaries and variety shows, the North 'features'.

Organizational problems went right to the top. Under the BBC's new constitution Reith was accountable to the Board of Governors; but a proud and sometimes prickly man who had already shaped the organization according to his own vision would never have found such accountability easy, and almost immediately he was at odds with one of its members, a Mrs Snowden, whom he regarded as officious and meddlesome. He also came to dislike the Chair, Lord Clarendon, believing him to be weak and vacillating for his failure to restrain Mrs Snowden, and it was not until Clarendon's departure in 1930 that Reith's relations with the board began to improve.

Nevertheless he was by temperament an architect and builder rather than a caretaker, and as the 1930s wore on and the Corporation became more systematic and settled in its ways, Reith grew bored. 'I am beginning to feel that I have organized and developed myself out of a job', he told his diary in 1935. In their different ways Reith and the Corporation were outgrowing each other, but if during his last years in office he could not live comfortably within the BBC, the subsequent thirty-three years of his life were to show that he could not live comfortably without it. There is some dispute as to whether the Chairman of the Board of Governors engineered his departure. What is certain is that his restlessness came to the notice of the government, by whom he was instructed to take the chair at Imperial Airways. Yet even though his departure from the BBC was pretty well inevitable, not least because Reith himself appeared to want it, the manner of that departure was characteristically painful. Reith rightly felt that his new job would not be so central to the life of the nation, he was excluded from the deliberations as to who his successor at the BBC should be, and his hope of joining the Board of Governors was thwarted by some of its members on the not unreasonable ground that he would make life impossible for his successor. Thus it was in tearful bitterness that he returned his wireless and television sets to the Corporation, and on 30 June 1938, the day of his resignation, made a symbolic trip to Droitwich to close down the high-power transmitter for the night.

Yet despite the organizational upheavals within the BBC, the 1930s were an era of continuing improvements in the quality and scope of its programmes, and as a result of the recommendations of the Ullswater Committee (1936) the government renewed the original ten-year Charter for a further ten years.

Developments in radio news

In its first years as a news medium, radio was obliged to declare that it was the prisoner of the press. 'This is London calling – 2LO calling,' the newsreader would intone – though not before 7 pm. 'Here is the first general news bulletin, copyright by Reuters, Press Association, Exchange Telegraph and Central News.' There followed a dry, sedate bulletin of 20 or 25 minutes, with no interviews, features or actuality.

It was the General Strike which showed that sooner or later broadcasting's ability to deliver the latest news would not be denied, and the 1920s and 1930s are a history of the BBC's gradual escape from the stranglehold of the press. The 1927 Charter recognized in principle the BBC's right to broadcast its own news, and thenceforth the Corporation made a continuous effort to reduce its dependence on agency material and establish its own news-gathering facilities. But in order to protect the circulation of the papers restrictions remained upon the time that the news could be broadcast: it was not until the outbreak of the Second World War that bulletins were heard before 6 pm. However in 1930 the BBC secured from Reuters the right to edit and write its own bulletins from the agency material on which it still largely relied, and was thus able to resume the attempt it had begun during the General Strike to transform news from something suited only to print into something that could comfortably be listened to.

To begin with, the production of the news was located within the large Department of Talks, but in 1934 a former economics professor, John Coatman, was appointed Chief News Editor and set about creating a separate news department. At first consisting of six people it had acquired a staff of thirty by 1939.

At about the time of Coatman's appointment the news gained new impact with the arrival of portable sound-recording machines. Some of them made use of Blattner steel tape which had to be edited with metal clippers and welding instruments, the joints clattering through the machine like a train over points, but most recording was on 9-minute 12-inch discs.

It was also from about this time that the newspapers began to learn how to live with radio, realizing that although it had dented their circulation somewhat, they still possessed strengths in news reportage which the sound medium lacked. Becoming less concerned with the recency of the news they began to exploit their special ability to amplify, contextualize, interpret and comment, an illustration of the point made in the introduction to Part I that old media are never entirely replaced by new ones: their roles may be altered, but they usually retain a distinctive and irreplaceable function. Because broadcast bulletins were briefer and sharper the newspapers reacted by reducing the amount of fine print, making bolder headlines, doubling columns, shortening sentences and paragraphs, and increasing the number of photographs.

Nevertheless radio news had some unrivalled successes. The last illness of King George V in 1936, a saga which developed from moment to moment, could be much more vividly rendered by radio than by the press, with Reith himself coming to the microphone to announce the king's death. The royal funeral was also broadcast, and the abdication statement made eleven months later by the new king, Edward VIII, was much more compelling to listen to than to read.

The BBC's first real scoop was the great fire which destroyed the exhibition centre at Crystal Palace in the same year. It occurred after the papers went to bed but before their morning appearance, thus emphasizing their relative inability to keep abreast of events. From the scene of the fire a young BBC reporter named Richard Dimbleby telephoned a live report which was accompanied by shouts, the roar of the flames and the clang of fire-bells.

Towards the end of the decade the press was still fighting a rearguard action against the BBC by getting certain news sources to embargo material as 'not for broadcasting', but it was the need to cover the 1938 Munich crisis by every means possible that finally enabled radio news to compete with the press on equal terms.

The cultural values of the BBC

Though widely admired, the BBC's output was not always enjoyed: indeed the Corporation was often accused of being undemocratic and elitist in its programming policy. How could this be, when through mixed programming it set out to provide something for everyone?

Part of the answer lies in the shifting and paradoxical notions of 'democratic'. One notion, to which the BBC broadly subscribed, was that democracy consists of giving all the people what they want; but this is undemocratic in the sense that within a limited resource such as broadcasting then was, and because people have differing tastes, nobody gets *enough* of what they want. The second notion, to which many of the Corporation's critics subscribed, was that democracy consists of giving the *majority* of the people what it wants – which is also undemocratic, positively despotic, in the sense that the minority gets nothing at all. The complaint against the BBC, then, was that the majority did not get enough of what it wanted – and a great deal of what it did *not* want.

Yet although, to take a hypothetical example, it might be 'undemocratic' that the great sport-loving majority was denied the amount of soccer it wanted because from time to time minorities of farmers or business people had to be catered for, it was hardly elitist. The question of elitism arose because as we have seen, the BBC's public service policy was to try to provide not just something for everyone, but the *best* of everything – and 'the best' is a notoriously difficult concept which is likely to cause controversy not simply about the merits of programmes within certain categories, but about where those categories should be drawn.

For instance, for all those listeners who liked music, what constituted 'the best'? Classical, as distinct from popular music? (After all, 'classical' is a value-judgement: 'serving as a standard of excellence', as well as a merely neutral description.) Or was there a separate category of popular music with its own distinctions of good and bad (as even within classical music there might be good or bad performances of the great works)? The same question applied to drama. Was 'the best' Shakespeare and Ibsen and 'the worst' music hall – or was the latter a separate category with its own qualitative differences?

From the number of programmes it devoted to them the BBC evidently took the view that 'the best' works were the classical ones. This was especially true of music. Its Music Department dealt only with classical music, while popular music was seen merely as an adjunct of light entertainment and consigned to the Variety Department. The assumption was that if you liked music you could not be displeased with Bach or Beethoven, and that if you liked the theatre you could not be discontented with Shakespeare.

But many listeners did not greatly care for these things and felt that the amount of air-time they occupied was not just undemocratic but elitist in the sense that unlike programmes on farming or sport, where 'the best' derived from other criteria, programmes of classical music or drama simply reflected the values of those at the higher end of the social scale. The BBC, it was thought, regarded the likes of Bach and Shakespeare as the best only because they were preferred by the middle and upper classes.

The BBC's case was that Bach and Shakespeare were preferred by these classes only because they were the best. Certainly it reflected their judgements in the matter, but this was almost inevitable. Where else should judgements about artistic and intellectual merit come from, if not from the most highly educated, the most fully informed and the most widely travelled? And since these qualities generate wealth and are themselves sustained by it, where else would these people be found if not on the upper echelons of the social scale?

But the Corporation also held that there was no *inherent* connection between cultural values and social class. Given the opportunity, everyone – not just the elite – could appreciate Bach and Shakespeare, and this opportunity it was determined to provide. Hence the aim of public service broadcasting was to give to the public a 'better' service than it asked for. Reith himself was famously explicit on this. 'It is occasionally indicated to us that we are apparently setting out to give the public what we think they need – and not what they want', he wrote, 'but few know what they want, and very few what they need' (1924: 34).

Such apparent arrogance must be seen in its historical context. In pre-war Britain universal education ended when children reached the age of about 14. Those temples of high art, the concert halls, opera-houses and theatres, were beyond the pockets of the great mass of people, and within the tiny minority who underwent higher education there was much more consensus than there is today about what in cultural terms was good, significant or worthwhile. Wireless was a new, and in terms of the number of frequencies available, a relatively scarce medium. Its potential was huge: in these early years nobody was sure what it could or could not do. To use it for less than those who were the fittest judges of these things acknowledged as 'the best' was a needless limitation – or as Reith put it more bluntly, a prostitution – of its powers.

Thus what Reith and the BBC were actually positing was a *third* notion of democracy, based, unlike the others, on considerations which were more than merely quantitative: for the aim was to open up to all those who had been denied them by a limited education, low social status and small income the great treasures of our culture.

From a modern viewpoint 'treasures' perhaps begs the question, but they were regarded as such by those classes who embodied the prosperity and wisdom that set the standard for the other members of society. For the latter, Reith's BBC offered a chance of spiritual if not material enrichment, a policy which was surely less cynical than providing only what they would certainly have enjoyed, but which would neither have broadened their horizons nor raised their aspirations.

In practice, however, the BBC was rather more responsive to mass taste than Reith's words imply, for the logic of its cultural position would have been to broadcast no popular music, popular drama, light entertainment, or anything else which had a highbrow equivalent. It was aware that even with its virtual monopoly there were limits on how far it could edify or 'improve' listeners who might not wish to be improved: they could always switch off. The Corporation therefore broadcast a fair amount of popular culture. For instance, according to figures it gave to the Ullswater Committee, it provided during 1934 nearly three times as much dance and light music as 'serious' music. Nevertheless it was always ready to discriminate on the listeners' behalf between 'the good' and 'the inferior' in popular culture – often on moral rather than aesthetic or intellectual grounds, as we shall shortly see in the case of jazz.

What would modify its cultural elitism was that as the 1930s progressed, the political and indeed cultural tide in Britain ran ever more strongly in the direction of that notion of democracy which is based on the will of the majority; and the media historians Paddy Scannell and David Cardiff (1982) have detected a softening of the BBC's didactic approach during this period and an increasing sensitivity to popular taste.

Classical music programming

In the debate about cultural value and popular taste, music assumed a central position simply because a sound-only medium such as radio would almost inevitably transmit a great deal of it. On classical music the BBC's policy was twofold: to broadcast a wide range played to the highest standards, and to help the mass audience to understand and enjoy it. In its aim of combining quality and popularity it had been anticipated by Sir Henry Wood's annual Promenade Concerts, which ever since 1895 had provided London audiences with a cheap and informal blend of established works, adventurous new compositions and popular favourites. However in 1927 their sponsors, the music publishers Chappell, decided to pull out, and on the personal initiative of Reith the BBC took them over, and has ever since relayed them to the nation at large.

In 1930 the BBC founded its own symphony orchestra, and by the middle of the decade it was quite simply the most powerful music patron in the country – a huge concert-giving agency and the biggest employer of orchestral musicians. To ensure that the mass of its listeners would appreciate what they were hearing it engaged Percy Scholes and Sir Walford Davies to give talks on the rudiments and meaning of music – which they did clearly and without condescension. From 1927 to 1937 a 15-minute programme, *The Foundations of Music*, was broadcast five times a week, and some historians insist that the BBC succeeded in spreading a knowledge and enjoyment of classical music among those who were at the lower end of the social scale.

Nevertheless there was a sense in which its aim to broadcast the best performances of classical music was at odds with its aim to widen the public's access to it, because the former merged only too easily with its administrative policy of centralization. The BBC's cultural conservatism was typical of the time, in that broadly speaking it perceived the distinction between the good and the inferior as corresponding not only to the distinction between the preferences of the 'educated' and 'uneducated' or of those 'higher up' and 'lower down' the social scale, but to that which exists between 'capital city' and 'the regions'.

Something of this traditional association between culture and place can still be seen in words like *urbane* and *cosmopolitan*, which have the sense of 'cultured, educated'; for the former, like 'urban', comes from a word meaning 'belonging to the city', and the latter means 'a citizen of the world' in contrast to someone of merely local status or background. On the other hand the words *parochial* and *provincial* can, in addition to their obvious meanings, imply ignorance and narrow-mindedness. Implicit in all these terms is the suggestion that since it draws from a variety of sources and not from any one place, great art or culture is a world-wide phenomenon, or at least characteristic of the city rather than the regions.

The BBC therefore believed that the best performances of classical music should, like those of any other art form, be transmitted from London, for as the capital city London embodied the culture of the entire nation. However, its critics argued that at a fraction of the cost of hiring international artists to perform in the capital, the BBC should be encouraging music in the provinces – using the Regional Programme to introduce its listeners to their local orchestras and thus stimulate their attendance at local concerts.

Popular music

Rather less 'cosmopolitan' than its view of the classics was the BBC's attitude to popular music, for much of the latter originated from America, specifically that sought-after negro music called jazz, and the Corporation set itself against American influences as being vulgar in tendency. The question was not simply what 'the best' jazz was, but whether jazz had any merit at all, especially as it was widely denounced as 'jungle music', an unnatural sexual stimulant. Again, some knowledge of the historical context renders this view slightly less bizarre than it seems. Jazz had emerged only twenty or thirty years earlier from the brothels of New Orleans, the word itself deriving from negro slang 'to copulate'. Hence the music still seemed primitive and lewd: only in the 1950s would it come to be regarded as 'high art', sanctified by old age, a decline in general popularity and that growth of critical attention by which such decline is often accompanied.

In the early days the BBC's solution to what it saw as the problem of jazz was characteristic: it set out to 'improve' it, to make something decorously British out of this vigorous new art form. Though of unmistakably American provenance, jazz was mostly performed on air not by mere dance-bands but by smart hotel orchestras such as the Savoy Orpheans, and thus acquired something of the status and refinement of the native upper classes for whom they normally played. The more authentically American or American-influenced 'hot jazz' was alternately banned and either filtered through the rather sedate presentation of the first disc-jockey Christopher Stone, or broadcast not in 'jam sessions', where it might be merely enjoyable, but in 'recitals' of a more solemnly educative nature.

Yet whether as jazz or in some other guise, popular music was given an enormous boost by radio, the latter soon surpassing gramophone records and local shows and dances as its main outlet. At the same time the balance of power within the music industry shifted from the publishers and music hall impresarios to Broadcasting House – a shift which the BBC acknowledged in 1933, when it instructed the producers of its dance programmes to deal directly with the bandleaders and no longer with the managers of the theatres from which they broadcast.

For their part, the music publishers sought to turn the new medium to their advantage by paying bandleaders to play on air the songs they wished to promote from their lists, a practice known as 'plugging' and one which the BBC deplored as covert advertising. It therefore imposed a ban on the naming of songs so that the listeners would find them harder to identify, but the publishers' collecting agency, the Performing Right Society, responded by threatening to rescind the licensing agreement it had made with the Corporation. The latter was forced to back down, and plugging has ever since been a feature of music broadcasting.

At first it was not just the publishers and impresarios who felt threatened by radio; so, too, did the record companies – a rich irony in that records now make up virtually the whole of radio's output. Nevertheless there seemed at the time to be good grounds for their anxiety. Records were a mass medium which had preceded broadcasting in the successful exploitation of popular music, but the ownership of wireless sets was becoming even more widespread than the owner-ship of gramophones and records. The companies feared that the BBC would simply use their products as a substitute for live music, thus relieving the public of the need to continue buying them, and in 1935 they charged the Corporation several thousand pounds for the right to play records on the air.

What they perhaps underestimated was the durability of their products as against the evanescence of radio's, for broadcasting actually stimulated record sales. The BBC played relatively few records but it did broadcast live performances of many songs which, initially at least, were not available on disc. The companies were then able to offer contracts to the artists who performed them – and the public would buy their records on the strength of what they had heard on the air.

Thus radio helped to create the record-based star system, for 'stardom' came to be defined not so much by popularity in the music halls or the sheet-music sales of songs as by popularity on the wireless and the sales of records. The BBC became a source of talent rather than a mere staging post for it and the record companies grew to appreciate the promotional value of radio, even though they could not fully exploit it until the mid-1950s, when the more widely affordable cost of their products coincided so potently with the birth of rock music.

Of particular interest to the media student is the way in which broadcasting and records (whether discs, tapes, cassettes or CDs) have over the years wrought a change in the social consumption of music and in the status of popular musicians. When radio arrived, the traditional role of much popular music was as the setting or background for *dance*. People certainly bought the sheet versions of their favourite music hall tunes to sing and play at home, but band music, especially under the growing influence of jazz, was primarily dance music, and in the early years many people used the wireless or gramophone as a kind of domestic dance band, rolling back the living room carpet to do the waltz or the fox-trot.

But although radio and records could domesticate music, for reasons of space they could less easily domesticate dance, the effect of which was, as Stephen Barnard points out, that the music shifted from background to focus, the arrangements of the songs becoming steadily more elaborate to satisfy the inactive listening to which these media mostly gave rise. This in turn had the effect of raising the status of those bandleaders, popular singers and musicians who broadcast or made records to that which had long been enjoyed by classical virtuosi, and meant that they would mainly be watched and listened to even when audiences had the opportunity to dance to them.

This change in the consumption of popular music and the status of those who played it is well illustrated by the career of the early bandleader Jack Payne. In 1926 Payne got himself appointed as the BBC's Director of Dance Music, and in order to give the music a kind of corporate style he managed to form the BBC Dance Orchestra in 1928 – two years before an institution which was renowned for its cultural elitism created its first classical orchestra. His radio shows soon made Payne such a celebrity that in 1932 he left the BBC and took his orchestra on a national tour – not of dance-halls but theatres.

The change from bands as dance accompanists to performers of interest in their own right is traceable through the wartime shows of the great Glenn Miller Band to the gargantuan rock and pop concerts of the last thirty years; and a measure of this change would be the *lèse-majesté* of expecting any of the leading rock groups of our time to play at a mere dance. To repay our concentration on the music, their songs have become longer and more intricately arranged (the first rock songs of the 1950s lasted about 2 minutes, whereas most are now between 5 and 6 minutes); and to heighten the visual appeal of the bands there has been an increasing use of such accessories as light-shows, dry ice, moving rostrums, back projections, and onstage terpsichores to dance vicariously for the tightly-packed spectators. Rock videos have gone yet further by posing bands in improbable locations far removed from dance- or even concert halls.

Light entertainment

During much of the 1920s and 1930s the BBC's producers continued to think of light entertainment in terms of its original habitat, the theatre and the music hall, and wireless merely as a means of relaying shows from that habitat, or at best, as a place to re-create it. Because stage-shows had a chorus-line so might the BBC, even in the shows it originated. Its 1925 revue *Radio Radiance* featured a troupe of dancing girls who were rendered audible by performing on boards!

At first the BBC exploited the music hall fairly successfully, either by direct broadcasts of its shows or by using its stars, but not surprisingly it soon fell foul of the impresarios, notably the Society of West End Theatre Managers. Fearing a loss of custom, they periodically stopped shows from being heard on air and threatened to ban any performer who broadcast.

The performers themselves were scarcely more enthusiastic. Radio simply devoured their material. The two or three routines which in the halls could last them a lifetime now vanished into the ether and could never be used again. By the early 1930s the live theatres were no longer a rich source for the BBC, for it had all but exhausted what material had not been denied to it by the theatre managers.

In 1933 it therefore began to systematically develop its own material by creating a variety department under Eric Maschwitz. Nevertheless it continued to regard light entertainment primarily as a creature of the theatre, in imitation of which it established a live studio audience to whom the radio shows made concessions in both costume and staging. The very titles of these shows are telling. Among the first, yet one which survived until 1952, was *Music Hall*, a blend of singing and comedy acts, but also for a time including more invisible tap-dancers, the Eight Step Sisters. Another with a title which betrayed its derivative nature was *Songs from the Shows*; but perhaps most extraordinary was the adaptation of a genre whose visual essence is expressed in its very name: black-face minstrelsy. *The White Coons' Concert Party* ran from 1932 until 1936, its theme-tune beginning with the exhortation 'Come on and listen to the gay white coons'. But even more popular was *The Kentucky Minstrels* (1933–50), later revamped for television as *The Black and White Minstrel Show*.

The early wireless entertainers fell into two main categories. The broader comedians and singers included Will Hay, Gracie Fields, Wee Georgie Wood, and Elsie and Doris Waters, while a gentler, more sophisticated style was adopted by Gillie Potter, Ronald Frankau, Jack Hulbert and Beatrice Lillie, who incorporated into her act songs from cabaret and operetta.

Whether by inclination or necessity, the theatre impresarios and their artists gradually softened towards radio. The former came to appreciate the value of the publicity it gave to their shows, the latter to recognize that however greedily the medium swallowed their material it could, in a single show, provide them with an audience bigger than that acquired in a whole lifetime on the boards – and in any case, if they declined to broadcast they would soon be eclipsed by the home-grown stars of the BBC.

The evolving attitude of the music hall artists, along with that of the newspaper proprietors, theatre managers and owners of the record companies, illustrates a process which is a familiar feature of cultural history: those who in some way control traditional media or genres begin by opposing a new medium, and then make an accommodation with it which often provides them with a new and profitable role, albeit one which is changed or reduced somewhat.

A final word on the broadcasting of sport. Before 1927 the BBC was unable to offer full running commentaries on sports events because the Newspaper Proprietors' Association had persuaded the government that these were another form of news reporting. The restriction was lifted when the company became a corporation, and thereafter such national events as the Derby, the Cup Final and the Boat Race were successfully covered.

Educational, features and documentary programmes

Most of the BBC's *educational* programmes were for schools. These ranged from attempts at direct teaching – the giving of on-air lessons – to story-readings and dramatizations whose didactic aims were rather more oblique. Schools broadcasts had begun in 1924, when they were received by 220 schools. By 1927 they were being heard in 3,000 schools, and in 1939 up to 10,000 schools were listening to thirty-nine programmes a week.

Despite these figures schools broadcasting was attended by problems from which it has never altogether freed itself. Radio had already become so indelibly associated with leisure and entertainment that local education authorities could seldom be persuaded that it was an educational necessity and not a luxury. Second, in an era before off-air recording was possible it was hard to integrate this time-based medium into individual school timetables and curricula: lessons had to be adjusted to wireless broadcasts and not vice versa. And third, the temporal dimension was a problem even within individual broadcasts because despite the reinforcement of their teachers, children sometimes found it hard to extract learning points from a constantly changing text.

Its problems of blindness and evanescence mean that radio has always been more effective as an educative or informative than as a direct-teaching medium, and the BBC broadcast a wide range of educative talks. A measurable and gratifying effect of these talks was that in the shops and public libraries they would create an immediate demand for books on whatever subjects they were dealing with. The Talks Department was started in 1927 under Hilda Matheson and further developed from 1932 by Charles Siepmann, and among the distinguished speakers it used were the playwright George Bernard Shaw, the economist John Maynard Keynes, and the writers H. G. Wells and G. K. Chesterton.

Very different from educational and educative output was that strange category known as *features*, though as we shall see they tended to converge in a third category: documentaries. Features programmes, which date from 1928, occupied the large space between drama and current affairs and were often treated as a kind of broadcasting laboratory in which the aim was to test the limits of a sound-only medium. Many of them were montages of narrative, dramatic dialogue, music, verse, sound-effects and later, sound actuality. Many were also blends of fact and fiction, and though 'features' is a term we still use, albeit in the rather different sense of a human interest story or investigation, these early wireless features seem to be distant ancestors of the modern TV docudrama. Certainly one important generic contribution of radio and television, with their use of actuality and 'real' locations, has been their ability to equivocate very effectively between real-life and make-believe — a subject we shall return to later.

In essaying vast themes such as *The Sea* or *Speed: A Tragi-Comic Fantasy of Gods and Mortals* (1928) some of these early features were ambitious failures, but as Paddy Scannell (1986) points out, in the growing economic recession of the 1930s the programmes gradually acquired more social and political relevance, and were in this respect influenced by the contemporary cinema documentaries of Robert Flaherty and John Grierson. They thus became less easily distinguishable from the *documentary* genre.

The strength of the BBC's documentary output in the 1930s grew quite unexpectedly out of its organizational upheavals, in particular from Reith's desire for firm control at the centre and for radical and dissident members of the Corporation to be dispersed to its fringes. One able features producer of left-wing views was A. E. Harding, whose *Crisis in Spain* (1931), which recounted the events that had recently led to the formation of the Spanish Republic, showed how much he had been influenced by the cinematic techniques of Grierson. It has been suggested that his political leanings were the cause of Harding's later removal to the Northern Region, and that the removal was ordered by Reith himself.

At its Manchester headquarters Harding gathered around him a talented team of writers and actors. His work included more poetic features such as *The March of the '45* (1936), a chronicle of the Jacobite Rebellion, but he also devised a strategy for making programmes which would evoke the characteristic spirit of the north and its people. Harding and his associates interviewed ordinary people, among them the unemployed, and encouraged them to relate their experiences in their own words. Their accounts would be worked up into scripts by such writers as D. G. Bridson and Crawford McNair, and then returned to them to rehearse and broadcast at the Manchester studio. Before the war, almost all broadcast utterances were scripted, partly because the BBC felt a need to maintain tight editorial control, but mainly because of poor recording and editing facilities. This meant that Harding's interviewees could never sound as spontaneous and authentic as those in a modern documentary, but at least they were reading out experiences which were both genuine and their own.

In the second half of the decade the Northern Region enjoyed a flowering of radio documentary. Harding's best known creation was *Harry Hopeful*, a series which began in 1935. The eponymous character was an unemployed glass-blower's assistant played by Frank Nicolls, in real life a clock-mender from Irlam near Manchester. Its theme was that Harry Hopeful travelled through the north in search of work, meeting and talking to people in the places he visited – a blend of fiction and 'real life' which had been retained from the earlier features programmes.

The BBC had gathered its first sound actuality in 1934, using a recording van which had been hired from a film company. It was used in a documentary about cockneys hop-picking in Kent which was given the racy title *'Opping 'Oliday* to show that the BBC knew how the ordinary people talked. From 1937 Bridson was able to use a new but hugely unwieldy mobile recording unit to make such industrial features as *Steel* and *Coalface*, further blends of actuality, poetic narrative and music. Later, Olive Shapley incorporated actuality into her studies of lorry drivers, barge-people and other working-class folk.

As an informative genre, documentary could embrace both features programmes and talks on social, economic and political themes. During much of the 1930s Professor John Hilton spoke with chatty shrewdness, for the most part on economic matters but on a range of contemporary issues; but some talks embroiled the BBC in quarrels with politicians both inside and outside the government. Not surprisingly, the latter feared the power of the new medium to disturb the *status quo*. In 1931 the Liberal peer Lord Beveridge was accused of left-wing bias after delivering a series of talks on unemployment, and in 1933 *SOS*, another series on the same subject, caused further controversy despite being given by the genteel S. P. B. Mais, a former public school master.

In the same year Howard Marshall gave graphic reports of the poverty and squalor of the north in a series called *Other People's Houses*, and in 1934 even greater uproar attended a series called *Time to Spare*, in which the talks were delivered by the unemployed themselves. Fear of the subversive effects of the wireless perhaps reached its apogee in 1935, when the government forced the BBC to ban the communist Harry Pollitt and the fascist Sir Oswald Mosley from contributing to a series of talks it had planned on the British constitution. It was natural that politicians should fear that social unrest would follow such programmes: as Paddy Scannell (1980) observes, their effects were potentially the more radical because they were not reports for the initiated or sermons to the converted but heard by the broadest cross-section of the public. What was perhaps less clear was the grim possibility that an accumulation of these programmes would not incite their listeners but inure them.

Constructing the listener: the need for audience research

Whether its aim was to improve or entertain, the BBC had a lively consciousness of the listener, even if an uncertain impression of her or his identity. Such a consciousness was essential, for like most newspapers the new medium of broadcasting was received privately – by people in their homes. Yet whereas newspapers, which were targeted at particular socio-economic groups, could gauge their success in the finite terms of 'copies sold', broadcasting, which was aimed at everyone, could not.

In *Broadcast Over Britain* (1924) Reith manages to combine consciousness of the listener with a sense of the medium's indeterminacy when he writes of wireless entering both the rich person's mansion and the poor person's cottage, yet remaining freely available to the second however much it is used by the first.

In 1923 concern for the listener and for her or his needs was tangibly expressed in the launch of the *Radio Times*, which owed its existence to the newspapers' refusal to publish details of the BBC's programmes. As well as listing the programmes for the week ahead it contained articles and features, at first appearing under a deal with the publisher Newnes. Eventually the BBC took it over completely, and with its appeal to readers of all ages and its seven-day life, it became hugely popular and a very valuable medium for advertisers. By 1934 its circulation had climbed to 2 million, and it was especially important to listeners in the days before programming became routinized and hence rather more predictable.

But although the listener was provided for at this material level, the BBC remained largely in the dark as to her or his composite identity. In the absence of precise knowledge it was thus necessary to 'construct' the listener – and not surprisingly the BBC did so in its own image. Consistent with its conservative and elitist cultural perspective, it recruited most of its own staff from the educated middle class, and this provided the social background and moral values of the audience it constructed.

Implicitly it promoted the idea that contemporary social arrangements were the best ones possible, that family togetherness was cemented by radio listening, and that in the context of our vast European cultural heritage the influence of America was for the most part a vulgar irrelevance. In matters of family morality, the standards the Corporation set related not only to the nature of its output but the conduct of its employees: in 1929 Reith dismissed his much-valued chief engineer Peter Eckersley when the latter was cited in a divorce case.

Inasmuch as the BBC reflected what vast numbers of middle-class people were, and many working-class people aspired to be, its approach was successful: inasmuch as it neglected or misrepresented what working-class people were, it was not. One should not exaggerate its failings: much of its music and light entertainment was nothing if not populist, and many of the documentary and features programmes were attempts to express the problems and culture of working people. But it provided less than it might have done, for a number of reasons, social, geographical and cultural, which were mutually reinforcing.

In the first place the predominantly middle-class background of its administrative and production staff meant that within the Corporation there was a widespread ignorance about the realities of working-class life. But this ignorance was not simply social; it had a geographical dimension, too. The main centres of education and affluence from which the BBC most readily recruited were in London and the South East, whereas the great mass of the industrial working class was in the Midlands and the North. Moreover, middle-class ignorance of the latter was legitimated by the broad assumption we outlined above that what was culturally valuable or significant was not specific to regions or localities but urbane, cosmopolitan. In this respect, London, the capital city, did not count as a mere 'locality'.

As we have seen, Reith's policy of centralizing the BBC on London related to organization and administration, not to programmes. But as we also saw in the case of classical music, the cultural assumptions of the time enabled the process of centralization to extend to programe content, too. The Regional Programme was intended to convey regional affairs and regional culture, but the sustaining service from London that was provided for it suggested that the BBC regarded those of the metropolis as even more important, and when it came to a choice between the two, London normally prevailed.

This meant that to a large extent the limitations in regional programming were limitations in the programming that was provided for the working class. Folk songs and folk writings were given relatively little air-time, and according to Stephen Barnard (1989) there were two working-class crazes of the 1920s and 1930s, accordion playing and community singing, which the BBC neglected altogether.

Some other aspects of working-class life were even more glaringly overlooked: Curran and Seaton tartly observe that during 'a decade of hunger marches and "red united fighting fronts" the BBC regarded a succession of royal broadcasts as the triumph of outside broadcasting and actuality reporting' (1991: 145). This was not insensitivity pure and simple: though the 1930s were a period of economic slump and severe unemployment, the Corporation held the artless if well-meant belief that it could bring greater solace to working people by giving them a glimpse of the lives of their king and queen than by holding a mirror to their own. A similar belief presumably underlies the obsession of today's popular tabloids with the doings of the royal family, film stars, rock singers and other celebrities.

But it should be added that for most people during the 1920s and 1930s the monarchy provided more than glamorous escapism. It symbolized a nation which despite its economic and political difficulties was one of the wealthiest and most powerful in the world, at the centre of a diverse and far-flung empire, yet ethnically and spiritually much more homogeneous than it is today. With whatever justification, many – though by no means all – working people felt they had as much reason as any other social group to be proud of the monarchy and of what it represented.

The BBC's preoccupation with royalty and its rituals, which now strike us as anachronisms that say much less about the health of the nation than those marches and movements it largely neglected, perhaps expressed another aspect of its cultural conservatism, a belief that the most valuable things are not only 'placeless' or cosmopolitan but timeless, and therefore that since current affairs are ephemeral there is a sense in which they are relatively unimportant. That the BBC inclined, at least intermittently, to this view seems less far-fetched when we reflect that even today that conservative and highbrow network Radio 3 carries almost no news or current affairs.

Hence we can conclude that although working people did not necessarily feel excluded by programming which did not address their circumstances, they were clearly less well provided for than those who were higher up the social scale. However from the early 1930s producers felt a growing need to identify rather than construct the national audience and discover just how effective their programmes were. By 1935 98 per cent of the population were within reach of at least one network, and 58 per cent could reach two. But the other available figures, though broadly encouraging, were not very revealing. The number of homes with wireless sets rose from less than 4.5 million in 1931, to almost 8 million by 1939. What did the myriads of mouthless, faceless listeners actually think of what they were hearing? Was public service broadcasting effective? Were the serious programmes edifying and the lighter ones entertaining? Was the Corporation overlooking anything which its listeners considered valuable?

Unfortunately, that more articulate section of the population whom we term the intelligentsia was of no help in these matters. In Gorham's words, 'serious criticism of broadcasting was rare, mainly because serious people did not take broadcasting seriously' (1952: 102). Such people tend to be suspicious of new media because agreed critical standards for them have not yet been established (later on, television was for many years dismissed as 'the idiots' lantern', while radio came to be regarded as a serious medium); and so in 1929 the BBC began *The Listener*, a periodical of essays and reviews for the more critically minded and analytical within the audience.

The only things which were known about the identity and tastes of the listeners came from the casual letters they wrote to the BBC or the press. But these were not truly representative of the audience as a whole: they came from a tiny fraction of it and were written by untypically literate people with untypically strong views.

For a long time Reith resisted the demand for audience research. In pursuit of public service aims he did listen to the views of such bodies as the National Advisory Committee on Education and the Religious Advisory Committee, since both had been appointed to speak on the audience's behalf. But he knew that a comprehensive investigation of listener tastes would influence and eventually dictate broadcasting policy, and that worthwhile programmes for minorities would be sacrificed to the ratings.

Nevertheless the advocates of research eventually had their way, and in 1936 the Listener Research Section was set up within the Public Relations Department. Its first head was Robert Silvey, who conducted his research by a technique of random sampling and was soon gathering reassuring evidence that the BBC was being listened to by a broad cross-section of the population.

This in itself suggests that the programmes could not have been wholly displeasing, but what, more precisely, did the listeners think of them? The general verdict seems to have been that they were substantial, reliable, sometimes highly enjoyable – but circumscribed. That many listeners did not get exactly what they wanted, or in sufficient measure, did not create frustration pure and simple. There was doubtless a measure of that, but just as we are apt to despise those who pander to our every whim and respect those who do not, there was a certain esteem for the BBC and pride in it as an august national institution. What the audience often had to take from it was rather like medicine: it was not altogether pleasurable but it sometimes made them feel better.

The converse of this is, of course, that a diet mainly of cakes and sweets can often result in disgust and nausea, but what made popular taste seem increasingly authoritative was the growing political status of that form of democracy which favours only the largest number. The most disquieting discovery of the audience researchers confirmed Reith's fears that the BBC could not withstand competition from populist, commercial stations. Such competition had been harrying it since the beginning of the 1930s, but that is a story for another chapter.

Sources/further reading

This chapter owes a comprehensive debt to the three authorities on broadcasting during the 1930s: Asa Briggs, Paddy Scannell and David Cardiff. Briggs (1965) provides a general account of 'the extension and enrichment' of broadcasting between 1927 and 1939, and Scannell and Cardiff (1991) have written a history which is particularly illuminating on the social impact and cultural implications of broadcasting. A fascinating account of the unique social entity that was created with the establishment of the British Broadcasting Corporation in 1927 is provided by Burns (1977).

For an excellent summary of the BBC's statutory position, its relations with government, and the mixed programming output of its first networks see also Scannell and Cardiff (1982). A defence of the BBC's monopoly and its public service policy is in Reith (1924).

A brief, illustrated history of BBC external broadcasting is Walker (1992). For the first ten years of the Empire Service see MacKenzie (1987), and for an account of external services up to the 1950s see Paulu (1956), which is extended to 1974 in Briggs (1995) and to 1980 in Paulu (1981). The standard history of the first fifty years of BBC external broadcasting is Mansell (1982).

Briggs (1965) and Scannell and Cardiff (1982) deal at some length with the early organizational problems of the BBC, and the latter summarize the dilemmas of regional programming, on which Gorham (1952) is also illuminating. A useful sketch of the way in which regional expression was accommodated within the BBC's policy of centralization can be found in Harvey and Robins (1994).

For various versions of the relations between Reith and the first Board of Governors, Reith's role in the BBC during the 1930s, and the events leading to his resignation, see Reith (1949), Boyle (1972) and Stuart (1975).

Good general accounts of pre-war programming categories and individual programmes are to be found in the standard works of Briggs (1965) and Scannell and Cardiff (1982; 1991); also in Gorham (1952), Paulu (1956), Parker (1977), Briggs (1981), Gifford (1985) and Donovan (1992).

In addition to all these, the following are illuminating on particular programme categories: Pegg (1983) on the impact of radio news on press news; Reith (1949) on radio coverage of the death of George V and the abdication crisis. Scannell (1981) provides an authoritative account of the BBC's pre-war policy on classical music. For similar accounts of its policy and practice on popular music, see Frith (1983) and Barnard (1989). Frith also covers contemporary light entertainment.

A general survey of early radio comedy is in Took (1976), and Cardiff (1988) explores its origins and social basis. Pickering (1994; 1996) is useful on the origins and development of 'blackface' comedy on the radio.

In the field of educational talks and information presentation Cardiff (1980) detects a drift towards populism in the 1930s, but Crisell (1986; 1994) argues that radio is in any case of limited effectiveness as an educational and talks medium. For an understanding of early radio features, see Sieveking (1934). Bridson (1971) offers personal recollections of making features and documentaries for the Northern Region, and for a lucid and detailed account of pre-war features and documentaries see Scannell (1986). A transcript of some of John Hilton's 1930s talks is in Hilton (1938).

For the BBC's approach to the economic problems of the 1930s and the political controversies it provoked, see Scannell (1980). Curran and Seaton (1991) argue that as far as possible the BBC avoided contentious political issues during the 1930s as a way of consolidating itself as a national institution.

On the broadcasters' consciousness of the listener see Reith (1924). Pegg (1983) is especially useful on early listener reactions and on the birth of audience research. For the early methods and discoveries of audience research, see Silvey (1974).

Chapter 3

Keeping the Sabbath, waging a war and building a pyramid

Keeping the Sabbath, waging a war and building a pyramid

Breaches of the BBC's monopoly

As we have seen, the efforts of the Corporation to inform, educate and edify would be ineffective if the audience had the option of ignoring it and tuning to stations which catered solely to popular taste. Since as a monopoly broadcaster the BBC did not depend for its survival on maximizing its audience it could maintain a varied and balanced diet of programmes and cater to minorities.

But the arguments against monopoly were equally powerful. By any standards it was undemocratic, because even for those whose tastes were being met by the varied programming it was a denial of choice. Who was to say that the varied programming provided by a competitor might not delight them even more?

Lack of choice was also a problem for those who had something to broadcast. If the BBC refused them access to the air no other outlet was available, and the audience might be worse off for not being able to hear what they had to say.

In the event the monopoly lasted less than ten years. Its demise was largely a result of the 'Reith Sunday', the grimmest of the Corporation's attempts to 'improve' its listeners rather than provide the kinds of programmes that most of them wanted. Sunday was a day on which nearly everyone had the free time to listen to the radio, and after what was not uncommonly a working week of six days people felt especially in need of output which was lighthearted and relaxing. What Reith decreed they should get were programmes which did not begin until 12.30 pm and consisted entirely of religious services, serious talks and classical music.

It must be acknowledged that during the 1920s and 1930s Britain was a more uniformly Christian country than it is today, and that among the faithful there was rather more observance of the sabbath, whether through church-going or in a fairly sedate and reflective lifestyle. Nevertheless the Reith Sunday was a serious misjudgement of the national mood – or at best an indifference to it.

Inevitably, certain entrepreneurs saw a profitable way of delivering programmes which the great bulk of the wireless audience would enjoy: they would make money out of advertising – either by creating programmes which advertisers would pay for, or by selling them air time in which to broadcast programmes of their own. One such entrepreneur, whose surname proclaimed his faith in the power of advertising with the improbable aptness of a character in a fable or children's card-game, was Captain Leonard Plugge, later a Conservative MP for the Medway towns. Since under the agreement between the BBC and the Post Office no commercial stations could be established in Britain itself, the solution was to beam programmes into it from stations located in Southern Ireland or the European mainland.

Running his International Broadcasting Company from an office in insolent proximity to Broadcasting House, Plugge bought air time on several foreign stations within reach of Britain – Toulouse and Paris in France, Athlone in Ireland – and simply sold it as advertising space to British companies, leaving the actual programme content to be determined by the presenters he engaged. But in 1931 he also founded Radio Normandie, which broadcast from Fécamp on the northern coast of France and provided the clearest signal of all. Southern England was its main reception area, where listeners were regaled mostly by American-style dance music. Within twelve months twenty-one firms were sponsoring broadcasts, and by 1934 Normandie was taking £400,000 a year in advertising.

On 4 June 1933 another station opened, the continentally owned Radio Luxembourg, broadcasting from the tiny principality of that name situated between France, Belgium and Germany. Ignoring the International Broadcasting Union, the body which had been set up to allocate wavelengths, it began by pirating a long wave frequency and offered, like Normandie, output which was unashamedly populist. It declared its competitive intentions by at first broadcasting only on Sundays, but throughout its pre-war years it always reserved its strongest programmes for this day, featuring such major stars as George Formby and Gracie Fields. The BBC made strong representations to the IBU to get both Normandie and Luxembourg taken off the air but to no avail, and by 1934 ninety companies were advertising their products on the commercial stations.

Luxembourg was a highly professional enterprise, for sound commercial reasons exercising little control over its own output. It sold its air-time to any advertiser on the basis that it was the latter, and not the station, which provided the programmes. This meant that Luxembourg gained revenue from the sale of air time without having to spend money on providing entertainment. Its attitude was that those best qualified to make programmes were the advertising agencies, the biggest of which had their own radio production departments. The two main agencies were J. Walter Thompson and the London Press Exchange, which would find a programme format and a presenter to suit the brand image of each client.

Since the Post Office's agreement with the BBC precluded it from supplying overseas lines for the agencies, they pre-recorded the programmes on disc and sent them out to Luxembourg for transmission. The quality of reception back in Britain was variable, but the station could be picked up nearly everywhere and was especially popular in the working-class areas of north east England and south Wales.

Programmes consisted mostly of variety shows, dance band half-hours and personality showcases in which the artists were closely associated with the products they advertised. Thus Joe Loss and his orchestra were heard thanks to Meltonian Shoe Polish, Geraldo and his orchestra by courtesy of Cadbury's Chocolates. One of Luxembourg's most successful pre-war shows was a children's programme sponsored by the makers of the malted drink Ovaltine, and punningly titled *The Ovaltineys' Concert Party*. As a by-product of the show a club called the League of Ovaltineys was formed in 1935, and by 1939 had enrolled some 5 million members.

What the BBC's audience researchers discovered in 1936 was that on Sundays a vast number of its listeners (its rivals put it as high as 82 per cent) were defecting to the commercial stations, and that of these Luxembourg had by far the largest single audience. Both Normandie and Luxembourg were eventually closed by the exigencies of the war, but the latter resumed in 1946.

It is true that before 1939 the BBC was not able to compete with the commercial operators on altogether equal terms because its transmission hours were limited by the government. Except during the General Strike it was never able to begin broadcasts before 10.15 am. But the real cause of its Sunday problem could not be disguised.

Nevertheless, the subtler change in listening habits which was taking place during the rest of the week was even more ominous, for the researchers found that even when the BBC's programme mixture included many lighter and brighter elements, a slowly growing number of people were abandoning it for the often weaker signals of its rivals. In his dour way, Reith was right: if the listening public had a choice between continuous light programming and a mixture of serious and light programming it would gravitate towards the former, and his concept of public service broadcasting was therefore at risk from the moment the Corporation's monopoly was broken.

Trimming some sails

It is possible to exaggerate the effects of competition on the BBC, especially before it initiated audience research in 1936: we saw in the last chapter that for much of the pre-war period it fashioned the listener very largely in its own image and planned its programmes accordingly.

Nevertheless the historians Scannell and Cardiff (1982) have detected a tendency in its programmes during the second half of the decade towards popularization, that notion of democracy which favours the majority. Not surprisingly it was a tendency which grew more marked after 1936 and gathered further strength with the departure of Reith some two years later.

The earliest sign of a shift towards lighter programme content dates from about 1934. David Cardiff argues that after the Corporation's disputes with the government about their political content, its broadcast talks became generally less serious in subject matter and more entertaining in tone. Paddy Scannell suggests that from about the same time there was some falling away from the public service ideal in the sphere of classical music. We have already seen that there was a general policy within the Music Department to educate the mass audience into an appreciation of such music. However, the Department came under growing pressure from the administrators not so much to raise popular taste to the level of the music as to 'jazz it up' – in effect to lower the music to the level of popular taste.

The other signs of popularization were those which occurred in the *sequence* and *format* of the programmes, notably the development of routinized or 'fixed point' scheduling. It will be remembered that one of the aims of Reith's concept of mixed programming was to combat lazy or routine listening. Frequently there were pauses between programmes to enable listeners to adjust to a change of stimulus or even to switch off (in the *Radio Times* they were actually urged to 'give the wireless a rest' from time to time).

During the early 1930s fixed point scheduling – the transmission of the same or similar programmes at the same time every day – was generally avoided. Apart from news and special items like religious services and charity appeals, the great bulk of the programmes dodged about from week to week. Even popular series had only short runs and were replaced by something of quite different appeal. Programme under- or over-shoots were common and continuity was leisurely.

Reporting the inroads which were being made into the BBC's audience by the European stations, the Listener Research Section confirmed what by the late 1930s must have been the observations, if not the intuitions, of many programme producers: that except at moments of national crisis, mourning or celebration, or during big sporting events, radio was treated by most people as little more than 'a cheerful noise in the background', a mere domestic utility.

It is difficult to determine what influence listener research had upon the scheduling and format of the BBC's programmes, but these began to change at about the same time as it was making its findings, and Scannell and Cardiff (1982) observe that by 1937 there were as many as forty fixed points in the weekday output of each week. Just as significantly, there was a growth in the number of series and serials, which strengthened continuity from one day's fixed point to that of the next, and in the case of soap operas (*The English Family Robinson* began in 1938) mirrored something of the domestic continuity of the listeners' own lives. Thus because wireless broadcasts were received in the home, the scheduling, and even to some extent the content, of the programmes came increasingly to reflect daily routine rather than offering entertainment which broke with it as the theatre and cinema did.

The series or serial format could of course characterize not only drama but talks, features, concerts, or almost any other kind of programme. But it had a further significance for the Corporation. As Scannell and Cardiff (1991) so shrewdly point out, it was the most efficient way of meeting the unrelenting demands of the daily programme schedule, providing a fixed structure which could accommodate changes of content, locating novelty and surprise within the familiar and predictable. Moreover the problem of generating fresh material, a problem which was made harder by the disparate cultural backgrounds of the national audience, was alleviated by the shared culture that could be built up within the series itself, in the form of signature tunes, catch-phrases, stock characters and past themes. (In passing, we might add that programmes of all kinds could increasingly draw upon the broader culture which was developing within broadcasting: the common knowledge of other programmes and personalities and of the ethos and idiosyncrasies of the BBC.)

Of course, routinized and formatted programming was not an invariable sign of popularization: highbrow themes could also benefit from this treatment, and often did. But there is no doubt that it was especially suited to those kinds of output which did not require close attention or could be assimilated without too much effort, and which were therefore preferred by the great majority of listeners.

Two cheers for democracy

Those who condemn Reith for being arrogant and patronizing and for force-feeding the public with highbrow culture are just as likely to come back from other countries thankful that British television offers something more than an unvarying diet of populist entertainment: game shows, chat shows, soaps, sport, action movies, and news bulletins in which two presenters swap jokes in case the viewers are not finding the items exciting enough. Yet it is hardly an exaggeration to say that if in Britain we are aware that the media are capable of more than these things, it is thanks to the drag-anchor of Reith's influence – a man who quit broadcasting nearly sixty years ago.

In fact Reith's essentially conservative and elitist BBC was founded in a society whose commitment to democracy was already considerable and growing steadily. In 1918 all women over 30 were given the vote for the first time. In 1929 their minimum voting age was lowered to 21, and here as in certain other countries the democratic ideal has prevailed ever since, sometimes shining the more brightly amidst totalitarian regimes. In 1970 the franchise was widened yet further when the minimum voting age of both sexes was reduced to 18.

It was suggested in the last chapter that since Reith's policy of public service broadcasting strove to cater for each person's needs, it could also be seen as in some sense democratic; but it was not a policy in which its beneficiaries were given any say. That more orthodox version of democracy which considers the individual herself to be the best judge of what is good or right has long roots which are traceable to the religious and political conflicts of the sixteenth and seventeenth centuries. The Protestant Reformation exalted private judgement over the received authority of the Catholic Church, which it held to be arbitrary and unnecessary, and in the gradual disentanglement of politics from religion we can see the Civil War as a secular development of this, since it was largely a struggle to establish parliamentary democracy.

The United States prides itself on being a nation which was founded in democracy. The first white settlers in America sought to escape the religious and civil persecutions of their native Europe, and at the end of the eighteenth century the American War of Independence, fought on the principle of 'no taxation without representation', was a struggle to escape a British political system which denied them suffrage. Indeed the furtherance of the democratic ideal – the emancipation of black slaves – was a major cause of the American Civil War, which was to take place in the middle of the following century.

Historians have commonly linked the rise of democracy with the rise of capitalism and the development of a competitive, consumerist society, a common denominator being the sovereignty of individual taste or preference. As we might expect, these tendencies have gone rather further in America than here: not only in religion, politics and economics but in the arts and in intellectual matters generally, the customer is always right. As Scannell and Cardiff (1991) have pointed out, the classless and informal nature of American culture that the BBC tried to resist expressed the developing spirit of British democracy much better than the BBC did. The BBC sought to educate the masses: the American media catered to them on their own terms, giving them what they wanted.

Which of us, at some time, is not grateful for living in a democracy – in a society which allows each of us to judge and choose for herself? Even those who are living under a government which did not receive their vote know that it nevertheless owes its existence to votes, to the principle of popular choice. And in our daily lives, within what are fairly broad limits if compared with those of other socio-political systems, we can live as we like, believe in what we like, say, read and watch what we like. Perhaps one of the healthiest features of democracy is scepticism: we can impugn or ignore received wisdom, expertise or values; we can come to our own conclusions.

Indeed it is hard to resist the idea that the rise of democracy has owed something to scepticism and agnosticism, to an intellectual exhaustion after the futile religious and civil upheavals of several centuries; for the principle of one person, one vote seems to rest upon the assumption that one person's judgement is as good as another's, that there is no such thing as authority or expertise.

The conflict between the status of authority and the rights of the individual, between the fact that some people know more or better than others and the idea that each of us should be empowered or free to choose, is a central problem for political thinkers. Even though it should be wrong that the most sophisticated intellectual has no more than that single vote which is also the birthright of the ignoramus, in a democracy it seems right. The paradox troubled Reith, although he expressed it in terms which are characteristically moral as well as intellectual:

> There must be some principle of ethics or economics to justify equality of electoral power to an intelligent, responsible, respectable citizen, a producer by hand or brain, contributor in large or small measure to the wellbeing and wealth of the State; and to another unintelligent, irresponsible, a lifelong charge on the State.
>
> (Reith 1949: 170)

Thus while democracy elevates individual judgement it also, in a sense, debases it. If one person's view is as good as another's, then they are equally worthless. And what if the views differ? The consequence in a democracy is that qualitative criteria are replaced by, or become identified with, a merely quantitative one. In matters of culture we might say that terms like 'excellent', 'high quality', 'valuable' or 'worthwhile' are likely to be regarded either as meaningless or simply as synonymous with 'that which is preferred by most people'.

Most of us would rather watch such television programmes as game shows, soap-operas, rock videos, and soft porn and action movies than serious discussions, documentaries, operas, ballets, classical dramas and symphony concerts. Sometimes we may also be ready to cite their greater popularity as proof that they are better than the programmes we have rejected. But often what we reject is what we regard more highly. As the Roman poet Ovid put it: 'I see better things and approve them: I incline towards the worse.' Indeed among those who are keen to preserve highbrow television programmes are many who never watch them at all. What we avoid is often demanding and difficult, and what we watch is a soft option which we sense is less good for us, just as toffee may be sweeter but less nourishing than fresh fruit.

The point, then, is that even when we find ourselves in the majority we generally feel that democratic preference is a poor guide to cultural value, not least because we are aware that at some time or other each of us might find herself in a minority. Instinctively we feel that cultural value is something to be determined on rational or intellectual grounds, even though there seems to be no general, or at any rate absolute, agreement on what is or is not culturally valuable. Instinctively we defend our tastes not by claiming that most people share them but by some exercise of reason or logic, however limited or inarticulate. Even our verdicts 'programme A is rubbish' or 'programme B is brilliant' have some rationale implicit within them: we are unlikely to revise them simply because we are told that the former programme is popular or the latter unpopular.

In fact precisely because although the human impulse to reason and justify is universal, the ability to excel in it is rare, there abounds a kind of intellectual snobbery which sees an *inverse* relationship between cultural value and popularity. Some of us will cite a programme's popularity as evidence that it is *bad*, or choose to approve another because nobody else does.

Those of us who were alive when rock 'n' roll was born in the mid-1950s will remember that the music was nothing if not populist – innocent of all pretensions to cultural value. This of course invited the judicious disapproval of our parents. Yet critics have long since sprung up who claim to be able to make qualitative distinctions within rock music. Using criteria which elude some of us, they have a tendency to esteem the obscure and uncommercial and dismiss anything that gets into the charts.

The purpose of this discussion has been to suggest that even though Reith's concept of public service broadcasting has been gradually eroded by the tides of democracy and free competition, there is a sense in which nothing has changed, for people continue to determine cultural values not primarily by counting heads but by invoking reason and intellect. They thus make judgements which are, in their way, every bit as elitist as Reith's were.

The Home Service and the Forces Programme

The Second World War was the first total war: because of the Blitz, the bombardment of our major cities by the German air force, British civilians were as much in the battle zone as the troops were – and so, of course, was the BBC. It was also the first ideological war, a conflict of words in which radio played a greater part than did the medium of print. And besides these challenges the BBC had broadcasting duties which would be normal in any war: to provide an

extensive and credible news service and to raise and maintain national morale with a varied diet of entertainment.

To adapt to its wartime role the Corporation expanded rapidly. In 1939 it consisted of 4,000 personnel, but by the beginning of 1940 they had increased to 6,000, and by its end to 11,000.

During the war there was also an interesting development in the way that radio was listened to. Having been largely a domestic medium it became simultaneously domestic and public because there was a need to reach listeners in those collective situations that war required or created: workers in factories and canteens, officers in messes, soldiers in camps and barracks. When the war ended radio largely reverted to its domestic role, although it is still collectively listened to in many warehouses, shops and factories.

It was also during the war that the BBC was forced for the first time to learn a great deal about its audience. Since the war effort depended so much on the workers in the factories, shipyards and mines, as well as upon thousands of ordinary servicemen and women, their tastes had to be discovered and catered for; and as we shall shortly see, the populist tendency within the output became so strong that when war ended it was no longer reversible.

On the outbreak of hostilities in 1939 the BBC removed some of its operations to the provinces, notably Oxford, Evesham, Bristol, Bangor, Manchester and Glasgow, and combined its national and regional networks into a single *Home Service*. Broadcasting was certainly difficult while these organizational changes were being made, but at first the Corporation seemed to think that because life was serious its programmes should be dull, and it offered a leaden routine of public announcements, concerts by Sandy Macpherson at the BBC theatre organ, ministerial pep talks and gramophone records. Even members of the government joined in the protests.

By contrast, the broadcasts of the pro-German radio propagandist, William Joyce, attracted a good deal of interest. First heard from Hamburg in 1939, in the droning, hyper-refined tones which earned him the nickname Lord Haw-Haw, Joyce seems to have been treated by most listeners as a fascinating, slightly spooky joke. But the joke wore thin when the Germans invaded the Low Countries in 1940, and from that point his audience dwindled.

By this time there was more worthwhile listening at home, for in the same year the BBC launched a second network, the *Forces Programme*, which was intended to maintain the morale of the troops forming the British Expeditionary Force in France. Asa Briggs (1970) observes that the theory behind the contrast between the Home Service and the Forces Programme was not so much that civilians' and soldiers' tastes differed as that their listening conditions did. Certainly the kinds of programmes which the new network carried – variety shows, dance music, talks and the occasional classical concert – were familiar enough: it was the relative narrowness of the mixture and the lightness with which it was presented that were new.

What helped to shape the Forces Programme was pressure from the military authorities, who were hoping that a flow of entertaining and undemanding programmes would dissipate the boredom of the troops. Their hand was strengthened by a report on the troops' listening habits which was commissioned by the BBC from A. P. Ryan and entitled *Listening by the BEF*. Ryan observed that the great majority of service people lent a deaf ear to 'cultural' output, and he urged the Corporation to stop broadcasting 'the more austere kind of programmes' and to build on the respect which it already commanded from the public in order to win its affection.

The Forces Programme was intended just for the troops and just for the duration of the war: it was assumed that the civilian population would maintain its allegiance to the more serious Home Service. But by 1942 the former was being listened to by even more civilians than service people and commanding a total audience 50 per cent higher than that of the Home Service. By late 1942 the BBC was also providing the *General Overseas Service* for troops stationed abroad, and in February 1944, when the invasion of France was imminent and the bulk of the armed forces would be moved overseas, it combined the two networks to form the *General Forces Programme*.

The significance of the forces networks was that they began a process of cultural streaming within the BBC's output which would conclude only with the reorganization of Radios 1 to 4 in 1970. Before the war Reith and his successor F. W. Ogilvie adhered to the full mixed programming concept, seeing it as vital to the cultural improvement of the nation. As we have seen, its justification was that if programmes were stratified within separate networks the individual listener would no longer be exposed to the full range and richness of the BBC's output.

The forces networks were intended to be a temporary dilution, not an abandonment, of this concept – a dilution acceptable only in the peculiar conditions of wartime. They offered mixed programming of a sort, but the mixture was noticeably thinner. We have seen that there was less variety in its ingredients and a more uniform lightness of tone. When the war ended there would be a return to the *status quo*. But it soon became clear that their popularity would allow no simple return to the old mixed programming networks, and the BBC would have to find some compromise between its public service ideals and the consistently lighter tastes of many of its listeners.

The sounds of war: news

During the war the BBC's relationship with the government inevitably became even more delicate than before. Since the General Strike governments had made fitful attempts to bring the Corporation to heel, usually when they thought that those it invited to the microphone were politically too extreme, or that its treatment of issues like unemployment was likely to provoke social unrest. The wartime government shared the general belief that in the present situation broadcasting would be a powerful, possibly a decisive, weapon of propaganda, and therefore decided that the BBC should be made firmly accountable to the Ministry of Information.

The BBC, however, had other ideas. At the outset of the war it took the policy decision to tell the truth, as far as the truth could be ascertained, rather than create propaganda – perhaps the wisest decision it has ever taken. In pursuit of this policy, it succeeded in maintaining a measure of independence from the various government departments, though Curran and Seaton (1991) suggest that this was in large part due to muddle and incompetence at the Ministry of Information.

It was thanks to the war that radio at last came into its own as a rapid news medium. The newspapers were in any case handicapped by the shortage of newsprint, but at such a time the newness of the news was of paramount importance and this was something in which even a healthy press could never have competed with broadcasting. The BBC's 9 am bulletin reached huge and hungry audiences calculated at between 43 and 50 per cent of the population, and the pressure of events combined with important advances in technology to create a revolution in the way the news was presented.

Before the war, bulletins had consisted of little more than straight readings of a text, in which style was often given more attention than intelligibility. Now the priority was reversed: there was a new concern to use syntax and vocabulary which were more appropriate to the sound medium, and to find newsreaders whose accents were more broadly representative of the audience, less particularly associated with the privileged. One improbable recruit was Wilfred Pickles, who hailed unmistakably from Yorkshire.

As the war progressed bulletins developed from simple readings into something richer. News-gathering became much more systematic and efficient, and from 1944 the BBC began to appoint its own correspondents. Moreover the bulletins were supplemented by extended news programmes like *Radio Newsreel*, which began in 1940. As we observed at the beginning of Part I, 'newsreel' was a term borrowed from film, and hints at the BBC's eagerness to incorporate actuality into news presentation. In order to do so it needed to adopt new production techniques, to combine newsreading, correspondents' reports, actuality and comment in ways which would lend the news depth and perspective.

The use of actuality would, of course, have been all but impossible without some improvement in the ponderous technology of sound recording that had characterized the pre-war years. But quite apart from its use in the battle zones, recording became important to the studio production of news and its associated material. From about 1941 it removed the need to bring broadcasters into studios which were threatened by air raids and provided reserve material if programming schedules were disrupted. Furthermore, it allowed producers to clear in advance any material which government ministries might regard as 'sensitive', and it facilitated both the export of material (known as 'bottled programmes') to the Empire and the United States and the monitoring of German and Italian broadcasts.

Nevertheless it was in the BBC correspondents' reports from the battle zones that improved recording technology had a dramatic effect. The Germans had done most to develop this technology, yet used it to much less effect than did the British. Reporters such as Richard Dimbleby and Wynford Vaughan-Thomas were put through the same battle training as the soldiers and equipped with 'portable' disc recorders which were actually extremely heavy. Weighing forty pounds and carrying twelve double-sided discs, they could be used to send back front-line dispatches which with skilful studio editing enabled commentary and actuality to be powerfully integrated.

On D-Day, 6 June 1944, the BBC launched another extended news programme, *War Report*, which quickly commanded regular audiences of 10 to 15 million in Britain alone, as well as being heard in many other parts of the world.

The sounds of war: entertainment

As Stephen Barnard (1989) points out, the war was the first time in which broadcast entertainment was used for ideological purposes: to cheer people up and bind them together. Perhaps no single programme contributed more to these purposes than a wartime comedy show with a superficially bizarre title: *ITMA*.

In the last chapter we observed that during the 1920s and most of the 1930s radio producers continued to think of comedy and the other forms of light entertainment in terms of the conventional stage. When they were no longer able to broadcast live relays from the theatres, they frequently re-created the conditions of the theatre within the broadcasting studio.

The first realization that radio might be able to create its own distinctive kind of comedy came with the unpromisingly titled *Band Waggon*, which began in 1938. Though primarily conceived as a music show, it contained comic interludes featuring Arthur Askey and Richard Murdoch. These were a conventional blend of quickfire gags and sitcom − Askey and Murdoch were the occupants of an imaginary flat on top of Broadcasting House; but it lit the blindness of radio with a streak of surrealism. The flatmates were custodians of the pips in the Greenwich Time Signal, and on one occasion a grand piano was heard slipping down the back of their settee.

When *Band Waggon* ended in 1939, the Variety Department was keen to replace it with another show which would mine the radiogenic seam it had opened. The result, which was built round the comedian Tommy Handley, already a seasoned radio performer, was *It's That Man Again*, a title borrowed from a headline which was frequently used by the *Daily Express* to announce the latest activities of Adolf Hitler.

Soon known by its acronym *ITMA*, the show began slowly but was given an enormous boost by the onset of war. In every episode Handley acted as master of ceremonies and was visited by a motley sequence of characters – Mrs Mopp the cleaning woman, Colonel Chinstrap, Funf the German spy, Ali Oop, and many others. A special feature of the show was a door which was fitted with a variety of handles, locks and bolts. Each character would make an audibly different entrance, exchange rapid comic dialogue with Handley, and then depart with a slam.

ITMA was peculiarly suited to radio because it exploited the speed, surprise and unstable reality that are the inherent properties of a blind medium. The characters came and went as fast as could be imagined, but faster than could be seen: driven by puns and sound effects, situations would take unpredictable turns.

The formal innovation, catchphrases, word-play and surrealism were certainly popular, but what struck a universal chord were the jokes about the dreariness of wartime: the queues, the rationing (one character, a senior civil servant, was fittingly named Sir Short Supply), the black market, bureaucracy and bumbledom. At its peak *ITMA* was attracting audiences of 15 million a week, and although that figure must have included some repeat listeners (each show was broadcast three times) it amounts to almost 40 per cent of the entire population.

Though their timing and delivery are faultless *ITMA*'s jokes may now be so dated as to be scarcely comprehensible; it may also be true that during the war people were so desperate to laugh that they thought the shows funnier than they were: but when Handley died suddenly in 1949 he was mourned as someone who had brought mirth and joy to an otherwise dismal and tragic world, and he was the first comedian to be honoured by a memorial service in St Paul's Cathedral.

Radio comedy may have given particular enjoyment, but in terms of the amount of air-time it could fill it was clearly a less 'efficient' form of entertainment than music. Music, popular and classical, live and recorded, filled hour after hour, a banal yet comforting presence in millions of homes. The government and the BBC collaborated in certain quasi-scientific attempts to use music to raise morale and productivity. In June 1940 *Music While You Work*, a half-hour programme of band music which was broadcast twice a day, was launched for relay by loudspeakers in factories. Its aim was to keep mass production at a steady rate by broadcasting a non-stop sequence of jaunty, popular tunes, all of the same tempo. As Barnard points out, it was an early acknowledgement from the BBC of the background function of radio music. By 1944 the programme was being heard in over 8,000 factories with a total workforce of more than 4.5 million.

Another programme whose aim was to boost morale and production was *Workers' Playtime*, launched in 1941. It was the brainchild of the Minister of Labour, Ernest Bevin, and brought variety acts and audience singalongs to munitions and other factories. What is interesting is that both these shows outlived their original objectives – and indeed outlasted the war – by many years: *Workers' Playtime* survived until 1964, while *Music While You Work* died only with the Light Programme in 1967.

Also beginning in 1941 was *Sincerely Yours*, a showcase for the singer Vera Lynn which was especially aimed at the men in the armed forces. Curran and Seaton (1991) point out that the military authorities believed the show was a serious mistake because the unsexy persona of the singer and her sentimental songs would have an enervating effect on the fighting men. In fact, the idea of a homespun girl pining for her boy but proud that he was doing his duty provided just the antidote to the suggestions of German propaganda that back at home the soldiers' women-folk were being unfaithful to them. Vera Lynn became the great icon of the Second World War, 'the forces' sweetheart'.

Not all entertainment was 'light' entertainment. From June 1940 the writer J. B. Priestley delivered a series of chats to a nation at war under the title of *Postscript*. Their determined, stoical tone exactly caught the national mood, but they were dropped in October after the Conservatives objected to Priestley's evident socialist sympathies, only to be reinstated for a short run in 1941.

Even more stimulating was *The Brains Trust*, a highbrow discussion programme which considered questions that were sent in by the listeners, and was first heard in June 1941. The panel consisted of the philosopher C. E. M. Joad, the zoologist Julian Huxley and – a populist gesture this – Commander A. B. Campbell, a bluff naval officer with a penchant for tall stories. It is extraordinary to think that this programme, which wrestled with problems of philosophy, art and science, engrossed a third of the population; but perhaps because it reminds us of the fragility of our existence, war seemed to sharpen the enthusiasm for everything – comedy and variety certainly, but also serious things: as well as *The Brains Trust*, traditional drama and classical music.

One important feature of wartime entertainment was the growing influence of American culture, an influence which was felt in a number of spheres and in several ways. For popular music the BBC was obliged, for obvious reasons, to make increasing use of gramophone records. But as Stephen Barnard points out, the shortage of raw materials meant that no British records were being made, and so most of the wartime releases were American.

As the war progressed increasing numbers of US military personnel were stationed in Britain, and to cater for their needs the *American Forces Network* (AFN) was set up in London in 1943 – the first, and temporary, domestically based breach of the BBC's monopoly. In fact, the low-power transmissions it beamed to the US bases were all but inaudible to more than 10 per cent of the native population, but it was to have an important indirect effect on British broadcasting.

Removing the commercial breaks, the American Forces Network simply re-broadcast the most popular music and comedy shows of the US domestic networks: it is not surprising that by comparison American service personnel had a low opinion of the BBC. But the AFN's slick, tight mode of presentation had an important influence on the British Forces Programme. Because from 1944 the latter was also broadcasting overseas, where its listeners would have no *Radio Times* but would still expect to hear their favourite programmes, it developed a greater regularity of scheduling and sharpness of timing.

We have already seen that fixed point scheduling was developing on the British networks before the war began, but this tendency was now strengthened not only on the Forces Programme but the Home Service. It is interesting to note that on the Home Service the hugely popular *Saturday Night Theatre* had routine built into its very title. Moreover it was at this stage that the continuity system – in which a single announcer is in charge of an entire evening's output, rather as a conductor is in charge of an orchestra – was introduced on both networks in order to eliminate pauses which during wartime could be alarming.

By 1944 American variety shows were being syndicated to the BBC, and British listeners became captivated by such stars as Bob Hope, Bing Crosby, Glenn Miller, Jack Benny, the Andrews Sisters and Frank Sinatra. It is perhaps at this point that British popular culture began to be dominated by that of America, a dominance whose end is not yet in sight.

Broadcasting in wartime: an assessment

The war years are of significance to our history partly because they were the occasion of particular achievements by the BBC and partly because they demonstrated the nature and capabilities of broadcasting in general. These two things are, of course, connected: it was largely because of what the BBC achieved that the nature and capabilities of broadcasting became clearer; but they were also directly illuminated by the war inasmuch as broadcasting proved much less vulnerable to its effects than did the other modes of mass communication.

Perhaps the BBC's greatest wartime success was to honour its original wise decision to tell the truth as far as it could, rather than create propaganda. Because its sources of information were limited and because national security sometimes called for the suppression of certain facts, it could not tell the whole truth; but it consciously eschewed lies and distortions and thus gained an immeasurable advantage over the stations of the enemy. Since it told the bad news – and there was nothing but bad news until the victory at El Alamein in November 1942 – its good news could also be believed, and it came to be depended on in much of occupied Europe, where the penalty for listening could be death, as well as in other parts of the world.

But it was perhaps even more important that the BBC could be believed at home, because by telling the truth it matched the nation's concept of itself as fighting a just war, waging a moral crusade against evil and tyranny. Surveys suggested that by the end of the war people placed much more trust in wireless as a news medium, presumably because the BBC's willingness to tell unpleasant truths meant that it could not be as closely associated with the government as, fairly or unfairly, it had been in pre-war years.

What also increased the public's esteem for the BBC was the fact that whether it wished to or not it shared their experiences of fighting on the home front. Many of its operations were moved out to the provinces, but its core was still in London, and six of its employees were killed when Broadcasting House was bombed in 1940 – the explosion causing a slight pause in a news bulletin. The building was bombed again later, but the Corporation soldiered on, radiating imperturbable good cheer from the thick of the Blitz.

Hence the BBC helped to sustain the nation's morale not just by telling the truth, nor merely by setting an example of courage in the face of danger, but by the very steadiness and familiarity of its output, which as Gorham (1952) remarks had a reassuring effect in an otherwise topsy-turvy world. However more can be claimed for its output than mere familiarity, for as we have seen its news and light entertainment were highly appreciated. Moreover they were increasingly conceived of in terms of the characteristics and resources of sound broadcasting itself: news was no longer seen as something that really belonged in the newspapers, nor comedy as something that had to be adapted from the stage.

The huge audiences for its programmes certainly did credit to the BBC, but also reflect the fact that radio was almost the only medium of information and entertainment which could survive in wartime – and this, too, was thanks to those characteristics which set it apart from the other media. Most of the cinemas, theatres, concert halls and sports stadiums were closed down, and although George Bernard Shaw deplored this act as 'a masterstroke of unimaginative stupidity' it is difficult to see how they could have remained open during the Blitz. People felt safest in their homes, or at any rate preferred to be bombed there than elsewhere, and to rely for their news and entertainment on those two domestic media, the newspapers and the radio. But aside from the hazards involved in distributing and delivering them, the newspapers were severely reduced in size by the shortage of newsprint. That left radio.

As Scannell and Cardiff (1991) observe, what radio actually did was to locate public within domestic life, probably more so than newspapers could ever have done, since it brought the *sounds* of the public sphere, not simply descriptions of it, into the privacy of the home. Moreover because of the scarcity of the other media and the momentousness of wartime events, it gave the individual an unprecedented sense of herself as part of the larger community. She became aware that she was one of countless others, all listening to much the same thing. As Eric Hobsbawm puts it, radio:

> though essentially centred on individual and family, created its own public sphere. For the first time in history people unknown to each other who met knew what each other had in all probability heard . . . the night before: the big game, the favourite comedy show, Winston Churchill's speech, the contents of the news bulletin.
>
> (1994: 196)

In this respect radio was very much like a party host who helps strangers to become friends by referring them to experiences they have in common. The point, then, is that when the BBC's role in uniting the nation and raising its morale has been freely admitted, there was something conducive to that end in the very nature of broadcasting.

The war was not an unalloyed success story for the BBC. As we have seen, it soon discovered that the full Reithian diet of mixed programming did not command the absolute support of its listeners, and that when the war was over it would have to find a new, more acceptable expression of its public service ideals.

Post-war reconstruction

In the light of its experiences with the Home Service and the Forces Programme the BBC laid its plan for post-war broadcasting in 1943, well before hostilities ended.

This would consist of a new, tripartite system. The General Forces Programme would be replaced by a *Light Programme* which would resemble it in style and content. The *Home Service* would continue as in essence a London-based network, which a federation of regional services – Scottish, Northern, Midland, West, Welsh and Northern Irish – could draw upon. And there would also be a *Third Programme*, a highbrow network dedicated to the arts, philosophy, serious discussion and experimental programmes.

Taken as a whole, the three networks were an attempt to provide for popular tastes without abandoning the old Reithian seriousness of purpose. They were a continuing expression of his idea of public service broadcasting in the sense that their combined output embraced the same range, catered for the same miscellany of interests, as BBC broadcasting always had. And within each network there was still a mixture of programmes, albeit somewhat attenuated – a variety of genres and content.

However, the new system was populist in the sense that the 'improving function' was transferred from the networks to the listener. She could *choose* to be 'improved' rather than having improvement thrust upon her; and the choice was real, because although all the networks carried a mixture of programming they were to a considerable extent stratified or banded into highbrow (Third), middlebrow (Home), and lowbrow (Light). As a way of sharpening listener choice, the Home and the Light, in particular, were expected to compete with each other.

For several years after Reith's departure from the BBC those who followed him as Director General were undistinguished. Then in 1944 William Haley, a former editor at the *Manchester Guardian*, was appointed. Haley's first important task was to 'sell' the new tripartite system to the government on the one hand and the general public on the other, especially as the Corporation's Charter was due for renewal at the end of 1946. The influential sections of the nation, many of them in or close to the government, had largely accepted Reith's premise that broadcasting should be serious and improving; but the mass of the people inclined to the opposite view, and there were even demands in some quarters for a new inquiry to consider the introduction of competition.

Haley's explanation of the new system illustrates the tightrope the BBC was trying to walk:

> Before the war the system was to confront [the listener] with the necessity for pendulum-like leaps. [S/He] was deliberately plunged from one extreme to the other. The devotees of Berlin (Irving) were suddenly confronted with Bach. Many listeners were won for higher things in this way, but many were irretrievably lost. For the weakness of the system was that so many intolerances were set up.
>
> (Smith 1974: 83)

What Haley is regretting here as a 'weakness' is precisely that element of serendipity, of being exposed to valuable things by chance, that Reith envisaged as the strength of his system. Henceforth, thanks to stratified programming the listener would be exposed to no more surprises. In this respect the new plan was a significant dilution of Reith's original concept of public service broadcasting. Indeed it was in his sense of the word 'undemocratic', because in not automatically exposing the less educated listeners to at least some highbrow content it reinforced social and cultural divisions. Reith denounced it in his diary as 'an absolute abandonment of everything I stood for'.

Nevertheless Haley's approving reference to listeners being 'won for higher things' illustrates the extent to which Reith's philosophy still held sway in broadcasting. Some mixture of programming would be retained within each network, but more than this, listeners would be encouraged to work their way up through the network system. The idea was that there would be a degree of overlap between the Light and the Home (indeed these differed more in tone than in substance) and between the Home and the Third, in order to give the overall system an edifying purpose. Haley perceived it as a 'cultural pyramid':

> This pyramid is served by three main Programmes, differentiated but broadly overlapping in levels and interest, each Programme leading on to the other, the listener being induced through the years increasingly to discriminate in favour of the things that are more worth-while. Each Programme at any given moment must be ahead of its public, but not so much as to lose their confidence. The listener must be led from good to better by curiosity, liking, and a growth of understanding. As the standards of the education and culture of the country rise so should the programme pyramid rise as a whole.
>
> (Smith 1974: 83)

Hence though diluted, the public service concept was far from being discarded, and the tripartite system heralded an Indian summer of sound broadcasting which would partly overlap with the rise of television in the 1950s.

On 29 July 1945 the General Forces Programme was replaced without a break by the very similar Light Programme. After the wartime discoveries of the audience researchers, it was here that the concern with listening figures was most acute, and perhaps best typified by the rise of the music request programme. *Forces' Favourites* was replaced by *Family Favourites*, and the latter was complemented by *Housewives' Choice* – a new vein of radio populism in that listeners determined programme content.

The Third Programme was launched on 29 September 1946 and gave prompt and stern notice of its highbrow preoccupations. Amid much classical music its early listeners were treated to an eighty-three-part series on the ideas and beliefs of the Victorians and a six-part translation of Goethe's *Faust* by the poet Louis MacNeice. It was also on the Third Programme that Bertrand Russell was allowed to question the existence of God.

The new tripartite system not only settled the long-term future of broadcasting but secured the BBC's immediate objective. A new Labour government was elected in 1946, with many other and far graver problems to face than broadcasting. Mindful of the BBC's strong war record and that the newly completed network reforms would need some time to bed down, it renewed the Corporation's Charter without appointing a committee of inquiry, though for only five years instead of the usual ten.

Sources/further reading

For the circumstances leading to the foundation of Radios Normandie and Luxembourg and for their early development see Briggs (1965), Baron (1975), Barnard (1989) and Chapman (1992). A broadcaster's memories of pre-war commercial radio are in Plomley (1980). Gifford (1985) and Donovan (1992) provide vivid accounts of Luxembourg's programming, and Gifford also gives details of Normandie's. The importance to the commercial stations of the first attempts at audience research is stressed by Pegg (1983).

The trend towards popularization in BBC talks during the latter half of the 1930s is in Cardiff (1980), and Scannell (1981) traces a similar tendency in its approach to classical music. A more general account of the growth of popularization and of cultural and social streaming is given by Scannell and Cardiff (1982), who as well as Silvey (1974) also outline the early findings of audience research which coincided with it. For the cultural significance of the development of fixed point scheduling and of series and serial formats see Scannell and Cardiff (1982; 1991).

The last-named book explores the ways in which the early BBC expressed corporate national life, but also explains why the American culture that the BBC tried to resist better expressed the new British democracy. For his meditations on the problem of reconciling democratic rights with intellectual and moral inequalities see Reith (1949).

The standard history of wartime broadcasting is Briggs (1970), but for a brilliant résumé of the unprecedented nature of the Second World War and of the role of radio within it see Cardiff and Scannell (1981). The characteristic flavour of wartime programmes is captured in Black (1972a) and Parker (1977), with more factual descriptions in Gifford (1985) and Donovan (1992).

As well as giving a helpful general account of broadcasting and the Second World War, Curran and Seaton (1991) indicate how successfully the BBC's music and light entertainment output expressed the popular mood. For the origins of radiogenic comedy see Cardiff (1988). A more general, theoretical discussion of its evolution is in Crisell (1986; 1994). Took (1976) describes *Band Waggon* and *ITMA*, and for a detailed account of the latter written by the show's producer, see Worsley (1948).

An excellent account of the BBC's wartime music policy and of the growing American influence on British popular culture is in Barnard (1989). Another valuable account of programming during the war, including the American influence on the development of fixed point scheduling and improved programme continuity in the British networks, is in Gorham (1952).

That assimilation of public to domestic life which is a general feature of broadcasting but which became particularly significant during the war is acutely described in Scannell and Cardiff (1991) and in Hobsbawm (1994).

For particularly helpful accounts of the establishment of the BBC's tripartite network system at the end of the war see Barnard (1989) and Curran and Seaton (1991). The latter proposes the interesting argument that the social philosophy which underlay this system was essentially that which inspired the government's educational reforms of 1944. Haley's explanation of the cultural pyramid is quoted in Smith (1974), and Carpenter (1996) gives a full history of the Third Programme and its successor, Radio 3.

Chapter 4

The golden age of radio and the rise of television

The golden age of radio and the rise of television

Listeners' harvest

Between 1945 and about 1960 BBC radio enjoyed what was probably its greatest era, broadcasting distinguished programmes of every kind, many of them regional in origin, to audiences of several million. The pioneering *Radio Newsreel* continued into peacetime: one of its achievements was an eyewitness report of the assassination of Mahatma Gandhi in 1947. Among special interest programmes the long-running *Children's Hour* was joined soon after the war by *Woman's Hour* on the Light Programme and, since the BBC seemed to take horticulture more seriously than it took women, by *Gardeners' Question Time* on the Home Service.

From 1948 *Any Questions?*, which was first heard on the West Region, complemented *The Brains Trust* as a discussion programme which managed to be both serious and popular. Features continued to thrive, and though they might just as easily have taken a turn in the direction of documentaries or current affairs, became closely associated with radio drama, examples of which regularly won the BBC the Italia Prize for Drama between 1947 and 1955.

Radio drama included adaptations of classic stage plays, but also many plays which were especially written for the medium by such established writers as Giles Cooper and Henry Reed, some of them now widely regarded as part of the literary canon. Perhaps the three most famous of these made-for-radio plays are Louis MacNeice's *The Dark Tower* (Home Service, 1946), Dylan Thomas's *Under Milk Wood* (Third Programme, 1954), and Samuel Beckett's *All That Fall* (Third Programme, 1957).

But much drama was not highbrow. There were hugely popular serials on the Light Programme – crime (*Dick Barton*, *Special Agent* began in 1947) and science fiction (*Journey into Space* blasted off in 1953) - as well as two enduring soap operas, from 1948 *Mrs Dale's Diary*, and three years later, *The Archers*, subtitled 'an everyday story of country folk' and still thriving on Radio 4.

We now hear and watch so many examples of soap opera that we are no longer aware of its formal and cultural originality, something it owes entirely to broadcasting: for the same reason we overlook the oddity, even obscurity, of its name. Since 'soap' refers to advertising it is clear that the genre came from America, where because of their domestic themes the early radio serials attracted the sponsorship of detergent makers. The facetious 'opera' was added presumably because these serials share opera's predilection for story-lines which are slow-moving yet somewhat melodramatic.

Soap opera clearly has its roots in cultural forms which pre-date the age of broadcasting, notably the sentimental novel, serial magazine fiction and even serial films. Nevertheless it is a genre peculiar to broadcasting, and we shall look at its original features when we come to consider the even greater popularity of soaps on television.

At the end of Chapter 3 we noted a new strain of programming which showed a greater awareness of the circumstances of the listener, and in some instances sought to give her more of a 'presence' on the medium. *Family Favourites* and *Housewives' Choice* began with the Light Programme, while *Music While You Work* and *Workers' Playtime* were carried over from the war. They were soon joined by *Have a Go!*, a quiz show which started in the North Region and under its Yorkshire compère Wilfred Pickles, whose heart was as warm as his accent was broad, travelled the length and breadth of the country 'presenting the people to the people'.

Of all the BBC's attempts at demotic radio this was the most successful, attracting an audience during the 1950s which was estimated at 20 million. The 'ordinary folk' who came to the microphone were asked a few simple questions and their answers were always followed by Pickles' catch-phrase 'Give 'em the money, Barney!' – little more than a week's house-keeping but enough to make the programme a touchingly innocent forerunner of the big prize shows on ITV.

As always the BBC provided a vast amount of music of all kinds, but it was perhaps in the field of comedy that its greatest achievements lay. What is astonishing about this post-war period is not just the number and variety of comedy shows it developed, but their durability: most lasted five, many ten years or more. In any one year of the 1950s the listener could enjoy episodes of no fewer than five different shows.

In popularity the rival and immediate successor to *ITMA*, which ended in 1949, was *Much Binding in the Marsh* (1947–53), though it eschewed surrealism for a more conventional sitcom format. Other popular sitcoms were *Ray's a Laugh* (1949–61), starring the wise-cracking Liverpudlian Ted Ray; *Life with the Lyons*

(1950–61), which featured a real-life American family; and the extraordinary *Educating Archie* (1950–60), in which the star, Archie Andrews, was a dummy and the sidekick his ventriloquist, Peter Brough. A topical blend of sketches, skits and songs, *Take It From Here* (1948–59), was the first creation of those prolific scriptwriters Frank Muir and Denis Norden, and featured Jimmy Edwards and Dick Bentley.

Within this galaxy two shows managed to outshine the rest, and between them neatly typified the two main strands of radio comedy which had developed in the medium's short history. The first was the highly surrealistic *Goon Show* (1952–59), a fusion of the crass and the clever, of naivety and knowingness, which is the essence of all great clowning. Peter Black shrewdly referred to its 'explosive and bloodless violence . . . in which childlike anarchy was overlaid with the whiff of something less innocent' (1972a: 193). One could also see it as an endless, consummate celebration of the power and limitations of radio itself. Whatever the source of its appeal, it convulsed millions, many of the younger listeners using its catch-phrases as cultural passwords and attempting endless, mostly feeble imitations of the characters created by Spike Milligan, Peter Sellers and Harry Secombe.

The other great show, a sitcom which had its roots in the conventional theatre and which was therefore able to run concurrently on television from 1956, was *Hancock's Half Hour* (1954–61). But in its way *Hancock* was innovatory too, for its scriptwriters Alan Simpson and Ray Galton were interested not in creating a gag-show, but in using comic dialogue to explore and illuminate character. Its star, Tony Hancock, had previously had an undistinguished career in radio, but at different times supported by Sid James, Bill Kerr, Kenneth Williams and Hattie Jacques, now proved himself to be a great comic actor rather than a comedian. The lower middle-class character he created was idle, pompous and tetchy, with aspirations to nobler things which were constantly thwarted by the earthiness of his companions. Peter Black (1972a) writes of his 'seedy grandiloquence and unavailing pretensions' (191) and of a 'comedy of longing and failure' (196) from which pathos was never far away.

What lends poignancy to this era is that even as radio was producing programmes of unprecedented range and quality, fewer and fewer people were listening to it: by the second half of the 1950s it had already been supplanted as the major mass medium by a younger rival, whose birth and infancy we must now consider.

The early years of television

The search for ways of sending pictures over distances began almost as early as the efforts to transmit sound. The problem for scientists was to break down a sequence of images into units of information which could be transmitted by wireless, and the first attempts at a solution were mechanical – by the German, Paul Nipkow, and then by several others including the American Charles Francis Jenkins.

In 1884 Nipkow created a revolving disc with perforations which were arranged in a spiral pattern. A beam of light shone through these perforations as the disc was turned, causing the light to 'scan' an image. This device formed the basis of television experiments for many years to come because it was seen as a means of transmitting images in the form of a sequence of dots.

The other strand of research into the scanning of images was electronic: the cathode ray tube was developed by Karl Braun in 1897 and the photo-electric cell by Julius Elster and Hans Geitel in 1905. A major figure in this strand was Vladimir Zworykin, a refugee from the Russian Revolution who emigrated to the United States in the 1920s and worked for the Westinghouse Company and then, when its research was transferred to RCA, for the latter. His discoveries were later combined with those of an unlikely genius in Philo Farnsworth, a farmer's boy from Idaho.

However as Roy Armes (1988) points out, romantic tales of lone inventors and brilliant eccentrics should not blind us to the mundane fact that the major developments in television were the result of well-funded and systematic research by the major communications companies such as Marconi and RCA. Indeed the most romantic of the lone figures, the Scotsman John Logie Baird, pursued his ideas down a dead-end, persisting with the mechanical method of image scanning long after its limitations had become generally apparent.

Nevertheless Baird achieved one or two firsts and several publicity coups. He began demonstrations of his system at Selfridge's in 1925, televised moving images in the following year, and in 1928 sent the first intelligible TV signal across the Atlantic and began regular experimental transmissions in London. But much more productive were the $9 million which RCA invested in research during the 1930s.

The BBC became involved in developing television from about 1929 and was pressed by the Post Office to provide the facility for Baird to continue his transmissions, the first of which was received by about thirty sets. Initially, sound and vision occupied a single wavelength: the speaker was first seen without being heard, then heard without being seen. However in 1933 the BBC resolved to end Baird's experiments because the rival electronic technology seemed to be making more progress in the form of the American-originated EMI system.

In 1934 the government appointed the Selsdon Committee to consider the future of television broadcasting, and the latter recommended that a regular public television service should be operated by the BBC, using both the Baird and EMI systems on a weekly, alternating basis until the superiority of one or the other had been proved. It also recommended that the service should not carry advertising but be paid for out of the existing licence fee, although some form of sponsorship might be considered.

The government accepted these recommendations and the BBC Television Service opened on 2 November 1936. According to Roy Armes (1988) it was not the first regular TV service in the world: the Germans had begun theirs in March 1935. But since the latter was transmitting only 180-line pictures, the BBC could fairly claim credit for the first high-definition service. It transmitted from Alexandra Palace in north London and was received within a radius of 40 to 100 miles by a few thousand viewers in about 400 households. Early broadcasts ran for two separate hours a day, excluding Sundays, and the weekly programme budget was £1,000. In the first week viewers were treated to a comedy featuring Ben Lyon and Bebe Daniels, excerpts from a West End play called *Marigold*, a demonstration of tap dancing, and a talk from a bus driver on how to build model boats.

The service sounded the knell of the Baird system, and perhaps of the man himself since he lived only a few years longer. While research into picture composition was at the level of 60 to 100 lines, Baird could hold its own. But the high-definition pictures proposed by Selsdon had a threshold of 240 lines, the uppermost limit for Baird. The EMI system, using all-electronic, mobile cameras, delivered a picture of 405 lines, and in February 1937 the Baird system was dropped.

By modern standards even the EMI picture was dim. It was, of course, monochrome, as all television pictures would be for the next thirty years or so. The average TV screen was about eight inches by ten, and the pictures lacked definition and detail and would often distort or roll. Receivers could cost up to £100, the price of a small car at that time, although the cheapest could be had for about £35.

Nevertheless, even in the 1930s there were faint hints of the universal spell that the new medium would cast. By 1938 about 5,000 sets had been bought, and it is estimated that by the time the service closed 18,000 to 20,000 sets had been sold during the three years it had been running.

In this time of its infancy, television reflected the ambivalence which was felt towards it. On the one hand, because it was a new, expensive and not altogether reliable medium there was a tendency to regard it as frivolous, a toy for the rich. As Stuart Hood puts it:

Pre-war television was aimed at a small and affluent audience in London and the Home Counties, which had not been affected by the depression and mass unemployment. In the South-East prosperity based on the boom in building and light industry and in consumer goods like refrigerators and radios and the car industry financed the purchase of sets. The programmes the viewers wanted were dominated by the concept of the West End show, of the revue and the kind of entertainment which was the middle class audience's idea of a night out.

(1980: 60)

In response to this the BBC included Noel Coward's *Hay Fever* and Brandon Thomas's *Charley's Aunt* among the two or three plays a week it was broadcasting by 1938. The lack of gravity was confirmed by the Gaumont-British and British Movietone newsreels which the BBC offered instead of any news output of its own – exactly the same newsreels that were watched by cinema audiences.

On the other hand the service was a child of the BBC, and to that extent imbued with the same public service principles and obligations which John Reith had established in respect of radio. Just as long as television was new and there had to be more concern with its technical reliability than with its content, some lack of range and seriousness in the latter might be permissible. Even so, as well as light comedies, viewers were presented with plays by Beaumont and Fletcher, Shakespeare and George Bernard Shaw.

The major televised event of these pre-war years, and indeed television's first outside broadcast, was the coronation procession of George VI in May 1937. Coverage was provided by three fixed-point cameras at Hyde Park Corner: one viewed the procession as it approached, the second as it passed, the third as it receded. Despite poor weather the broadcast was accounted a great success and seen by between 10,000 and 50,000 viewers, some as far away as Ipswich and Brighton.

The beginning of the war brought the television service to an abrupt end in September 1939.

The BBC's post-war television service

The television service resumed in 1946, initially to about 15,000 households; but bolstered by a new combined radio and TV licence, price £2, it began to grow. In 1949 it was extended to the West Midlands, in 1951 to Manchester, and in the following year parts of Scotland, Wales and the West were covered. By 1954 the BBC was broadcasting about six hours of television a day, most of it live.

Nevertheless the service was fraught with problems, not all of the Corporation's making. There was the familiar opposition to a new medium from the controllers of old media and cultural genres. A boycott of television was variously imposed by the British film industry, the music halls, the West End theatre managers, and the controlling bodies of boxing and, except in respect of the Cup Final and certain international matches, of soccer. But the real problems were internal. For the next eight or ten years there was little understanding within the BBC of television's potential: indeed it is hard to avoid the conclusion that during this period the Corporation was in two minds about the medium.

On the one hand it was the monopoly broadcaster and felt that it should naturally assume responsibility for what was a new kind of broadcasting. On the other hand, as a culturally conservative organization the BBC did not warm to its task. Radio, an essentially verbal medium, was something that its staff, with their typically literate and literary backgrounds, could deal comfortably with. But television was pictures – and their suspicion that pictures were mindless and vulgar drew strength from the fact that cinema, a medium which was both new and popular, was widely regarded as lowbrow. Grace Wyndham Goldie describes their dilemma thus:

> . . . their speciality was the use of words; they had no knowledge of how to present either entertainment or information in vision, nor any experience of handling visual material. Moreover, most of them distrusted the visual; they associated vision with the movies and the music hall and were afraid that the high purposes of the Corporation would be trivialised by the influence of those concerned with what could be transmitted in visual terms.

> (1977: 18–19)

The post-war Director General, William Haley, shared that misunderstanding and dislike of television of his great predecessor, John Reith. Just as before the war Reith had thought of 'integrating' radio and television (Briggs 1965: 608), Haley insisted in 1949 that television was merely 'an extension' of sound broadcasting and that TV and radio were 'parts of one whole' (Paulu 1981: 54). He seems to have had in mind a service in which television would be a mere adjunct to radio rather than one whose essence would be visual: in the case of drama, for instance, it would mean bringing cameras into a radio studio to watch actors reading into microphones rather than shooting a 'television play' on purpose-built sets or in suitable locations.

What lent some respectability to this reductive view of television were the likely costs of a full-blooded service. In 1937 the BBC calculated that one hour of television was twelve times as expensive to produce as the costliest hour of radio, a ratio which has surely not diminished over the years. But it meant that after the war the service resumed not so much with the expectation that it would develop as that it would need to be curbed. Television programmes were the added responsibility of radio production departments, they were not produced from a separate source, and a rough indication of the funding they received is that in 1947–8 television accounted for less than one-tenth of total BBC expenditure. Even in 1950 the budget for television was only half that of the Home Service. This niggardliness prompted the resignation of two Television Controllers, the first in 1947 and his successor in 1950.

Nevertheless the BBC's brief monopoly of television was not without its achievements. Paddy Scannell points out that in the realm of politics the Corporation's radio and television coverage was limited. It saw politics as little more than a matter of politicians and parliament, while its treatment of current affairs was distanced, non-committal, even non-political: but with *Special Enquiry* (1952) it made a first attempt to create documentary programming which was telegenic.

By extreme contrast two frivolous yet durable TV shows originated at this time: *Come Dancing* in 1950 and *What's My Line?* in 1951, the latter a quiz game in which the winning contestants received not prizes but certificates. The first TV soap opera, *The Grove Family*, dates from early 1955, and perhaps the BBC's two most notable dramatic achievements were a science-fiction thriller, *The Quatermass Experiment* (1953), and a powerful adaptation of George Orwell's novel *1984* (1954), with Peter Cushing.

The BBC also achieved much in outside broadcasting. Those public events to which it was admitted – Wimbledon, the test matches, the Lord Mayor's Show – it covered well. In August 1950 it forged the first live television link between two countries when it transmitted from Calais to Britain. This was not a truly international broadcast since because of different line-standards it was not seen in France; but the first real Eurovision link followed in July 1952.

Without doubt the Corporation's greatest television triumph was its coverage of the coronation of Elizabeth II on 2 June 1953. It is widely regarded as having been the first ever 'media event', in the sense that although not created or prompted by television it seemed tailor-made for the medium, and was the first event to be watched and enjoyed in many parts of the world. It was recorded as it was televised, and the films were then flown for rapid re-broadcasting to Canada, the United States and elsewhere.

The BBC's coverage, for which it gained permission only after delicate negotiations with both Church and State, was impressive even by today's standards. Transmission began at ten in the morning and continued till eleven-thirty at night. Beginning with the service in Westminster Abbey, on which a hushed, reverential commentary was supplied by Richard Dimbleby, it continued with the procession to Buckingham Palace, which was covered by cameras at every vantage-point along the way and a further seven commentators. Some 56 per cent of the nation watched the service, 53 per cent the procession.

The coronation usefully symbolizes the point when television surpassed radio as the major mass medium. In itself it prompted a boom in the sales of TV sets, and 1953 was the first year in which more television than radio sets were manufactured, at an average unit price of about £85. But the coronation merely quickened a trend that had been apparent for some time, and the fact that television's ascendancy was established two full years before the arrival of commercial TV suggests that the nation did not find the BBC's programmes wholly unappealing.

One or two figures outline the trend. In 1951 nearly three-quarters of a million television licences were issued. In 1955 viewing began to exceed listening for the first time, and by 1958 9 million licences were held. Radio's figures are in their own sad way just as eloquent. The BBC's average evening audience in 1949 was almost 9 million: by 1958 it had shrunk to less than 3.5 million, three-quarters of whom had no access to a television set.

Yet although the coronation trumpeted not only the power of television but at last the ability of the BBC to make television of high quality, the Corporation's monopoly of the medium was about to end. This seems all the more surprising when we learn that only two years previously the monopoly had been approved by a government-appointed committee. What, from the Corporation's point of view, had gone wrong?

The Beveridge Report and its aftermath

In 1949 the Labour Government did what had become customary when the BBC's Charter was shortly to expire: it appointed a committee to enquire into the present state of broadcasting and make recommendations for the future. The chair was Lord Beveridge and the committee presented its bulky, thoughtful and well-reasoned report in January 1951. Though sensitive to the dangers of mono-poly and by no means uncritical of the Corporation, it recommended, but not unanimously and not without safeguards, the continuance of the BBC's broadcasting monopoly. It also opposed the introduction of advertising into the BBC's programmes. However, among its appendices was a minority report by the Conservative politician Selwyn Lloyd advocating competition in the form of a service paid for by advertising or, failing that, by some form of public funding.

The Beveridge Report was immediately made irrelevant by a general election and the return to power of the Conservatives, who extended the BBC's Charter for a further six months (later renewed until 1962) so that they could take their own look at broadcasting's long term future. But Curran and Seaton (1991) point out that Beveridge was not a total waste of effort and paper: it was to have two marked effects on the commercial broadcasting it disfavoured. First, its alertness to the danger that advertising would influence programme content ensured that ITV would carry 'spot' commercials and not sponsorship; second, its disapproval of what it termed the excessive 'Londonization' of the BBC provided the inspira-tion for ITV's regional structure.

Hence it was the Conservatives, or at any rate a well-organized minority thereof, who reopened the monopoly debate. But the monopoly had been safe under previous Conservative governments: why should it be questioned now?

Three reasons suggest themselves. The first and most obvious was the deficiencies of the BBC's post-war television service, at least until about 1950, and the general feeling that it was being held back by radio. This feeling was confirmed by resignations among senior television staff, especially that of the Controller of Television, Norman Collins, in 1950. Collins had argued within the Corporation that television was the medium of the future, in competition with which radio was bound to decline in importance. Among those this argument failed to impress was Haley, who appointed to a new post, Chief Executive of Television, not Collins but a candidate with a background in the Third Programme and speech output.

In doing so Haley handed a piece of heavy artillery to the Corporation's enemies. Collins promptly resigned and devoted himself to masterminding the campaign for commercial television, something he did with great skill.

A second threat to the monopoly grew out of changes occurring in the socio-political climate of the time. There was a renewal of the process of democratization that had been gathering pace before the war, of the campaign 'to let the people decide for themselves'. Asa Briggs (1979) points out that in its evidence to Beveridge the Incorporated Society of Advertisers had suggested that it might be advisable to have a network which the public did not associate with a 'semi-official service'. He adds that this was to prove an immensely powerful argument in the Britain of the 1950s, when there was a reaction against the wartime system of managed information and bureaucratic paternalism.

The BBC, in particular, was seen by many Tories as self-righteous and arrogant, and their party battle-cry 'set the people free' had certainly impressed the people at election time. Indeed, back in 1946 the BBC had been dealt a shrewd blow by one of its own former Director Generals, Sir Frederick Ogilvie. 'Freedom is choice,' he declared in a letter to *The Times*, 'And monopoly of broadcasting is inevitably the negation of freedom, no matter how efficiently it is run' (Smith 1974: 85). There was a growing democratic revulsion against 'someone else knowing best': people craved diversity and choice.

The third and least obvious challenge to the monopoly, yet perhaps the most powerful, was economic. After the hardships of the war and post-war years the nation was once more on the verge of prosperity. More goods were being made and there was more money to buy them with. By the early 1950s people were looking to replace a multiplicity of household objects which had had to last them through a long, lean period. Food rationing would end in 1954; new washing machines and refrigerators would reduce the need for human effort and cool weather. Between 1951 and 1955 the manufacture of television sets leapt from 1 million to 5 million, the number of private cars from 2.25 million to 3.25 million. During the same period the ownership of telephones increased from 5 million to 6 million.

The growth in production created a corresponding growth in the demand for advertising: newspapers and magazines experienced a bonanza. By 1954 there was a three-month waiting list for selling space in the quality journal *Vogue*. More outlets were needed, and the advertising potential of television, much greater than that of radio, was never more apparent. This largely explains why the monopoly debate focused on television rather than radio, although there was another reason for this as we shall see shortly.

It is true that those for and against the continuance of the BBC's monopoly did not neatly divide along party lines. But since it was certain that the public would not support a large increase in the licence fee, the BBC's only conceivable rival would be commercial; and the reopening of the debate at this stage is attributable not only to the Conservatives' belief in individual choice but to the fact that, in general, they felt more enthusiasm than their opponents for the commercial principles of private enterprise and free competition.

The campaign for commercial television

The commercial TV lobby consisted of a relatively small group of Tory back-benchers and almost nobody in the Cabinet: the party leadership was largely indifferent, if not actively hostile, to its aims. In fact the leaders agreed to support the campaign only if it was confined to television, for they felt that the BBC's performance in radio had been so good, especially during the war, that its mono-poly therein should be left alone. The party chair, Lord Woolton, believed in any case that radio was by far the more important of the two media.

However, the BBC had no ally in the Prime Minister, Winston Churchill. Churchill's wartime speeches on BBC radio were highly successful and he was generally contemptuous of television, 'that tuppenny Punch and Judy Show'. But he held a grudge against the Corporation. He and Reith had always disliked each other, and Churchill had been so outraged by what he regarded as the BBC's 'soft' attitude to the strikers during the events of 1926 that he had urged the government to commandeer it. In the 1930s he had been denied the opportunity to broadcast his opposition to the government's appeasement of Hitler, and he also believed that the BBC had contributed to his defeat in the 1945 general election.

The commercial TV campaign was orchestrated from outside Parliament by Norman Collins, and enjoyed strong backing from business – among others, Pye Radio, the West End theatre managers and the advertising agency J. Walter Thompson – as well as the support of the *Daily Mirror* and the *Financial Times*.

Bernard Sendall (1982) suggests that the campaigners were concerned not so much with television content as with its *distribution*: many wished to be able to offer their services to more than one broadcasting organization. Calling themselves the Popular Television Association, they included performers and scriptwriters, manufacturers of equipment, advertisers and market researchers, pragmatic politicians and some journalists.

Their opponents Sendall (1982) sees as having been more concerned with *content*. Led by the Labour MP and BBC broadcaster Christopher Mayhew, they were known as the National Television Council, and among their number were churchmen, educators, moralists, ideological politicians and some journalists. They also enjoyed the less principled backing of most of the main newspapers, who were fearful that commercial TV would steal their advertising revenue.

The debate centred on the vexed issue of 'quality' in broadcasting and whether competition would raise or lower it. The elitist view was that quality programming consisted of what the intelligentsia broadly agreed was good or valuable; the democratic or populist view was that quality programmes were whatever was preferred by the greatest number. As was suggested in the last chapter, it is an issue on which most of us take a different view at different times, and for just this reason it has recurred again and again in the history of broadcasting. Even today it occasions debates that are every bit as passionate as they are inconclusive.

Those who sought to preserve the BBC's monopoly took the elitist view, invoking a cultural version of Gresham's Law: that competition would drive out quality. To capture the audience the commercial broadcasters would have to offer populist (that is, inferior) programmes, and the BBC would be obliged to abandon its public service ideals, its aim of elevating the masses and catering for special interests, and do likewise. It could not decline to compete because if it did, it might lose so big a share of the audience as to deprive it of all claim to a universal licence fee.

As a monopoly it could devote broadcasting to the most serious purposes, cooperating with such civilizing forces as the schools and universities. It could maintain editorial independence, since it was a creature neither of government nor commerce. This distrust of commerce seems to have struck a chord with the public since it was part of an anti-American feeling that was quite widely shared at this time. Stephen Barnard shrewdly observes that:

> Behind [it] lay a sense of national economic inferiority, exacerbated by Britain's dependence on American finance for post-war reconstruction, and a feeling that Britain's cultural 'superiority' over the United States (and the values reflected in its history and traditions) was under threat.

> (1989: 29)

As their official name implies, the campaigners for commercial TV took the democratic or populist view: that competition would force up quality. It would produce programming whose excellence would be declared in the fact that it was preferred by the majority of the people. The BBC's monopoly discouraged efficiency and denied choice, and in a democracy broadcasting should be as unrestricted as possible. Why should it differ from the press, where competition produced diversity and prevented the concentration of power into a single organization? Even in a competitive system some minorities would be large enough to target, so the BBC's highbrow programming would remain for those who preferred it, just as, even under competition, quality newspapers continued to exist for those who wanted them.

The commercial supporters could add that in any case the BBC had accepted the principle of choice and abandoned the aim of elevating the masses when it devised the cultural pyramid; for the cultural pyramid allowed the listener to opt out of highbrow content if she wished and hear nothing but populist programming.

In effect the pro-commercial campaigners were nudging the BBC's public service concept further along a path it had already taken – away from the idea of the audience as a single entity and towards that of a number of separate audiences with specialist or minority interests. The new concept would be less coloured by values, by the hierarchical belief that one set of interests was 'better' or more worthwhile than another and should therefore be imposed on the majority.

Between 1952 and 1954 the fortunes of battle favoured first one side and then the other. The anti-commercial campaigners scored a great victory with the coronation, partly because the BBC covered it so well as to suggest that its standards in television were now no lower than its standards in radio; and partly because the public was horrified to hear that when the coronation was re-broadcast in the States, NBC had punctuated the service in Westminster Abbey with commercials for deodorant, tea (sold by J. Fred Muggs, a famous performing chimpanzee) and Pepperell's Bed Sheets.

On the other hand the pro-commercial campaigners won ground when they convinced many waverers that commercial broadcasting did not have to mean advertisers controlling programme content through sponsorship – a practice which had a notorious and American reputation. Editorial integrity could be safeguarded through separate, 'spot' advertising – a practice which was subsequently adopted.

It seems true to say that despite occasional setbacks, the inherent advantage lay with the pro-commercialists. In any age it is possible to make an appeal to an audience's sense of status – to an intellectual, moral or cultural superiority which may be real or imagined; but in a democracy the advocates of monopoly would always find it harder to sell an argument that was essentially anti-democratic.

This is why Peter Black (1972b) insists that when the debate finally reached the Commons, that forum of democracy, the result was never really in doubt. The harder the champions of the BBC argued for the retention of its monopoly, the more priggish and patronizing they sounded. How could Christopher Mayhew and his allies approve democratic choice when it produced such principled politicians as themselves, yet abhor it when it was applied to broadcasting? As the beneficiaries of popular choice MPs were bound in logic to affirm their faith in its wisdom, for in the Lord Chancellor's words: 'Must we not give people what they want because they might want something that is not good for them?' (Hood 1980: 65). Such a fear was surely groundless.

But in the Upper House there was one man before whom people of all views would pause and listen with respect. Lord Reith, stout old Canute to the last, got to his feet, and in its likely effects on civilization compared commercial television with dog-racing, smallpox and bubonic plague.

With voting broadly though not exactly on party lines the Television Bill was carried in 1954. Nevertheless in order to placate its opponents and critics, who were by no means united in their objections to it, the plans for commercial television underwent many modifications and refinements, and as Peter Black (1972b) points out, the system that emerged was a practical compromise between those who wished merely to break the BBC's monopoly, those who sought new sources of profit and those who feared the worst excesses of American television.

Sources/further reading

General details of the BBC's post-war radio programmes are in Parker (1977), Gifford (1985) and Donovan (1992). Drakakis (1981) contains academic studies of some of the major radio dramatists of the 1940s and 1950s. For a discussion of the relationship of radio drama to the mainstream of English literature see Lewis (1981). Fink (1981) is useful on popular radio drama, including soap opera. Black (1972a) and Took (1976) include accounts of post-war radio comedy and light entertainment, while Crisell (1986; 1994) attempts a close analysis of the *Goon Show*.

For the early development of television see Barnouw (1977). To brief accounts of this development, Gorham (1952), Briggs (1965) and Armes (1988) add a description of the establishment of the BBC's pre-war television service, the blue-print for which is in Selsdon (1935). Hood (1980) offers some discussion of the economic and cultural background of the first viewers, and information about the programmes is in Davis (1976) and Day-Lewis (1992).

Various descriptions of the BBC's post-war television service are in Gorham (1952), Briggs (1979) and Paulu (1981). Illuminating accounts of the particular economic, administrative and creative problems it had to deal with can be found in Goldie (1977), Hood (1980) and Curran and Seaton (1991). Its achievements in entertainment are outlined by Day-Lewis (1992), in current affairs by Scannell (1979), and in international and outside broadcasting by Davis (1976). The devastating impact of post-war television on radio listening is summarized in Paulu (1961) and Briggs (1979).

For the findings of the Beveridge Committee and the minority report of Selwyn Lloyd see Beveridge (1951). A summary account of the development of the BBC during the 1950s and the establishment of ITV is in Paulu (1981). Curran and Seaton (1991) provide a perceptive discussion of the political issues raised by the Beveridge Report, the problems of the monopoly television service and the factors behind the introduction of commercial television. Smith (1974) quotes from the contemporary debate on the BBC's monopoly, and Seymour-Ure (1991; 1996) contains a brief but useful discussion of the issues of public service, monopoly and competition in broadcasting.

The question of 'quality' in television broadcasting, which the debate about commercial TV really ventilated for the first time, is discussed at length by Mulgan (1990), Corner, Harvey and Lury (1994) and Corner (1995), each of which offers possible definitions. Though all of these discussions are in the context of broadcasting in the 1990s, their relevance to the 1950s debate shows how intractable the question is.

The general political and economic background to the campaign for commercial TV can be gleaned from Briggs (1979), Hood (1980) and Gable (1980). For the particular events which triggered the campaign, some of them occurring within the BBC, see Black (1972b) and Sendall (1982). Together with Briggs (1979), these also contain the best accounts of the campaign itself and of the Parliamentary debates which led to the establishment of Independent Television.

Television: the first years of competition

Chapter 5

Television: the first years of competition

The structure of commercial television

Commercial television began, with suitable fanfares, on 22 September 1955. Agog, viewers watched among many other offerings the first ever British TV advert, for Gibbs SR Toothpaste, and the evening was generally judged a success although somewhat upstaged by the BBC. In that day's episode of its radio soap opera *The Archers*, the much-loved Grace Archer was killed in a stable fire. Competition had got off to a flying start.

It is a measure of the strength of the Reithian values which still pervaded broadcasting, and perhaps of a more general distrust of unfettered money-making, that commercial television was set up as an extension of the public service concept. It was to be supervised by the Independent Television Authority (ITA), a public body constituted rather like the BBC's Board of Governors. The government retained the power of appointment over its members – its first Chairman was Sir Kenneth, later Lord, Clark and its first Director General Sir Robert Fraser – and the 1954 Television Act gave it an initial life of ten years.

Though it owned and operated the television transmitters the Authority did not itself make programmes but allocated a number of regional franchises on a fixed-term basis – initially nine years – to various programme-making companies ('the contractors'). The regional concept was an interesting though not wholly practicable response to Beveridge's complaint about what, in the hands of the BBC, was the excessive 'Londonization' of broadcasting.

The ITA required the contractors to inform, educate and entertain – to produce programmes of balance, quality and variety in accordance with the promises of performance they had made in their competitive bids for the franchises. The contractors were also responsible for selling air-time to the advertisers and for supporting the ITA through a levy raised on their revenue. However, the nature and quality of advertising were strictly controlled by the Authority, and programme sponsorship was forbidden. Advertisers could only buy time within different 'slots' situated within and between programmes, slots which varied in price according to their place in the daily schedule, but there could be no more than an average of 6 minutes of advertising in any one hour.

This rigid separation of advertising from programme content was designed to prevent commercial interference in the latter, thus allaying another of Beveridge's fears. It has traditionally been regarded as one of the great virtues of British commercial television. As Burton Paulu puts it:

> The model followed [for ITV] was the press, in which news and editorial material are kept entirely separate from advertising copy, rather than American commercial broadcasting, in which advertisers often provide programmes, or at least participate in their development.

> (1981: 63)

The term 'independent', said to have been thought up by Norman Collins, was a mischievously clever one. It damaged the BBC, Collins's former employer and sworn enemy, since if ITV was so called because it was independent of government control the implication was that the BBC was not. In practice, too, 'independent' became a handy euphemism for 'commercial', which had connotations of greed and vulgarity.

The original plan for ITV was that there should be three regional franchises, London, the Midlands and the North, each occupied by more than one contractor. Hence there was to be competition *between* contractors, as well as between the whole ITV system and the BBC. But because of the government's failure to allocate enough frequencies to enable this to happen the ITA adopted another plan. In order to maximize the number of contractors and create as much competition as it could the Authority split franchises on a weekday/weekend basis. The first franchises were allocated thus:

LONDON   Weekdays: Associated-Rediffusion
                Weekends: Associated Television

MIDLANDS   Weekdays: Associated Television
                Weekends: ABC Television

THE NORTH   Weekdays: Granada
                Weekends: ABC Television

For its first few months ITV could be seen only in the London area, but it spread quite rapidly. Broadcasts began in the Midlands in February 1956, in the North in May, and after the establishment of the four original contractors further regional franchises were allocated – in Wales, Scotland, Northern Ireland and the Channel Islands, together with other regions of England. By 1962 the system was complete, but the main population areas were connected before 1960.

However, it became clear well before the end of the 1950s that the system could not survive without networking, since on their own most of the regions could not deliver big enough audiences to the advertisers. Hence a cost-sharing carve-up swiftly developed in which the four contractors who held between them the three original and most profitable franchises were guaranteed access to the network for agreed amounts of their programmes. This meant that the only real competition was between all the contractors and the BBC. It should be added that under the contractors' joint ownership the ITA also set up a separate organization, ITN, Independent Television News.

Where did the contractors' finance come from, and what experience did they have which was relevant to the unprecedented business of running a television company? One source of both was the entertainment industry: theatre and cinema (two notable examples of shareholders with show-business connections were Lew Grade at ATV and Sidney Bernstein at Granada). Another, as in the case of Associated-Rediffusion, was the radio and TV rental business. And a third, rather more controversially, was newspaper money, which overlapped with regional finance. Other financial backing came in the usual way from banks, pension funds and investors on the stock market.

Press interest was controversial because while it was not unreasonable that one mass medium might seek to protect itself by investing in another, a Conservative-dominated press could thereby lead to a Conservative-dominated television industry, and in any event to media outlets which were concentrated in too few hands. Somewhat surprisingly, however, it was the pro-Labour Mirror Group which until 1990 was the largest single newspaper conglomerate to be continuously associated with ITV.

A dissection of the complicated structures of the different ITV contractors would take up too much space in a book of this kind, and perhaps leave the reader scarcely the wiser. Suffice to say that the contractors were highly miscellaneous groups of businesses – perhaps more accurately, business coalitions. One random example might be Associated-Rediffusion, first holder of the London weekday franchise. Rediffusion, formerly Broadcast Relay Service Ltd, was a company founded in the 1920s to operate the wireless relay exchanges. In 1947 it became a division of British Electric Traction, a vehicle manufacturing group, and later expanded its radio and TV rental business. Before making its bid for one of the franchises Rediffusion had agreed to form a partnership with Lord Rothermere's

Associated Newspapers, owners of the *Daily Mail*, which explains the name of the contractor.

To complicate matters further, the contractors used their television profits to diversify into other businesses, a prudent course of action since there was no guarantee that the ITA would renew their nine-year franchises. Granada, for example, had interests in book and music publishing, bingo halls, motorway services, cinemas, property and TV rentals, while ATV was involved in feature films, theatres, cinemas, music publishing, record companies and property.

In the red – then in the pink

ITV got off to a shaky start. In order to receive it, viewers needed to fit a special aerial and either to buy a new television or to have their existing set adapted. Since in the first franchise areas only 33 per cent of households had taken these measures, the medium was not especially attractive to advertisers in terms of cost per thousand. Understandably, they remained cagey.

The first contractors were not allowed to broadcast more than fifty hours per week, but their rental charge was considerable: it was fixed by the ITA at about ten pence per head of the *total* population within their respective franchise areas. Nevertheless in order to attract new viewers and advertising, they were obliged to spend big money on programmes. The start-up and running costs were, in a word, enormous, and there was an early panic that the entire system might fail and that the first programmes were insufficiently populist. Among the contractors, the programme controller of Associated-Rediffusion expressed a common view:

> Let's face it once and for all. The public likes girls, wrestling, bright musicals, quiz-shows and real-life drama. We gave them the Hallé Orchestra, Foreign Press Club . . . and visits to the local fire station. Well, we've learned. From now on, what the public wants, it's going to get.

> (Sendall 1982: 328)

ITV was soon seen, not altogether accurately, as consisting of little other than quiz games, known as 'give-away shows' because of the big and rather easily won prizes they offered, variety spectaculars, soap operas and American film series, and described by its apologists as 'people's television' (another artful term).

By the second half of 1956, barely a year after it started, the tide began to turn. Whereas in September 1955 only 188,000 homes had been equipped to receive ITV, the number in September 1956 was 1.5 million. During the autumn and winter of 1956 viewers were rising by 50,000 a week, networking among the contractors was helping to cut production costs, and advertisers were having to queue for air-time. But not everyone's nerve held. Between 1955 and 1957 Associated-Rediffusion, holder of the London weekday franchise, lost nearly £3 million. One of its key shareholders, Associated Newspapers, decided to sell out. Two years later Rediffusion began to turn annual profits of £5 million. In 1958 the number of homes which could receive ITV had reached five and a quarter million and by 1960 that number had almost doubled.

However, it was not merely that many homes could receive ITV: millions of viewers were glued to it. As recently as 1953 the status of the BBC as the national broadcasting institution, a status it had acquired during the General Strike back in 1926, seemed to have been confirmed by its television coverage of the coronation. Now, the audience, especially its working class segment, was deserting it in droves. By July 1957 the BBC was admitting that in homes with a choice, three adults watched ITV for every two who stayed with the Corporation. Two months later the Chairman of the ITA, Sir Kenneth Clark, claimed a 79:21 ratio in favour of ITV.

As we shall see, the BBC's programming was by no means weak: indeed most of the memorable programmes which date from this era are the Corporation's. Part of the problem lay in the way they were scheduled. Under the Director General Sir Ian Jacob the policy was partly to compete with ITV, to match like with like, but true to its old public service philosophy of providing range and catering for minorities, the BBC also tried to offer contrast by scheduling some of its more serious output at peak viewing hours – with predictable results. Not surprisingly, morale within the Corporation sank: its creative staff either felt disgust at the public's lack of taste and discernment or formed the belief that the lack of popularity of its programmes implied a lack of quality. But as Peter Black (1972b) points out, the BBC had to respond to a changed world. The public could no longer be patronized: through programme promotion, shrewder scheduling, and a change in styles of presentation, it had to be courted.

Technological developments in television

At this relatively early stage of television's history the most important developments were in the technology of recording – important because they had far-reaching consequences for the viewer as well as the broadcaster. They are also of importance to the media student since they help to sharpen our understanding of television's essential nature. As we might expect, these developments were interconnected and not always easily distinguished from one another.

The first related to television's use of material which had been recorded for screening in the cinema. The second related to television broadcasters' recordings of their own material, recordings which could be made before or during transmission. These were known in the 1950s as 'telerecordings'. And the third related to the broadcasters' use of recording technology with an instant playback facility – a technology which soon became known as 'video'.

Until the end of the 1950s the essentially live nature of television was always apparent. Not least because of mistakes which were often made before the cameras, but also because the picture quality of film was never quite as good as that of a live transmission, the viewing public was in no doubt that most of what it was watching was happening presently – in 'real time'.

The historical reason for this liveness was that the technology which had been adopted for television was the EMI system, which as we will recall was based on electronic scanning. But despite its many advantages over the mechanical system of Baird, electronic scanning did not initially cope well with the transmission of film. According to Roy Armes (1988), the Baird system's comparative lack of sensitivity enabled it to deal better with the direct illumination provided by a film projector.

Despite its problems with film and its consequent reliance on other forms of programming, the visual (and moreover domestic) nature of television hit post-war cinema audiences hard, and as the custodian of an older medium the motion picture industry fought that rearguard action against a clever new upstart which is by now familiar to us. In Britain the Cinematograph Exhibitors' Association opposed the showing of all movies on television. Nevertheless, the major studios and distributors in America came to accept that what could not be resisted should be worked with, and after 1955 made their film libraries available to the TV stations. Moreover the contraction of the cinema, which left the film studios with surplus capacity, and the high cost of live television, from which nothing could be preserved and recycled, enabled companies such as Warner to do deals with the TV networks to produce whole series of films especially for television.

By 1957 over 100 such series were running on the US networks: cops-and-robbers and detective stories like *Highway Patrol* and *Dragnet*, spy and war dramas, and most of all westerns, of which *Cheyenne* and *Rawhide* were the most popular. These film series were cheap to make, predictable in structure, and bought in bulk by the ITV contractors, who used them as a heavy weapon in the battle for audiences. Though it relied on them less, the BBC soon followed suit.

Despite strong resistance from the British film industry, the BBC bought its first old cinema movies in 1957, a hundred of them from RKO, and twenty-four from the Selznick Corporation in 1959. These developments illustrate the ability of one medium to exploit the content of another. But though by no means alone in this respect, television is perhaps more obviously parasitic than the other media: besides originating content of its own it can appropriate that of both cinema and the live theatre.

In its early years television had difficulty not only in showing pre-recorded material – in screening films – but in recording or pre-recording material of its own. Technological weakness strengthened industrial muscle: at the end of the war the broadcasting unions were able to impose a virtual ban on recorded output, which explains not only why TV showed very few cinema films during most of the 1940s and 1950s, why its own content – its variety and comedy shows, quiz games, documentaries, outside broadcasts, plays and so on – were almost all live. As Roy Armes observes, 'If cinema can be said to have been shaped by the flexibility of celluloid as a carrier base for its images, television was equally defined by its initial *lack* of an adequate means of recording' (1988: 58).

However, the development during the 1950s of telerecording meant that broadcasters could pre-record and edit more of their own material. This had a number of important consequences which would in one way or another transform the experience of the viewer. As Bakewell and Garnham (1970) point out, television aesthetics grew closer to those of the cinema. Instead of being performed in a single sequence as they would be in a theatre, plays could be shot in the manner of movies – discontinuously and in a number of takes from which a final version would be assembled and edited. They also became like the movies in making greater use of actual locations rather than being confined to not wholly believable studio sets. (We might add at this point that despite the formal enmity between the cinema and television industries, there was some fruitful interchange between their employees: several cinema directors got into television, and one or two TV directors such as John Schlesinger and Ken Russell made a highly successful move to cinema.)

Bakewell and Garnham further observe that television's ability to record 'encouraged the economic development of the programme factory. Recording was exploited because it offered management the maximum use of scarce resources' (1970: 14). It also favoured the production of series and serials over single plays: like the made-for-TV movies which were being imported from America these series and serials were often formulaic, providing a blend of familiarity and surprise, at its most obvious in the soap opera, which gave new satisfactions to the audience.

Telerecording had another economic consequence which was of benefit to the viewer. It enabled television broadcasts to be turned from mere ephemera into physical objects which could be preserved and re-used, as a result of which repeats of favourite programmes came to occupy a significant part of the schedule. As Asa Briggs (1995) points out, the real impetus to all this was the arrival in Britain of magnetic recording technology. The first Ampex videotape machine was imported from America by Rediffusion in June 1958, but others arrived at the BBC soon after. The long-term consequence of the video revolution is that the great majority of programmes are now pre-recorded. Yet nothing has changed: they should not blind us to the essentially *live* nature of television. Television can show films just as cinema can, but in cinema there is nothing within the medium which is of a live nature. TV programmes, even if they are all pre-recorded, exist within a live 'envelope' which is part of the medium and which we feel distinguishes broadcasting from all the other modes of mass communication. Because of this capacity for liveness we also feel that the programmes which best express the essential nature of television are those which are least susceptible to pre-recording, whose value depends on their up-to-dateness or topicality: news (even though it usually contains filmed inserts), current affairs and outside broadcasts, especially of sport. Adapting Roy Armes's remark, we might affirm that despite the advances in recording technology, and despite its grossly parasitic behaviour, television *still is* defined by the lack of a carrier base for its images.

In fact the great irony about video technology is that it was first wanted in order to emphasize the vivid, *live* nature of the medium, its ability both to convey and keep up with a detailed yet fast-moving reality, rather than as a new way of making films; for in the beginning, editing on video was all but impossible. Cutting and splicing were dangerously imprecise, and since tapes were about £100 each and not re-usable the cost of failure was high. Producers wanted video primarily because it could be used in a live context – to provide an instant review of material which was being recorded as it was being broadcast and a rapid return to the action that was taking place in 'real time'.

As we might expect, the Ampex machines were especially in demand for sport, and are yet another instance of the way in which the viewer's experience of television was transformed by recording technology. Video not only enhanced sport as a spectacle but improved the viewers' knowledge and understanding of it, especially when slow-motion replay was developed. It also enabled the decisions of referees and umpires to be questioned. As Asa Briggs pertinently remarks: 'Through technology as much as through ideology, authority in sport, as in politics, was becoming more open to doubt' (1995: 838).

News and current affairs

One field in which the BBC's failure to match ITV was a matter of quality rather than mere scheduling was the news. We noted in the last chapter that a major reason the Corporation's television monopoly was unsatisfactory was that its production staff were more comfortable with words than with images, which they tended to distrust. Their faith in the former was embodied in a department of 'Television Talks', which had been created as a kind of catch-all for everything that did not fit into such traditional programme categories as drama, sport and light entertainment. As Stuart Hood puts it:

> The name continued in use for a very long time and is an indication of how difficult the BBC found it to come to terms with the fundamental difference between radio and television, how many of the concepts of radio were taken

over and imposed on television and how little the top echelons of the television service understood the new medium.

(1975: 40)

This mentality seems to have persisted longer in news than in other kinds of programming, for TV news continued to be presented in a way which was much more appropriate to sound broadcasting. Hence it was in this field that the BBC would be hit hardest by the competition: funded by the contractors, Independent Television News was a networked organization which was concerned with the news to the exclusion of all else, and whose approach to it was entirely uncluttered by preconceptions carried over from radio. It could be argued that in the form of ITN, independent television's greatest contribution to the history of broadcasting was to make TV news into something truly telegenic.

The BBC's backwardness in this field has been attributed to the New Zealander Tahu Hole, who was head of its news throughout most of the 1940s and 1950s. Hole held a view of the news which was impossibly purist. He deplored the fact that in contrast to the apparently authorless and objective medium of print, broadcast news was unavoidably 'tainted' by the personality of a reader. But if the evil of conveying the news through a human voice could not be avoided in broadcasting, the worse evil of conveying it through a visible presenter most certainly could. Between 1946 and 1954 the BBC offered no television news as such, merely a late evening relay of the radio news during which viewers were obliged to stare at a single photograph of Big Ben. Apart from this there was only a 10-minute newsreel five evenings a week, whose format – a sequence of items accompanied by a voice-over – exactly resembled that of its counterpart in the cinema. In 1954 a new combined daily bulletin and newsreel was launched, the former using film and still photographs with captions or voice-overs. But the newsreaders remained in purdah, coyly concealed behind the caption cards: there was no visible reader on BBC news until three weeks before ITV went to air.

ITN had been set up in May 1955 under the editorship of Aidan Crawley, a journalist and former MP. This made a much more appropriate use of the medium. Crawley recognized that if the element of personality could not be eliminated from television, it should be used to best effect. The ITN presenters, Robin Day, Christopher Chataway and Barbara Mandell, were more than merely visible; they were authoritative and journalistic and known not by that rather passive term 'newsreaders' but as news*casters*, which implied – accurately – that they had something to say in their own right. They helped to gather and select the news and wrote the scripts to suit their own style of delivery.

ITN's mission was 'to make significant news more interesting, more comprehensible and more acceptable'. It used an unprecedented quantity of film in its bulletins and incorporated as much informed comment as possible to give viewers a better perspective on events. Like a newspaper it also set out to get scoops and exclusives. It managed to send back the only film – shots of Port Said – from the 1956 Suez War, and in the following year gained an exclusive interview in Cairo with Britain's arch-enemy, President Nasser.

On the not infrequent occasions that the importance of the news justified it, the ITN bulletins would overrun. Its news-gathering units used lighter film cameras, for whose lack of studio quality the dramatic impact of their location shots more than compensated. As a former politician himself Crawley encouraged a more persistent questioning of public figures, which contrasted with the deferential style of BBC interviewers perhaps over mindful of who fixed the licence fee. ITN also favoured the spontaneity and human interest of vox pops, informal interviews with people in the street which were then assembled into a tightly edited package.

Two episodes serve to illustrate the much more 'televisual' approach of ITN. At an open-air meeting of the boilermakers' union, reporter Reginald Bosanquet climbed on to a platform to question the leader Ted Hill against a background of 3,000 shouting strikers; and during a 'Keep death off the roads' campaign the Minister of Transport was interviewed beside a main road to the coast just before the Whitsun Holiday rush. Crawley's early resignation in January 1956, on the ground that the contractors were seeking to curb ITN's budget, served only to strengthen the organization he had helped to set up, and because the contractors were regionally based their local news operations gave them a further advantage against a more centralized and metropolitan BBC.

In both ITV and the BBC current affairs were organizationally separate from news, which is not to deny that the former were strongly influenced by the presentation of the latter. In ITV current affairs were the responsibility of the contractors, not of ITN, and because BBC current affairs occupied a department of their own they were able to respond to ITV news more promptly than the Corporation's news department did.

Part of their response had its origins in the demise, at the end of 1956, of the 'toddlers' truce', an extraordinary instance of Reithian paternalism which had been conceived by the BBC. This was a shutdown of television between 6 pm and 7 pm so that parents could put their younger children to bed and persuade the older ones to do their homework. Only too aware that this period was valuable in advertising terms, the ITA argued that the responsibility for children lay not with broadcasters but with parents – and it and now the BBC both realized that whichever captured the viewers during this period had a fair chance of holding them for the rest of the evening. From 1957 the six-to-seven slot therefore saw the fiercest competition of the entire schedule.

For five nights a week the BBC filled it with the *Tonight* programme, a current affairs magazine which by 1960 was commanding an average audience of 9 million.

Its items varying in mood, pace and style, yet each lasting no more than a few minutes, *Tonight* offered an original blend of political and current affairs with light entertainment. Yet underlying it was a serious philosophy. The programme was meant to be 'on the side of the viewer'. Using Cliff Michelmore as the presenter, and as interviewers and reporters the former print journalists Fyfe Robertson, Trevor Philpott and Alan Whicker, who adapted very well to their new medium, the producer Donald Baverstock encouraged a more incisive style of questioning than the bland and often obsequious approach that had been common hitherto.

Tonight aimed, in Grace Wyndham Goldie's words, to show that: 'It was not always necessary to be respectful; experts were not invariably right; the opinions of those in high places did not have to be accepted' (1977: 216). Its approach chimed well with an informal, sceptical, even irreverent *zeitgeist* which was beginning to develop during the second half of this decade – perhaps a manifestation of that broader democratizing trend we mentioned earlier, more certainly an effect of the familiarizing, demystifying effects of television itself, on whose innate iconoclastic tendencies we shall have more to say later. For the BBC at any rate, *Tonight* was a beneficial consequence of competition in the sense that the casually authoritative style of ITN allowed it to treat current affairs in a way which might have seemed too flippant in a monopoly broadcaster.

Whereas *Tonight* was lightly sceptical, the BBC's other major current affairs programme, the weekly *Panorama*, seemed more serious and weighty. Presented by the sedate and magisterial Richard Dimbleby, it had started in 1953 as a mainly arts and cultural programme, but from about 1957 its concerns became more exclusively political. Its contributors included Woodrow Wyatt, Ludovic Kennedy, John Freeman and Robert Kee, and Christopher Chataway and Robin Day were later lured from ITN. *Panorama* attracted some early competition from Associated-Rediffusion's *This Week*, an approach to current affairs which has been described as 'tabloid but serious'.

It was not until 1958, when Tahu Hole was replaced as head of news by Stuart Hood, who formed a team of presenters consisting of Robert Dougall, Richard Baker, Kenneth Kendall and Michael Aspel, that news on BBC television stood comparison with that of ITN and with the Corporation's own current affairs output. But what finally established television, whether BBC or ITV, as the main news medium was the Cuban missile crisis of 1962. With the world on the brink of war, only radio and television could keep people fully abreast of events – and only television could show the pictures taken by US reconnaissance planes of the Soviet missiles on freighter decks. Whereas in 1957 the ratio of media which people chose as their main news source stood at 30 per cent for newspapers, 46 per cent for radio and 24 per cent for television, by 1962 52 per cent were treating television as their main news source, with only 31 per cent opting for newspapers and 17 per cent for radio.

Some other programming milestones

In other kinds of programmes – notably drama, comedy and light entertainment, pop music shows and sport – the impact of competition was highly variable: much depended on the foresight of the BBC's individual heads of department and the energy and originality of their commercial rivals.

In drama the BBC persisted long after the arrival of ITV with a policy which one might expect of a public service broadcaster: it tried to be as eclectic as possible, offering classic plays, adaptations of great novels, original series and serials, and single plays by modern authors. Its Head of Drama, Michael Barry, prided himself on an ability to encourage talented new playwrights such as N. F. Simpson, John Mortimer and Johnny Speight.

The BBC also offered much popular drama – science fiction and detective stories (its outstanding adaptation of *Maigret* began in 1960), and of course, soap opera. But though the BBC was first in this field, the earliest successes were ITV's: the hospital soap *Emergency – Ward Ten* (ATV) lasted for ten years from 1957 and Granada's *Coronation Street*, launched in 1960, is still running.

At first most plays were broadcast live, but as we saw earlier the increased use of recording moved them away from the ambit of the theatre and closer to that of the cinema, since it gave TV producers some of the flexibility of the film director. Commendable as the BBC's drama policy was, it perforce became more sharply focused when in the late 1950s ABC introduced a Sunday night series shrewdly entitled *Armchair Theatre*: all the delights of a vivid public experience brought to you in the comfort of your own sitting-room.

The series was soon entrusted to a Canadian director, Sydney Newman, who saw contemporary British drama and society with a fresh eye. He realized that the theatre was a largely middle-class sphere which failed to reach a working-class and regional audience. He therefore concentrated on plays of social realism, many of them reflecting a changing Britain.

After 1958 Newman was able to stockpile plays with the aid of the new video technology. The series format, which recording made easier, had an obvious economic appeal to broadcasting institutions; but it also commanded audience loyalty, and by the end of the decade *Armchair Theatre* could boast 12 million viewers. Moreover the series was a success with the critics, and when its own head of drama resigned in 1962 the BBC brought in Newman as his replacement – its first appointment of a senior figure from ITV and thus its first, if tacit, admission that it had a competitor.

In the field of comedy and light entertainment ITV mounted a formidable challenge by exploiting the showbiz connections of Lew Grade and Sidney Bernstein. It did particularly well with variety spectaculars like *Sunday Night at the London Palladium*, but the BBC held its own in straight comedy shows, many of which proved more enduring than ITV's. The BBC's Head of Light Entertainment, Eric Maschwitz, ascribed this to a recognition that the strength of comedy, even television comedy, lies in the writing: that however important its visual elements they must grow out of the dialogue. Yet he also stressed that the shows were written for television, not for the theatre: they respected and made use of the intimacy of the medium rather than striving for big visual effects.

The force of these arguments becomes apparent when recalling one's experience of the early ITV variety shows. Largely theatrical in concept (many were actually relayed from theatres), they seemed in some respects too vast, too detailed, for the small screen. The very term 'spectacular' reveals their predominantly theatrical concerns, and as the theatre has existed far longer than television there seemed to be something oddly old-fashioned about them, which is not to deny that they were hugely popular with the TV audience.

In this respect, then, the BBC's concentration on comedy series was more progressive, more telegenic. The excellent *Hancock's Half Hour* transferred from radio in 1956 to reveal an artist whose facial expressions and physical posture were just as variously expressive as his vocal delivery. Moreover the show was one of the first to use Ampex videotape, its producer realizing that if Hancock could be freed of the strain of a live performance, and if the show were recorded in discontinuous segments, the range of shots (especially of Hancock's comic reactions) could be extended, and the overall pace and finish of the programmes improved.

Asa Briggs (1995) has made another important point about the television comedy of this period, whether on ITV or BBC: that although both imported US shows (the former offered *I Love Lucy*, the latter *Sergeant Bilko*), the bulk of it was still British — neither American nor Americanized. The BBC featured not only Tony Hancock but Michael Bentine, Billy Cotton, Charlie Drake, Jimmy Edwards and Benny Hill, while ITV's hugely popular sitcom *The Army Game* focused on a very British experience: national service.

In the field of light entertainment, ITV had another and yet heavier weapon than the variety spectacular: the competition show offering big prizes of cash or consumer durables such as fridges and TV sets. ATV provided two of the most popular: *Double Your Money* (1955–68), featuring the ersatz sincerity of quizmaster Hughie Green and a top prize of £1000; and *Take Your Pick*, presented by Michael Miles, who in the words of one TV critic looked like a public-school boy gone wrong.

The shows were banal and trite, but had the virtue of being cheap — cheaper than full variety shows — and of pulling big audiences. Moreover as ITV realized, these were all the bigger for the fact that give-away shows were a kind of programming in which the BBC, inhibited by the anti-materialistic nature of its public service ethos if not by the actual dictates of its Charter, would decline to compete.

Pop music shows began only with the era of competition, because pop music as we now know it did not exist before the birth of rock'n'roll in the mid-1950s. Today's pop music is the recognizable descendant of rock'n'roll, just as rock music was a recognizable relative of the jazz-based popular music which preceded it. Like 'jazz' its name was a sexual euphemism. But the kinship of rock to jazz was more like that of niece or nephew than offspring: the change of musical direction in the 1950s was abrupt, and the extraordinary popularity of the new music quite unforeseeable. Rock's own parents were black rhythm and blues and white country music, and its novelty, as the name suggests, lay in a heavy, plangent beat.

Yet the simple, rural background of rock'n'roll was deceptive. Whereas the vehicle of jazz had been the old labour-intensive orchestra or big band, its driving-force the human breath of trumpet and saxophone, rock was performed by a modern, labour-saving 'group', its driving-force the electricity of guitar and bass.

Within twenty years rock music had been eagerly adopted far beyond America and the English-speaking world. In its modern form it is an accompaniment to activities both public and private, pervading everyday life in a way which is barely noticed; it is a staple of both radio and television; and with its panoply of stars, bands, singles and album charts, videos, vast concerts and unending tours, it has become a major preoccupation of people all over the globe.

As we shall see, it was radio which played the major part in spreading rock music, but television also made early if faltering attempts to feature it – attempts which would reach their apotheosis some thirty years later with MTV. The records of the first great rock stars, Bill Haley and the Comets and Elvis Presley, reached Britain in 1955–6, and Associated-Rediffusion was the first to present rock music on television with *Cool for Cats* (1956–9).

The BBC followed in January 1957 with *Six-Five Special*, which replaced the toddlers' truce on Saturdays; but at the same time as it tried to target teenagers, the main fans of the new music, the show was hampered by a residual public service impulse to appeal to everybody else. Consequently there were interludes for sport, comedy and even classical music.

One important aim of pop music shows on both channels was to develop British versions of the American rock stars, and Cliff Richard made his debut on ABC's *Oh Boy!* (1958–9). But there was also an assumption that when the young rock'n'roll idol 'grew up' he would develop into something called an all-round entertainer – a fate which, to universal relief, soon befell Tommy Steele.

In its early years rock music was so potent that it was hugely popular on television even though producers had not yet succeeded in making it telegenic. The BBC's *Juke Box Jury*, for instance, in which viewers watched a panel of celebrities merely listening to the music, ran from 1959 to 1967 despite its almost complete lack of visual interest. As Asa Briggs (1995) observes, the popularity of this show was a means by which figures from rock culture were assimilated into mainstream entertainment. Nevertheless, by the mid-1960s rock music, in all its rebellious and anti-social posturing, had *become* mainstream. To their great credit, coarsely arrogant bands like the Rolling Stones have never felt a need to develop into 'all-round entertainers'.

In its television coverage of sport the BBC had already reached high standards which its new rival was unable to match until after the end of the decade. This was thanks to a rare act of providence by the Corporation. At the start of ITV it retained its Head of Sport, Peter Dimmock, by increasing his salary, and Dimmock then secured all its most important sporting contracts for the next five to seven years.

Until 1958 the BBC's main offering in this field was *Sportsview*. For Saturday afternoons it then launched the hugely successful *Grandstand*, whose title well evoked the privileged perspective of the viewers. However Dimmock had his struggles within the Corporation. He had to fight hard for modern cameras, for the use of the expensive new video equipment, even for priority over children's programmes so that *Grandstand* would not be superseded at that climactic point when the afternoon's results were coming in. But under Dimmock, the BBC's great achievement was to exploit the dramatic possibilities of sport, and in so doing bring it nearer to other, more conventionally theatrical kinds of entertainment.

With respect to programme innovation, whether in the form of new genres or of new developments to old genres, the BBC took most of the honours, which is perhaps to be expected of an organization not solely concerned with maximizing its audience. In 1959 it launched *Monitor*, a fortnightly arts programme presented with infectious enthusiasm by Huw Wheldon. Sir Brian Horrocks brought a similar quality to his accounts of the battles of the Second World War. No modern TV producer would risk such a series with the meagre visual aids available to Horrocks: enthralled by the power of his narrative, no viewer felt the slightest need of them.

Also dating from this period were the pioneering nature series *Zoo Quest*, and from 1959 to 1962, *Face to Face*, a series of interviews of public figures tactfully yet searchingly conducted by John Freeman. Among his thirty-five guests were Evelyn Waugh, Bertrand Russell, John Osborne, Tony Hancock and Lord Reith.

It is a measure of the range of programming that the BBC and ITV were providing between them that the government decided to increase transmission from fifty to sixty hours a week – a move which gave ITV extra revenue from more advertising time but brought the BBC only extra expense.

Television and advertising

It is now difficult to understand the nervous excitement that the first TV advertisements created in a nation largely unused to commercials, even on the radio. The public felt deeply ambivalent about them. Adverts were associated with the glamour and prestige of America, whose way of life seemed a triumphant vindication of business enterprise and sales promotion. On the other hand the decade was marked by widespread if rather naive fears of 'brainwashing', mainly as a result of the traumatized state some fifty Allied prisoners were found to be in after their Communist captors had attempted to indoctrinate them during the Korean War. Could TV adverts be a form of brainwashing? After watching them, would we all be reduced to automatons, helplessly buying toilet rolls and pots of jam by the gross?

For their part, the creative and production staff of ITV could draw upon no received wisdom in order to cope with the 'commercial breaks', as the advertising slots were called – many of them within as well as between programmes. Writers of documentaries and plays were likely to be the most frustrated by them. Suspense points had to be devised just before the breaks in order to hold the viewers until the programme could resume. On the other hand the breaks might fatally halt a narrative or drama as it hastened towards its climax. The impact of commercial breaks on artistic and narrative structures in television is a fascinating subject that has hardly been explored.

Technical staff also faced a challenge. They had to 'package' commercial breaks in a way which would render them neither too similar to, nor too incongruous with, the adjacent programme content. One unhappy instance of accidental continuity dates from the earliest days of ITV when a boxing match was being screened. A commercial break between rounds concluded with the shot of a man downing a glass of Watney's beer. Viewers then cut straight to one of the boxers spitting copiously into a bucket.

After an initial uncertainty, commercials became enormously popular. Viewers gleefully quoted advertising jingles and slogans at one another, using them as cultural passwords. For young and old alike they provided a whole new treasury of nursery rhymes:

You'll wonder where the yellow went
When you clean your teeth with Pepsodent . . .

Esso sign means happy motoring . . .

Murraymints, Murraymints,
The too-good-to-hurry mints . . .

Oxo gives a meal man-appeal . . .

> Carpets at prices you can afford
> From Cyril Lord!
> (Mr Lord, however, could not: his business failed.)

For the advertisers themselves, TV was a much more attractive medium than street hoardings, cinemas, stadiums or public transport because, like newspapers, it was essentially domestic. But sound and moving pictures gave it obvious advantages over the latter. In 1957, a mere two years after the beginning of ITV, £13.7 million was spent on television advertising, and by the following year ITV's total advertising revenue had already surpassed that of the press. The commonest products to be advertised were soaps and detergents, soft drinks, beer, petrol and lubricants, sweets and toothpaste.

In theory, advertisers could not buy into a programme but only into time-slots which were more or less expensive according to their proximity to peak viewing periods. In practice, however, the contractors sold many advertisers slots in or next to programmes which were appropriate to their products. This is why children's television has always been punctuated by comercials for toys, games, soft drinks and snacks.

Though extraneous to programme content, commercials can be seen as 'distilled television' not only because in needing to make their point – in a matter of seconds and often through a complete dramatic narrative – they are a compendium of shooting and editing techniques, but because they constitute a magpie genre, borrowing freely from TV programmes in the form of pastiche and parody. Even our awareness of their similar borrowings from cinema films derives largely from seeing those films on television. But in their techniques of shooting and editing, commercials have influenced other genres, notably the travelogue, the pop video and certain forms of full length drama.

We might take TV advertising's continuing popularity with viewers as proof of its infallible power to increase sales and change behaviour. In many cases this has certainly happened. After a television campaign in 1960 sales of Kennomeat dog-food rose by 53 per cent in nine months. TV commercials for toothpaste have been credited with the vast improvement in dental hygiene which has occurred over the last forty years or so: in 1959, when ITV was still an infant, only two out of every five households actually possessed a toothbrush.

Yet despite those early fears of brainwashing there are evident limits to the power of TV advertising. One reason for its popularity is, of course, nega-tive: the commercial breaks give us the chance to make a cup of tea or answer a call of nature without missing any of the programme we are watching. But even when we sit through them we might enjoy the commercials without feeling impelled to buy the products they feature, or even being able to recall their brand-names.

Of itself TV advertising is powerless to reverse certain social trends. Some products which were once intensively advertised have all but disappeared. Among them was starch, which since the middle of the 1960s has succumbed to collar stiffeners and the fashion for more casual clothing. Another was shoe polish, whose sales have declined as leather has yielded to synthetic materials needing less care.

As all this might suggest, the real interest of TV commercials to the media historian lies in the keyhole view they offer into the social conditions of a particular era. In the late 1950s, for instance, a fierce advertising war broke out between the two main detergent manufacturers, Procter and Gamble and Lever Brothers, a war from which ITV derived one quarter of its entire advertising revenue. Their new or newly-promoted products, with brand-names like Omo, Surf, Persil, Oxydol, Daz, Tide and Fairy Snow, combined soap with grease-dissolving agents. But what explains the number of brands that were marketed, and the intensity of the competition?

Automatic washing machines were beginning to sell during this period, but for the majority of housewives laundry was the most burdensome of all the domestic chores. Many families lived in houses which lacked a permanent hot water supply. Water had to be specially heated and with the aid of soap powder clothes were washed by hand, but with the additional use of bar soap for heavy stains. White clothes and linen had to be bleached. The weekly wash could occupy a whole day, even if the weather was good enough for outside drying. Ironing and putting away could occupy much of another, and in wet weather the house would be festooned with drying clothes for the best part of a week.

Any product which would lighten this burden was likely to sell well. One such, fashioned from the new 'man-made' fibres and frequently advertised on television, was the drip-dry, non-iron Rael-Brook shirt. But even more crucial were the new detergents, which were depicted, in Jo Gable's words, 'like laundering Sir Galahads come to free the housewife from wash-day tyranny' (1980: 58). Even in an era of washing machines the TV soap war has rumbled on, brandishing newer weapons with names like Ariel, Bold and Radion. Other and more recent commercials which offer similar social clues have been for foreign package holidays, photographic goods, cars, mobile phones, and reflecting the greater competitiveness in financial services, banks and building societies.

The history of television advertising is also of significance in reflecting the changes that have occurred in public morals and mores. The 1954 Television Act carefully defined those products and services which could not be advertised, and though many prohibitions have remained constant, some have been lifted and fresh ones imposed. The Act forbade advertising with a political or religious aim, or on any public question on which there could be more than one opinion, such as abortion or capital punishment. No commercials could be broadcast for money-lenders, matrimonial agencies or fortune tellers. On the grounds that they might offend public taste there could be no adverts for condoms or, until the late 1970s, for female sanitary products. Cigarette commercials were not banned until August 1965, yet before 1971 no female could be seen modelling underwear except in silhouette.

Since 1955 two important changes have occurred which pertain not to commercials for individual products but to the overall relationship between advertising and programme content. The first was the early abolition of what were called 'ad-mags', 15-minute sequences of dialogue set in shops or pubs, whose purpose was to promote a whole range of products. The most notable ad-mag was *Jim's Inn*, which began in 1957.

The problem posed by ad-mags was that the more interesting they were made to seem, the more they came to resemble straight programmes, thus threatening the principle that advertising and programming should remain absolutely separate. Moreover they clearly exceeded the amount of advertising per hour which had been permitted by the Television Act. They disappeared in 1963, at the behest of the Pilkington Committee.

Of an opposite tendency was the relaxation in 1988 of the rules governing sponsorship, for it eroded that acclaimed distinction between advertising and programming which had been maintained for over thirty years. News and current affairs were among the few genres to which this relaxation did not apply, and viewers soon learned that they were to be grateful to Croft's Port for *Rumpole of the Bailey* and to PowerGen for disclosing the secrets of the next day's weather.

'A licence to print your own money'

The major shareholder of Scottish Television, the biggest ITV contractor north of the border, was the Canadian news magnate and businessman, Roy Thomson. At its launch in August 1957 he announced, in a famously indiscreet phrase, that owning a commercial TV franchise in Britain was 'like having a licence to print your own money'. Uttered less than two years after ITV started, it is a measure of the speed with which the service turned its fortunes round.

Yet its very success would render it vulnerable. By 1959 questions about the size of the contractors' profits were being put to the ITA by members of the Commons Public Accounts Committee, doubtless with Thomson's words ringing in their ears, and two years later the government introduced an 11 per cent excise duty on television advertising, payable by the contractors. Had their profits accrued from a programme diet of opera, ballet, documentaries and discussions, they might well have been ignored or even applauded; but the contractors were seen as having made their pile from nothing but 'wiggle dances, give-aways, panels and light entertainment' (quoted in Briggs 1995: 16).

This was not altogether fair, but as we noted earlier the contractors' initial financial problems certainly pushed them further along the populist road, a move the ITA could block only by risking the future of the whole system. When their fortunes improved the Authority pressed the contractors to produce more serious programming, but not entirely successfully. In January 1957, for example, the ITV network was running no less than ten give-away shows a week. The consequence was that by 1960 it was easily winning the ratings war, but losing the battle for the support of the nation's opinion formers – the members of parliament and the press, those in academia and the arts.

In these circles there was anxiety about cultural standards, the erosion of 'British civilization', and the lack of a public service ethos on ITV. More specifically, its programmes were seen as mostly trite, the game shows – along with the commercials, which were attacked for being too frequent and often misleading – as encouraging crassly acquisitive attitudes. Above all, there was dismay that such a programme diet could attract and hold a great majority of the viewing public.

These strictures helped to place ITV and the BBC on much more of an equal footing. Commercial television had won the lion's share of the audience, but the BBC retained a moral and cultural superiority – and the rivals still had much to play for. The BBC's Charter was now due for renewal in 1964, the same year in which under the terms of the Television Act of 1954 the progress of ITV would be reviewed.

In 1960 the Conservative government therefore set up a committee under the industrialist Sir Harry Pilkington to appraise the performance of both organizations and to consider the future of British broadcasting. The government also intended to authorize a third television channel and there was every chance that it would be awarded to the organization that Pilkington preferred.

The BBC believed strongly that it needed the third channel in order to provide a comprehensive public service: on its present channel it could fight the ratings war with ITV and on the new channel it would cater for otherwise neglected minorities. Under its Director General Sir Hugh Greene, who had succeeded Sir Ian Jacob on 1 January 1960, it strove to become more competitive, aiming to increase its audience share to 50:50 by 1962, the year the Committee was to report.

One of Greene's first acts was to revamp the news and encourage the new Controller of Television, Stuart Hood, to reschedule the Corporation's programmes to meet the challenge of ITV head-on. But Greene was also an astute public relations man and a clever political lobbyist, and while ITV counted its profits the Corporation carefully assembled the case it would put to Pilkington.

Sources/further reading

The standard history of the birth and early years of commercial television is Sendall (1982; 1983), but useful summary accounts of the establishment and structure of ITV and of the birth of competition are in Paulu (1981) and Tunstall (1983). The political and cultural implications of competition are explored by Curran and Seaton (1991). Seymour-Ure (1991; 1996) is generally useful on broadcasting during this period and, along with Hood (1980), particularly illuminating on the economic composition and overall business interests of the ITV contractors.

For the first years of competition I am generally indebted to Briggs (1995), which is brilliantly researched and highly detailed, though primarily written from the perspective of the BBC. For another, more compact, more journalistic yet also enlightening account of this period, written primarily from the perspective of ITV, see Black (1972b).

On technological developments in television Armes (1988) is invaluable, especially on the historical relationship between live and pre-recorded television content. Bakewell and Garnham (1970) are shrewd on the ways in which the economics and aesthetics of television production were affected by recording technology.

Ward (1989) gives a useful account of how the US movie industry offset its own contraction by making films for television, many of which were soon sold on to ITV. Comparing British reactions unfavourably with those of the Americans, Buscombe (1991) describes the ways in which the motion picture industry tried to cope with the rise of television.

For the deficiencies of early television news on the BBC, see Hood (1975). Detailed accounts of the early years of ITN are in Sendall (1982) and Davis (1976), who also covers current affairs. The best characterization of the *Tonight* programme is in Goldie (1977).

In his editorial introduction to a useful collection of essays on other programme genres of this period, Corner (1991) gives an excellent synoptic account of television and British society during the 1950s. A briefer survey of the programmes of this time is in Day-Lewis (1992).

Caughie (1991) helpfully traces the transition of television drama from relay and rival of conventional live theatre to a genre whose nature and aesthetics more closely resembled those of film, one consequence of which was that TV plays became a kind of commodity. Goddard (1991) is fascinating on the way in which the new technology of Ampex videotape transformed the production of *Hancock's Half Hour*. Sendall (1982) is illuminating on the give-away shows, Hill (1991) on early pop music television, and Whannel (1991) on TV coverage of sport during the first period of competition.

The fullest treatment of television's first years as an advertising medium is Gable (1980), but my remarks on the aesthetics of TV commercials have been inspired by Corner (1995). The factors which led up to the appointment of the Pilkington Committee are described in Sendall (1983) and Briggs (1995).

Pilkington
and after

Chapter 6

Pilkington and after

Sir Hugh Greene: character and achievements

Sir Hugh Greene, whose period of office spanned the 1960s, is reckoned by many to have been the greatest Director General of the BBC since John Reith. However the two men, who managed only a brief and uneasy friendship, were cast in very different moulds. Whereas Reith had stamped himself upon the Corporation, Greene commanded the loyalty of his staff by being relaxed and liberal, affording freedom and flexibility to programme-makers and performers. He had his weaknesses, including a flippant, mischievous streak which prevented him from taking certain matters as seriously as his high office required: he finally fell out with Reith because he was unable to agree with the latter's assertion that dignity was the greatest quality to which humans could aspire. He could be contemptuous of his opponents, some of whom were influential, and he was rather more interested in news and current affairs than in other kinds of programming. But he was also tough and decisive, and a shrewd and unfailing champion of the Corporation.

Yet what were probably his greatest achievements date from the early years of his tenure. By the time the Pilkington Committee reported in 1962 Greene had raised the BBC's audience share to 50:50 for the first time since competition began. Under him the Corporation succeeded in justifying itself to Pilkington, in thoroughly discrediting the achievements of ITV and in capturing the third channel. It also ensured that it would be regarded for many years to come as, in Pilkington's fulsome phrase, 'the main instrument of broadcasting in the United Kingdom' (1962: 288). Indeed the enormity of its success was almost embarrassing: 'The BBC know good broadcasting,' the Committee concluded, as if with a nod and a wink, 'by and large they are providing it' (1962: 46).

Having had military experience of psychological warfare Greene was an adroit propagandist, and under him the BBC presented a much more painstaking and persuasive case to Pilkington than its competitors did. The ITA and the contractors mistook winning the war of the ratings for winning the war of words, and their approach to the Committee was complacent, sloppy and uncoordinated.

But if credit must go to Greene and the BBC for gaining the approval of Pilkington it has to be said that the Committee was predisposed in their favour. From the start many of its members held a severely Reithian view of broadcasting and were altogether reluctant to grant legitimacy to any other. Though Pilkington himself was an industrialist its dominant member seems to have been Professor Richard Hoggart, a working-class beneficiary of higher education and celebrated historian of popular culture.

Hoggart was inclined to be critical of the cultural standards of ITV, believing that it confined itself to entertaining people when it should also be improving and educating them. The Committee as a whole was highly sensitive to the enormous profits which were being made by the ITV contractors; the acquisitive attitudes encouraged by the big money prizes of the ITV give-away shows; the possible effects on young people of the frequent depictions of violence in TV films (ITV was also perceived as responsible for most of these); and more generally, to the possibility, at a time when TV sets were being bought in huge numbers, that television had become the most influential force in modern society.

The dilemmas of 'public service' and the BBC's case to Pilkington

The BBC would have to put its case to Pilkington as a public service broadcaster. However by the end of the 1950s 'public service' broadcasting was already acquiring different meanings, each of which presented a problem for the BBC. It might be helpful at this stage to summarize them.

First there was the original, Reithian notion of serving 'the whole person'. Minority interests were catered for, but it was not in serving these interests separately that public service lay: it was in the *range* of interests catered for, whether of a majority or minority kind. Each listener's or viewer's interests were as far as possible served, but she was exposed to others: to 'the best of every-thing'. The problem, as Reith saw from the outset, was that this form of public service broadcasting was sustainable only as a monopoly, a position which the BBC had lost some five years previously. When audience choice existed, populist programming would drive out all other kinds.

In focusing on a majority interest or interests – giving the people what most of them want – the second notion of public service broadcasting mirrors the modern democratic concept of 'rule by the greatest number'. For instance a great majority of people like soap operas, game shows, action movies and rock concerts, and on this basis the operators of populist TV channels sometimes claim that they are offering a public service. The claim has its own severe logic, though if you are a member of the public who prefers ballet or opera, such channels do not provide you with a service. Moreover the BBC could not easily adopt such a position because to do so would mean that it was providing at the cost of a licence the kinds of programmes that its commercial rivals could provide free of charge.

The third notion is that which targets a minority interest or interests, largely on the basis that it or they would otherwise be neglected. This is what most people now understand by the term 'public service broadcasting', though since it is a kind of reaction against majority preferences and since 'the majority' is seldom exposed to the specialized or esoteric fare it affords, it is almost as paradoxical an idea as that of the 'public' school. It is nevertheless one which the BBC has increasingly favoured, and is attractive because it shares with its Reithian fore-runner a recognition of the viewer's individualism of taste and (in many cases) accompanying desire for self-improvement.

However in other respects it clearly differs from Reith's notion: indeed, in acknowledging the right of choice and in seeking to serve minorities rather than the whole community, it is its opposite. And it, too, holds dangers for the BBC because the service of minorities cannot be too zealously undertaken by an organization that depends for its money on the entire viewing public.

This notion of public service thus helps to explain a dilemma in which the BBC often finds itself. If it produces a popular success, a soap opera or game show, its critics ask why it is spending licence money doing what its rivals do free of charge; but if it produces a ballet or grand opera, there are complaints that it is failing the vast majority of its fee-payers who prefer other things.

The case which the BBC made to Pilkington owed its success to the skill with which it equivocated between all these notions of 'public service'. In order to assert its superiority over ITV it pointed to the Reithian variety of its programmes. But to make too much of this variety might cause Pilkington to question its need for an extra channel. Hence it also claimed that the presence of ITV had forced it to schedule competitively – a situation in which serious and minority programmes were the first casualty. The award of a second channel would therefore provide it with the opportunity to complement its present service with programmes of a more diverse, distinctive or experimental nature.

This looked like the blueprint for a minority, special interest service, yet presumably in order to placate the great licence-paying majority who felt that they should not be expected to fund a service which held nothing of interest for them, the Corporation insisted that it would also carry popular programming. According to Asa Briggs (1995), Greene disapproved of the idea of BBC 2 as a narrowcast or specifically educational service, and Pilkington was duly persuaded to recommend that the third channel should not be specialized but carry a range of programming. Thus in addition to its Reithian rhetoric the BBC made a bow towards the notion of public service which is concerned with neglected minorities, and even managed a nod in the direction of that which is concerned with majority choice.

As well as its preoccupation with 'public service' the BBC professed concern about the social and moral effects of broadcasting, especially television, and this further endeared it to Pilkington since the latter happened to believe that their domestic situation made audiences peculiarly susceptible to television's messages. It began its report by accepting the premise that 'television is and will be a main factor in influencing the values and moral standards of our society' (Pilkington 1962: 15).

The ITA took the opposite view. It believed that despite the popularity and pervasiveness of television its effects had been exaggerated, that it was much more of a mirror than an influence on society – and this, perhaps more than anything, damned it before the Committee. 'The Authority's working assumption is that television has little effect. This is, in our view, a mistake', it announced tersely. 'Our general appraisal is that the Authority have too negative a conception of the purposes of broadcasting. In discounting the influence of the medium they scale down their responsibilities' (Pilkington 1962: 53–4).

The Pilkington Report: immediate impact and long-term effects

When the Report was published in June 1962 the BBC was vindicated and ITV blamed. Pilkington retained its pristine objections to commercial television, judging it by Reithian standards and refusing to allow it any of its own. Its undeniable popularity was simply perceived as vulgarity and turned against it. Claiming that the public service aims enshrined in the 1954 Television Act had never been fulfilled, the Report proposed that ITV should start all over again, with the Authority planning all the programming and selling the advertising time, and buying its programmes from the contractors for inclusion in the schedules it planned. It proposed that the maximum prizes in the give-away shows be greatly reduced. And most important of all, it recommended that the third channel should be given to the BBC.

Among the ITV contractors, some sections of the press and many Conservative MPs the Report caused outrage. As Bernard Sendall (1983) points out, it appeared to judge the achievements of the two services on unrepresentative evidence – on the basis of complaints received rather than the satisfactions implicit in the viewing figures. *The Economist* attacked its 'compulsive nannying' of British audiences, while the *Daily Telegraph* averred that 'this amazing document' was 'saturated by a haughty conviction that whatever is popular must be bad'.

But the real reason for Pilkington's disapproval had perhaps been identified some two years before by the Director General of the ITA, Sir Robert Fraser. His relaxed and humane view of the mass TV audience certainly makes a refreshing contrast to the weighty, moralistic pronouncements of the Committee:

> If you decide to have a system of people's television, then people's television you must expect it to be, and it will reflect their likes and dislikes, their tastes and aversions, what they can comprehend and what is beyond them. Every person of common sense knows that people of superior mental constitution are bound to find much of television intellectually beneath them. If such innately fortunate people cannot realise this gently and considerately and with good manners, if in their hearts they despise popular pleasures and interests, then of course they will be angrily dissatisfied with television. But it is not really television with which they are dissatisfied. It is with people.
>
> (quoted in Potter 1989: 85–6)

Still, the supporters of ITV had no fundamental reason to worry. Politically the Pilkington Report was a dinosaur. No government of any colour would attempt radical reforms to a service as popular with the electorate as ITV was, and the present Conservative administration, with its faith in commercial enterprise, was broadly unsympathetic to the Report. In a new Television Act it awarded the third channel to the BBC on 625 lines UHF, a standard to which all channels were to change, and it extended the Corporation's Charter from 1964 to 1976. It also empowered the ITA to take firmer control over the contractors and it imposed a levy on their advertising revenue; but the other proposals were ignored.

Indeed, like Beveridge before it and Annan later, the Pilkington Report was significant not so much for the substantive changes it wrought as for its broader role in shaping the values which would suffuse broadcasting in the years to follow. As Sendall (1983) points out, the term 'people's television' rapidly became pejorative, and by 1967 an aspiring contractor could impress the ITA with talk of 'producer's television'. It is significant, too, that when the Authority renewed Scottish Television's contract in 1968 its price was that Roy Thomson, author of the famous remark about an ITV franchise being like a licence to print money, should relinquish control. His shareholding was to be reduced from 55 to 25 per cent. Yet Thomson had the last laugh. He sold out at the height of the boom. A year later ITV was hit by recession and STV's survival was in doubt.

But by insisting on the public service responsibilities of ITV, what Pilkington did above all was to strengthen the non-competitive aspects of the British system of television: during the 1960s and 1970s the extent to which it was a duopoly became much clearer than it had been during its first five years. The BBC and ITV continued to compete for audiences, but as Ralph Negrine (1994) observes, neither had an absolute incentive to destroy the other because each had its own source of revenue. Clearly if ITV lost too many viewers it lost advertisers, and if the BBC lost too many its case for a compulsory licence fee was weakened; but a split of up to 60:40 was acceptable to both.

Hence an almost accidental virtue of the system was that while it kept both broadcasters on their toes the competition was not so cut-throat as to rule out all programmes which were experimental or of special interest rather than merely audience-chasing. As Colin Seymour-Ure so happily puts it, the system looked increasingly like 'an expression of the British genius for making practical contraptions which then turn into beautiful machines' (1991: 69).

As a result of Pilkington, then, ITV's programming over the next two decades became more like the BBC's. The Television Act of 1964 allowed the ITA to 'mandate' certain serious kinds of programmes and to require all the contractors to show them at prescribed times in the schedule. In the late 1960s, for instance, all contractors had to broadcast *News at Ten*, one weekday play, one weekend play and two weekly current affairs programmes.

News at Ten began in 1967 and epitomized for many ITV's renewed dominance in the field of news and current affairs. In using two newscasters, Alistair Burnet and Andrew Gardner, it followed an American practice which provided variation for the viewers and the opportunity to give fresh briefings to whichever of the newscasters was out of shot. It also used interviews within the programme not only to comment on news stories but to develop or even create them; it deliberately blurred the old distinctions between newscasters, interviewers and journalists; and it made greater use of on-screen graphics and of special reports and features.

Some of the contractors also won fresh acclaim for their current affairs programmes. Rediffusion's *This Week*, which was later continued by Thames Television, was joined in 1963 by Granada's *World in Action*, whose refusal to pull its punches gave the ITA as well as its targets a severe headache. The contractors renewed their efforts at high quality drama, and according to Curran and Seaton (1991) the 26 per cent of ITV programming which was 'serious' in 1959 had risen to 36 per cent by 1965, a figure that was maintained.

But convergence was not solely the effect of Pilkington. Despite the latter's praise for its serious output, the BBC had been badly shaken by the loss of its audiences during the late 1950s, and its programming now grew more like ITV's in the sense of becoming more populist: game shows and US imports, including soap operas, were every bit as likely to be encountered on the BBC as on ITV. For ITV, then, convergence meant moving 'up-market' – becoming less competitive, more duopolistic: for the BBC convergence meant going 'down-market' – becoming more competitive and less duopolistic.

The extent to which the organizations operated both in competition and as a duopoly was reflected in their various types of programming. Their bids for

Hollywood movies and major sporting events such as the Olympic Games and Football League matches were fiercely competitive, a reminder that one negative feature of rivalry is its inflationary effect on programme costs. In certain other fields, such as educational and religious programming, there were more or less firm agreements to offer complementary coverage. And in yet others, notably party political broadcasts, general elections and state occasions, duplication was acceptable and even enforced by legislation. The only element of competition here might be in style of coverage.

Sometimes too, the ITA pressed the contractors to create duplication through their programme schedules, albeit in a way which bore a semblance of competition. For those viewers in search of light entertainment, for instance, it could hardly be said that the scheduling of *This Week* against *Panorama* was an enlargement of choice. The question it raised was whether such scheduling was in the public interest or just an excess of paternalism.

The cultural convergence of the organizations was reflected in the movements of their top personnel. In 1967 Lord Hill, a former Conservative MP and typical champion of commercial broadcasting, was transferred from the Chair of the ITA, which he had occupied since 1963, to the BBC. At the ITA he was succeeded by Lord Aylestone, the Labour government's former chief whip, who in 1975 would be followed by another Labour Party member, Lady Plowden, previously a Vice-Chair of the BBC. It was also typical of the new *gravitas* of the ITA that when its Director General, Sir Robert Fraser, retired in 1970 he should be replaced by an educationist and intellectual, Sir Brian Young.

The birth and infancy of BBC 2

By the mid-1960s the morale of the BBC was, not surprisingly, high. The sale of TV sets had been rising steadily, and the government was prompted by the findings of Pilkington to restore the licence fee to the realistic level below which it had languished for some years. But the Corporation's biggest reward for impressing Pilkington was the third channel: BBC 2 was launched on 20 April 1964.

In all the Corporation's rhetoric about what the new network would offer there was a strong practical reason why its special interest, experimental flavour could not be over-emphasized – why it should have some 'mixed, popular appeal' and not be 'an intellectual ghetto' (Briggs 1995: 405). To receive it viewers would have to purchase new television sets, and with an existing choice of two channels they were unlikely to do so merely in order to watch minority programming.

Yet notwithstanding Greene's professed views on the new channel and the subsequent recommendations of Pilkington, BBC 2 did mark the hesitant beginning of television narrowcasting. There was a variety of programmes, but many of them – and their overall packaging and presentation – wore a rather more sedate and thoughtful air than those of BBC 1. They were not exactly recherché, but neither were they likely to win the ratings war.

Since it was the government's as well as the Corporation's aim that the channel should be used as a test-bed for new technologies, the programming strategy seems to have been to leaven the generally serious output with a sprinkling of populist programmes (*Match of the Day* made its debut on BBC 2). By this means viewers might be tempted to purchase new television sets, without which it would eventually become impossible to receive any of the networks.

New sets were needed because BBC 2 broadcast not on VHF with 405 lines but on UHF with 625 lines, a higher definition picture that would become the standard for all British television channels. Hence it was only on 625 lines UHF that colour would be introduced some three years later. In the event, the change to the new standard was to take just over twenty years: the manufacture of VHF sets ended in 1975, by which time UHF was available to 95 per cent of the population, and VHF transmissions were phased out by both the BBC and ITV between 1982 and 1985.

Because BBC 2 was at first available only in the south east of England, and further restricted to the few who had bought 625-line televisions, it took some time to make its mark. Nor was it helped by a catastrophic opening night during which it was deprived of a significant part of its tiny audience by a huge power failure in central and west London. Its early programmes attracted some very low viewing figures. After six months about 1.25 million people could actually receive it, though by 1966 it was within reach of nearly two-thirds of the population should they choose to buy the appropriate receivers. At first it broadcast for a mere four hours per evening, and even in 1974 was on air only 60 per cent as much as BBC 1. Eventually the typical viewing ratio between the three channels was ITV: 49, BBC 1: 39, BBC 2: 12.

Despite its modest start the new network managed some early successes both in traditional programme genres and in its experiments with new kinds of programming. At first it tried to liberate television from the straitjacket of the conventional programme schedule by having occasional 'themed' evenings – perhaps an extended debate on a major political issue or the celebration of a particular film genre. Unfortunately the idea was abandoned within three months, partly because the sustained coverage of a single theme made programme 'junctions' with BBC 1 difficult to achieve, and thus deterred viewers from switching into the new channel, and partly because viewers who were in any case uninterested in the theme were lost to the network for an entire evening.

The biggest triumph of its opening year was undoubtedly *The Great War*, an archive compilation in twenty-six parts of immense interest to both professional historian and casual, uninitiated viewer. Before this series the technical limitations of old ciné film had caused its subjects to move about at a frenetic, unintentionally comical pace, but BBC production staff now found a way to screen the contemporary footage of the war at a natural speed.

With *Late Night Line-Up*, presented by Joan Bakewell, BBC 2 also pioneered the 'talk show' – less vapid than the celebrity based 'chat show' of a later era, more relaxed and wide ranging than the old-fashioned studio discussion. Its aim was to provide an open ended critical review of the current output of BBC television.

From 1965 Johnny Speight's sitcom *Till Death Us Do Part* brought us the jingoistic cockney character, Alf Garnett, who gave great pleasure not only to those who regarded him as a caricature of prejudice and ignorance but to those who admired him as the last stronghold of traditional British values. He was thus an interesting though not unique instance of the way in which irony can rebound upon the ironist, yet make him popular with everyone.

In 1966 the channel began a magnificent twenty-six part adaptation of *The Forsyte Saga*, the series of novels by John Galsworthy. Its significance was twofold. It was the first great example of the way in which television could give serious literature a renewed and indeed unprecedented popularity, not only in the form of its adaptations thereof but by stimulating sales and readings of the original texts. And it was the last major television serial to be shot in black and white.

BBC 2 began regular colour transmissions on 1 July 1967, the first British – and European – network to do so. By no means all of its programmes were in colour, but their proportion steadily increased. Like the introduction of 625 lines UHF, they were part of the BBC's dual policy of using the network, with its relatively low audiences, as a test-bed for new technology, and using a new technology which would eventually become a beneficial and standard feature of television to lure more viewers to the network.

The United States had had colour TV since 1953, but British engineers had preferred to wait for a system which would offer subtler tones and a wider range. Nevertheless, whether because of teething troubles in the technology itself or because it was difficult to fine-tune the first colour receivers, many early pictures revealed people with unhealthily green skins and soccer strips whose reds and oranges showed a menacing tendency to shimmer and flare. Nor were these receivers cheap. Their average cost was £350 – about £2,000 at today's values. However, by the time colour was extended to the other two channels in November 1969, its quality seemed to be consistently better. At the same time the cost of sets fell and there was a dramatic surge in sales.

The obvious effect of colour was to make the medium of television immensely more vivid and picturesque: costume dramas and natural history programmes were only two of its more obvious beneficiaries. But there were also negative implications. Those who worried about the effects and influences of television were not slow to point out that in its representations of violence, whether real or simulated, the blood would now run red.

There were several other fine monuments to the serious and educative intentions of BBC 2, notably three documentary series with almost encyclopaedic ambitions. In 1969 and fully exploiting the new colour pictures, there was *Civilisation*, a thirteen-part series on the history of art presented by the scholar and former Chair of ITA, Lord Clark. Three years later, in *Alastair Cook's America*, a veteran broadcaster brought shrewd insights to a historical and political account of the United States.

But perhaps most ambitious of all was *The Ascent of Man* (1972–3), a thirteen part history of scientific discovery and a philosophy of human nature presented by the eminent scientist, Dr Jacob Bronowski. In pushing television to its intellectual limits this series marked an important moment in the history of the medium, when it was of sufficient technical maturity to provide high picture and sound quality, yet still young enough to command concentration from its audiences. In daring to put that moment to its fullest use, BBC 2, and British television generally, can take a certain pride.

Three programme landmarks of the 1960s

There is probably less agreement among historians than among geographers about what constitutes a landmark. Nevertheless I have selected three programmes, all on BBC, which in their different ways broadened the range of TV output and caught the spirit of the age: *That Was the Week That Was* (or *TW3* for short); *Z Cars*; and at its very end, *Monty Python's Flying Circus*.

In an attempt to evoke its carefree hedonism the decade was known, even in its own time, as 'the Swinging Sixties'. Its driving force seems to have been the new economic and cultural power of young people, those in their late teens and early 20s. For them more than any other social group, post-war austerity had yielded to full employment and an affluence largely free of domestic or family liabilities. They thus had a considerable amount of money to spend on such things as clothes, records (by now a burgeoning industry), cars and the cinema.

The preoccupations of youth, all of which were interrelated, thus became the fashionable preoccupations, and during the 1960s Britain was seen throughout the world as a trend-setter in those fields where the spending power of young people was a significant factor. One was the arts and entertainment, especially pop music. The Beatles became famous in 1963 and were the first of many British bands to storm the American charts. Another was design. The millionth Mini, a hugely popular car developed by the British Motor Corporation, rolled off the assembly-line in 1965 and gave a prefix to the mini-skirt, one of the era's great icons. And a third was fashion, symbolized by London's Carnaby Street, where young Britons donned ceremonial military tunics and bought accessories covered in Union Jack motifs, partly to recall but mainly to ridicule their country's former imperial greatness.

The economic and cultural power of the young was also a manifestation of the general rise in educational standards which had resulted from the 1944 Education Act. More and more were going on to higher education, and it was during the 1960s that the universities underwent the first of their enormous expansions. Thus the natural tendency of young people to question 'the received wisdom' and get impatient with the pretensions of established authority was reinforced in some by the sceptical habits of study and learning. For one or two university students it was but a short step from scepticism to satire. The vastly successful Oxbridge stage revue *Beyond the Fringe* (1961) and the fortnightly magazine *Private Eye*, launched in the same year and also the work of Oxbridge graduates, seemed to set the tone of the time.

In a curious way this general trend was strengthened by television, a medium which the 1960s generation was the first to have grown up with. I suggested in the last chapter that with programmes like *Tonight*, a certain spirit of scepticism and irreverence was developing at the end of the 1950s; but even more important was the fact that there was something almost iconoclastic in the medium itself. Largely because written words obscure their object and sounds and photographs are limited, newspapers and radio represent public figures in a way which is unavoidably 'distant' or incomplete; and distance lends enchantment, a lack of familiarity breeds respect.

But television showed people in close-up, 'warts and all'. It revealed every mannerism, uncertainty and hesitation. Mystique evaporated. The great and the good – aristocrats, statesmen, 'authorities' and experts – turned out to be people like the rest of us, their average physical blemishes and peculiarities implying average fallibility. Thus despite the elitist tendency of Reith's broadcasting philosophy, there was a sense in which television was a leveller, an inherently democratizing medium. Like that great democratic process which has been continuing over several centuries and which we outlined in Chapter 3, it seemed to call into question the ideas of status, authority and expertise.

Since during the 1960s it was the young who were in the vanguard of this questioning and often debunking tendency, and since the young are naturally preoccupied with sexual matters, it was here that scepticism of traditional values seemed at its strongest. With the wider availability of reliable contraception (the Pill was on sale from 1961), there was a new concern with 'permissiveness'. The previous connections between sex and fertility and between sex and marriage were no longer as necessary as they once seemed. It was not surprising that a libertarian spirit was developing, though for many, perhaps, it was more a matter of images and dreams than of solid fact.

The characteristic trends and concerns of the time seemed to be expressed or at least symbolized by the Saturday night satire show, *That Was the Week That Was*, launched in November 1962. Fronted by David Frost and including Millicent

Martin, William Rushton and Bernard Levin, it had its roots in the gently flippant *Tonight* programme, but was actually the brain-child of Sir Hugh Greene: 'I had the idea that it was a good time in history to have a programme that would do something to prick the pomposity of public figures.'

TW3 thus became the first satire show to be seen on British television. That it was broadcast by the BBC, that a publicly funded institution should at the prompting of its own director general see it as part of its role to 'prick the pomposity of public figures', was remarkable – and most likely possible only because the Corporation was no longer the sole broadcaster.

Since *TW3*'s content was highly topical and the show had to be put together in great haste, often with last-minute additions and alterations, it had a freshness and informality which was quite new to television. The studio from which it was broadcast was largely bare, with obviously improvised sets and props and the cameras themselves sometimes in shot. But the show was so popular that its absence of style became a kind of style in itself and was imitated by other programmes. One effect of its irreverence and the obvious relish of the studio audience was, as Grace Wyndham Goldie (1977) points out, to make it less like a conventional television programme than a private party, at which the viewer was nevertheless welcome.

Not only was *TW3* the first television satire: the fact that at its peak 10 million were watching meant that for the first time in its history satire had become a genuinely popular art form. However, in running to only two series, *TW3* had a short life. It always provoked angry complaints, and in the second series there was some loss of quality; but the show remained popular and few were convinced by the reasons which were given for its sudden demise in December 1963.

However *TW3* had a further historical significance. It marked television's coming-of-age in the sense that many of its jokes and references depended for their effect on the audience's knowledge of a culture which had largely been created, or at least disseminated, by the medium itself. That such knowledge could be assumed is a measure of the extent to which television had embedded itself in the national consciousness.

The police drama series *Z Cars*, which also began in 1962, was another programme which seemed to capture the contemporary mood. Set in Merseyside, it responded to the interest in provincial, especially northern, life which, as Asa Briggs (1995) points out, was a feature of the late 1950s and early 1960s, and expressed in several cinema films such as *Saturday Night and Sunday Morning*, *A Taste of Honey* and *This Sporting Life*, as well as in the celebrated TV soap opera, *Coronation Street*.

In order to achieve a factual, documentary effect, *Z Cars* used the narrative techniques which television had borrowed from film. Briggs has perceptively brought out the extent of its originality by comparing it with an example of the traditional police series, *Dixon of Dock Green*. *Dixon* had been running since 1955 and was the BBC's most popular programme of this kind. It was set in an old-fashioned east London community where its hero walked the beat. His domestic life was idealized, and every episode moved to a neat ending in which the villains were apprehended and the moral was spelt out by Dixon himself in an address straight to camera.

Z Cars, on the other hand, was set in the wilderness of a modern housing estate which could be patrolled only in vehicles. Its policemen were human beings who lost their temper, might even quarrel with their wives, and were often outwitted by the villains. Its atmosphere was gritty and unsentimental, though there was sometimes pathos; and while every episode was morally suggestive, there were few neat endings.

Within a year *Z Cars* was attracting an audience of 16.5 million to *Dixon*'s 13.5 million and had the effect of making subsequent episodes of the latter slightly tougher and less cosy. But while *Z Cars* in its original form ended in 1965, *Dixon* comfortably outlasted it, perhaps proving T. S. Eliot's maxim that 'human kind cannot bear very much reality'. Both the series and its hero staggered on until 1976, by which time Jack Warner, the actor who played Dixon, was eighty years old.

By the late 1960s soldier-boy tunics and Union Jacks had yielded to hippies and flower-power, and, perhaps assisted by soft drugs, to a more knowing and self-absorbed mood. This self-consciousness permeated the mass media as much as any other area of life, and helps to explain the popularity of a surreal comedy show named *Monty Python's Flying Circus*. The show made an unpromising debut at the very end of the decade as the replacement for a late-night religious programme on BBC 2, yet became the only one of our three landmark programmes to be enjoyed around the globe.

Featuring John Cleese, Michael Palin, Terry Jones, Graham Chapman and Eric Idle, it continued into the early 1970s – a sequence of fragmented, anarchic sketches and disconcerting animated drawings which is of interest to the media student not simply because it was vastly popular and often explosively funny, but because it consciously followed *The Goon Show* in deriving much of its humour from broadcasting itself: in this case, television.

In drama and comedy, television, like radio before it, had vacillated between merely relaying or simulating the traditional forms of the theatre and seeing itself as the locus of new and distinctive forms. *Monty Python* was the first comedy show to think wholly in terms of television, but whereas *TW3* could be said merely to have marked the medium's age of majority, *Python* celebrated its maturity. It took as the material for many of its jokes not just the culture and content of television, as *TW3* had done several years before, but its very 'grammar': the forms, codes and conventions of the medium. These things are rather less consciously absorbed by viewers than the content they express, but they are still delightedly recognized when parodied, and it is small wonder that *Python* struck a universal chord.

Other developments in programmes and technology

In our more general review of programmes it seems appropriate to remain a little longer with comedy, since (on BBC especially) the 1960s were a continuation of that golden age which had begun in the previous decade.

From the creators of *Hancock's Half Hour* came *Steptoe and Son* (1962–74), in which the relationship between Hancock and Sid James was transposed to that between a dreaming, idealistic rag-and-bone man and his crude, exploitative father, yet broadened to take in farce at one extreme and something approaching pathos at the other. From 1965 viewers had the pleasurable company of *The Likely Lads* and its sequel *Whatever Happened to the Likely Lads?*, starring James Bolam and Rodney Bewes; and from 1968 until 1977 a delightful gallery of characters made up *Dad's Army*, tales of the wartime Home Guard.

ITV's strength lay less in sitcoms than in the straight comedy showcase, but by the end of the 1950s the old variety spectacular with its teeming, ornate stage had evolved into something better suited to television: a programme built round a single star or act. Moreover many of the stars now owed their fame to television itself rather than TV's exploitation of earlier stage success. As Jeremy Potter puts it:

> For the viewers the magic illusion which had to be created was no longer that of a seat in the stalls but of the studio as an extension of their living room. The most popular entertainers, like Benny Hill in *The Benny Hill Show* (Thames), were those who adjusted their timing and projection to this more intimate relationship with an invisible audience.
>
> (1990: 231)

Among the other stars around whom ITV created special shows were Stanley Baxter, Tommy Cooper, Les Dawson, Bruce Forsyth, Rolf Harris, Morecambe and Wise, and Jimmy Tarbuck.

Drama continued to flourish along a broad front. Under Sydney Newman the BBC's *Wednesday Play* commanded a regular audience of between 10 and 12 million. Typically, its productions tackled contemporary social issues in a realistic, uncompromising way – or, if you agreed with the 'Clean Up TV' campaigner Mary Whitehouse, offered nothing but 'dirt, doubt and disbelief'. The most famous play was *Cathy Come Home* (1966), directed by Ken Loach and credited with leading to the founding of the homeless persons' charity, Shelter, and with persuading the government to change its housing policy. In 1967 the aims of the series were rather better expressed in a new title: *Play for Today*.

In adventure series and serials honours were evenly shared between the BBC and ITV: from 1963 the former offered the long-running *Dr Who*, which soon became a cult with science fiction enthusiasts, while ABC gave us the chic detectives of *The Avengers*. But it was still ITV which held the lead in soap operas, though not altogether a qualitative one. The redoubtable *Coronation Street* was joined in 1964 by ATV's *Crossroads* ('highly popular and irredeemably shoddy') – a saga which was set in a motel. Its production values were so poor that despite its massive following the ITA stepped in to prevent the public from having too much of what it enjoyed by ordering ATV to reduce the episodes from four to three a week, as compulsive an act of nannying as anything in Pilkington.

Sport was an area in which its regional structure left ITV at something of a disadvantage to its rival. In 1968 its Saturday afternoon programme *World of Sport*, which had been launched by ABC with ATV in 1964, was taken over by London Weekend Television in order to give it a firmer metropolitan base; but in *Grandstand* the BBC maintained its exclusive long-term contracts with the governing bodies of a number of popular sports: athletics, swimming, cricket, rugby.

ITV's strategy was therefore to broaden the range of sports it covered as a supplement to the main diet of soccer and horse racing. Since the great majority of soccer matches could not be broadcast live it was a strategy which was largely adopted by the BBC too, and meant that many sports like hockey, badminton, basketball, ice-skating and motor-cycle scrambling gained an unprecedented if sometimes short-lived boost from television. However certain others were permanently transformed by the medium, many viewers coming to enjoy sports like show-jumping, snooker and darts which they had previously known little of.

The sport which benefited most was probably snooker. Until well into the age of television it was largely confined to working men's clubs, but given the nature of the game the factor that changed everything was colour. By 1985 the World Championship was able to hold a TV audience of 18.5 million until after midnight, and snooker is now so commercialized that its humble pedigree has been all but forgotten. With American football and Japanese sumo wrestling, television's popularization of sports which were little known in Britain was to continue into later decades.

Something in which ITV held a hugely popular monopoly was professional wrestling, but this was a tussle between sport and show business in which the latter generally came out on top. Among some of the combatants the acting was as bad as anything seen on *Crossroads*.

As well as adding good programmes to the traditional categories and creating other good programmes which seemed to be *sui generis*, both broadcasters achieved some original variations within the traditional categories. A sample from each must suffice. In 1962 Granada introduced yet another game show, but one which featured competitors of supposedly above-average intelligence and education, tested real knowledge and skills, and offered a trophy, not TV sets, to the winners. *University Challenge* was an ideal concept for people's television in an era of the Pilkington Report and the Open University, of mass education and individual self-betterment. It was a bright if modest instance of edifying programming, and one which drew big audiences.

One BBC programme which offered something different within an established format was *Nationwide*, born in 1966 and another offspring of the fertile *Tonight* programme. Like *Tonight*, whose tea-time slot it took over and which it resembled in style and structure, it aimed to capture the bulk of the audience for the rest of the evening. But it had a novel element. After a networked opening the programme divided into several versions, each providing 25 minutes of news and current affairs within a different BBC region. These regions then reunited with London to contribute local angles and views on national issues, and thus reach a wider audience. The programme was devised partly to counter criticisms that the BBC was still excessively metropolitan: as its title implies it was an attempt to match the regional strengths of ITV yet be of national interest.

We must now turn to what, notwithstanding the arrival of colour TV, was the most momentous technological development of the 1960s: satellite broadcasting. The Soviet Union had inaugurated the space age in October 1957 with its rocket-launched satellite, Sputnik, but it was the Americans who most quickly exploited the broadcasting potential of satellite technology. Using their satellite, Telstar, the first transatlantic transmission took place in July 1962, when viewers in sixteen European countries saw live pictures from Washington, Chicago and Ontario, and the first two-way TV link between the continents followed soon after.

Since Telstar was an orbiting satellite, the transmission 'windows' were relatively brief and did not always coincide with popular viewing times, but in 1963 longer transmissions became possible when the Americans launched a geo-stationary satellite, Syncom II. Its first extended transmission, in November 1963, marked a melancholy occasion, the state funeral of the recently assassinated President Kennedy.

From April 1965 the Intelsat series of satellites made transmissions possible for eighteen hours a day, and the first live global television event was the Mexico Olympics of 1968. In July 1969 live pictures of the American moon landings provided a fitting climax both to the space race and to the global satellite broadcasts which had been developing over the past decade: 12 million watched on BBC, 14.5 million on ITV.

Yet there are other and more dramatic figures. The global audience was 600 million, one fifth of the world's population. Whereas in 1965 forty channel hours of international television had been transmitted, the number of hours in 1970 would be 1,214 and rising rapidly. Thanks to satellites television could now provide live pictures of everything that the human race was capable of seeing, whether on this planet or on any other, and it could also capture a single audience of unparalleled size. Yet as a mass medium it was barely thirty-five years old.

Educational television

The first years of television, like those of radio, were attended by the very reasonable and powerful feeling that since the medium can reach so many, span such vast distances, and bring such new and varied impressions and experiences to its audience, it is not only educative in itself but should be put to the services of formal education. Yet in practice it has been difficult to integrate both media to the structured courses of the latter. Though partly offset by advances in audio and video recording, there are three main reasons. The first is the difficulty of adjusting the dates and times of programmes to individual school or college curricula and timetables. Second there is the problem of extracting learning points from a constantly evolving and – in television at least – a highly detailed and unavoidably ambiguous 'text'. And the third is the students' abiding perception of the broadcast media as primarily intended for entertainment and leisure, and therefore to be consumed only passively.

These problems can be overstated: they are less in some subjects than in others, and there have been notable successes at both school and tertiary level. But even the Open University, which has its own production facilities and takes great care to tailor programmes to individual courses, does not expect sound and television to take up more than about 10 per cent of its students' time. Thus, while not belittling the important contribution which broadcasting has made to education, the account of it in this section is necessarily summary.

It is perhaps surprising that the first regular TV series for schools – which reached about 100 institutions – was provided not by the BBC but by Rediffusion in 1957. With a tendency to specialize in different areas of the curriculum, other ITV contractors soon followed, but their output was particularly enriched by the arrival of Yorkshire Television in 1968. By the late 1970s ITV schools programmes were at some point reaching 22,000 primary and 3,800 secondary institutions, about 76 per cent of the total. The Authority allowed no commercials to be screened in or around these programmes.

By 1961 the BBC had eliminated ITV's early lead, and over the subsequent years showed, as one might expect, a more consistent commitment to educational broadcasting at all levels. In 1969 it launched the pre-school *Watch with Mother* on BBC 1 and *Playschool* on BBC 2. At the same level *Rainbow* began on Thames in 1972, and the American import *Sesame Street* has graced Channel 4 for many years. Latterly Channel 4 has become the main ITV outlet for the few educational programmes still made by the contractors and by one or two independent producers.

At the other end of the educational spectrum the future prime minister, Harold Wilson, mooted the idea of a 'university of the air' in 1963 – an idea which was of a piece with the expansion of the traditional universities that was taking place at that time, and which also chimed nicely with the edifying impulse behind the Pilkington Report. When Labour came to power it announced that the Open University, as it was eventually to be called, would broadcast on BBC 2. The university admitted its first students in 1971 and in that year collaborated with the BBC to make no fewer than 300 television programmes for four foundation courses. The Open University has, of course, marked a significant stage in the liberalization of Britain's system of higher education. Many regard it as the greatest single achievement of Harold Wilson's premiership, and it is to the credit of British television, specifically the BBC, that it has played a significant role in that achievement.

The ITV franchise awards, 1964 and 1967

The original ITV contracts ran for nine years, which meant that the franchises would be open to new or renewed bids in 1964. However the next contracts would run for only three years because there was uncertainty as to whether ITV would gain a second channel, when it would be required to convert to a UHF 625-line signal, and at what stage it would be able to switch to colour. All the existing contractors reapplied in 1964 and all were reappointed, not so much because the ITA felt that their performances could not be bettered as because it would have been unfair to offer any new contractor a franchise which might last no longer than three years.

The 1967 contracts were to be awarded for six years in the first instance, though quite unforeseeably they actually lasted for more than thirteen. However in allocating these, the ITA wielded the surgeon's knife, causing howls of anguish and fury, and there were many who felt that the commercial television service emerged from the operation in worse shape than it had entered it.

For the new round of contracts the Authority determined that it would increase the number of franchise holders and end the weekday/weekend split, except in London. In the north it therefore rolled Granada back to the west of the Pennines but extended its broadcasting time to seven days a week. The new franchise to the east of the Pennines went to Yorkshire Television, though its area – a large one – was not coterminous with the county itself. Associated Television, which had previously held the Midland weekday and London weekend franchises was now confined to the Midlands, but like Granada's its air-time was extended to the full week.

It was in London and the West that blood was shed. The London weekday contractor, Rediffusion, had an excellent record. As well as having a good portfolio of general programmes it had been first in the field of schools broadcasting. It had also pioneered the use of Ampex videotape in Britain. But in its renewal bid it struck the Authority as a shade complacent. It was prepared to argue, for instance, that public service broadcasting merely consists of giving the majority of the public what it wants, a view which after the strictures of Pilkington could hardly find favour with the ITA.

At the same time the Authority was bedazzled by a star-studded consortium including Aidan Crawley and David Frost which was bidding for the London weekend franchise, and which said exactly the right things about the need to educate and elevate popular taste even while satisfying it. Not the least attractive feature of this group was that it signalled a new era in ITV management, in the sense that its membership did not consist wholly of novices in the industry – businessmen, pioneers or moneyed amateurs – but included people who had already made a career in television. These were either home-grown or, like Michael Peacock and Jeremy Isaacs, from the BBC: they could stand on their record as programme-makers or performers.

The Authority's new dispensation for London was to grant the weekend franchise to the star-studded consortium, London Weekend Television (LWT), and the weekday franchise to a new contractor, Thames Television, which it created from a forced marriage between ABC Television and Rediffusion, with the latter as junior partner.

Further west, however, one contractor was axed altogether – merely, many thought, to demonstrate that an ITV contract was not a guarantee of everlasting life. It was true that the sacrificial victim, Television Wales and the West (TWW), had an undistinguished record. But it had managed to maintain an awkward franchise which shackled Bristol and the near south west of England to a nation whose advocates of a separate native-language service raised a clamour out of all proportion to their number.

When the axe fell the cold fury of TWW's chairman, Lord Derby, prompted a hand-wringing apologia from the head of ITA, Lord Hill: 'if promise is never to be preferred to performance, then every television company will go on forever'. TWW rejected an ITA offer of a 40 per cent interest in its successor, Harlech Television, and threw it the franchise four months early.

As a condition of the 1967 contracts the ITA required the new contractors to accept a single programme journal which would bear comparison with the BBC's *Radio Times*. Hitherto there had been several journals published by, or on behalf of, the individual contractors. As a result of the new requirement the *TV Times* was launched and soon became hugely profitable, attracting the largest readership in Britain (12 million adults, 2 million children). During the 1970s the *TV Times* and the *Radio Times* became the two largest selling magazines in the country, far outstripping the more specialist women's magazines and delivering an unusually wide readership to their eager advertisers.

From swinging sixties to sombre seventies

The 1967 franchise awards had damaging consequences for ITV. LWT, the new contractor whose lucrative metropolitan franchise was the cornerstone of the entire commercial system, lacked experience of its hard realities and in its efforts to elevate public taste got off to a disastrous start. Its business people had little understanding of television and its television people knew little of business. Its programming strengths – in current affairs, the arts and children's TV – were ill-suited to a weekend franchise, and it was hammered in the ratings by what was now the much more populist output of the BBC. Nor could the company count on goodwill and support within the ITV system, for in making its distinctively up-market bid to the ITA it had disparaged the programmes of the other contractors.

But the problems were not confined to LWT. The introduction of a fifth major contractor, Yorkshire Television, raised the cost of the whole system in facilities and staff while reducing the role of the other four. Moreover the franchise upheavals had left production and technical staff insecure and resentful. In August 1968 one of the unions, the Association of Cinematographic and Television Technicians, called a two-week national strike. Programme schedules were disrupted, production halted, future projects shelved or dropped: audiences plummeted and advertisers grew restive.

Yet even without the problems caused by the franchise awards, ITV would have faced difficulties. Its two principal growth factors during the first half of the 1960s had now disappeared. Since the ownership of television sets had just about reached saturation point, the audience was no longer increasing; nor could ITV hope to take a larger share of the existing audience – indeed its share decreased – because it was now competing against two BBC networks instead of one. On the other hand, ITV was faced with increased capital expenditure. The introduction of UHF 625 lines and of colour committed all the contractors to re-equipping their studios and post-production facilities. But whereas the BBC benefited when viewers switched from monochrome to colour because the colour licence was more expensive, the change-over brought no extra revenue to ITV.

When at Pilkington's prompting the government imposed a levy on ITV's revenue – a heavier imposition than a tax on profits – it had not foreseen that ITV could be affected by a recession: indeed it increased the levy in 1969, the very year that revenue began to fall. By 1970 revenue had declined by 12 per cent in real terms and successive governments were obliged to reduce the levy in 1970 and 1971.

Despite this, several contractors faced financial collapse, notably Scottish TV, Harlech Television and Tyne-Tees TV. To ensure the latter's survival the ITA had to allow it to affiliate with Yorkshire TV under a joint management company named Trident Television. But not surprisingly it was LWT which threatened to become the most spectacular casualty, until at the end of 1970 Rupert Murdoch's News of the World organization offered to buy into it and put it on a more businesslike footing. The ITA vetoed Murdoch as chair of the company because of his press interests, but it had little choice than to approve his bid – not the only occasion on which it would allow a contractor to stay afloat by throwing its weightier programme promises overboard. LWT was duly restructured and successfully relaunched in 1971.

Meanwhile life had not been altogether rosy for the BBC. It had launched its second channel and was competing directly and very successfully with ITV on its first. But its finances, like those of its rival, deteriorated during the second half of the decade, and for similar reasons. The launch of a second service and the conversions to UHF 625 lines and colour all imposed extra costs, but its income from licences levelled off because the ownership of TV sets had reached saturation point and the initial take-up of colour was slow. Indeed, with a sudden rise in inflation, its real income actually declined.

But if media institutions could suffer occasional bouts of sickness, the medium itself was unmistakably healthy. In January 1972 the government would lift all restrictions on broadcasting hours – an acknowledgement that television had passed the stage of being novel or exotic and had inextricably woven itself into the fabric of modern life. De-restriction was not wholly welcome to the BBC. Whereas extra air-time could mean more advertising revenue for ITV, it merely meant extra expense for the Corporation, which was already burdened with a second network. But it was a portent that could not be ignored. Within twenty years viewers would be able to watch television round the clock.

Sources/further reading

The standard histories of this period, to which I owe general and particular debts, are Briggs (1995) of the BBC and Sendall (1983) and Potter (1989; 1990) of ITV.

An account of his years as Director General of the BBC is included in the biography of Sir Hugh Greene by Tracey (1983).

A wide-ranging discussion of public service broadcasting is in MacCabe and Stewart (1986), while McDonnell (1991) charts its historical development through the deliberations of the various broadcasting committees.

The Pilkington Report (1962) makes interesting reading: as a conservative view of broadcasting it is elegantly and eloquently written. Curran and Seaton (1991) usefully summarize its overall philosophy and its impact on subsequent broadcasting. Other accounts of its attitudes and findings are in Hood (1980) and Black (1972b), who also describes the public reactions to it.

Seymour-Ure (1991; 1996) and Negrine (1994) both contain shrewd comments on the partly competitive, partly duopolistic relationship between the BBC and ITV, and Hood and O'Leary (1990) point out that Pilkington created buoyancy at the BBC and tighter controls over ITV.

Within a concise account of the fortunes of both BBC and ITV during this period, Lambert (1982) outlines the case for the third channel which the BBC made to Pilkington. Briggs (1995) provides an excellent description of the birth and early years of BBC 2 and of the introduction of colour transmissions.

For helpful attempts to characterize the spirit of the 'swinging sixties' see Booker (1970) and Levin (1972). There are analyses of *That Was the Week That Was* in Goldie (1977), Wilmut (1980), Sherrin (1983) and Crisell (1991). On *Z Cars* see Laing (1991). For the comparison of *Z Cars* with *Dixon of Dock Green* I am heavily indebted to Briggs (1995). Wilmut (1980) outlines the genesis and evolution of *Monty Python's Flying Circus*, and there are remarks on its telegenic nature in Nathan (1971).

A general survey of the TV programmes of this period is provided by Day-Lewis (1992) and an illuminating discussion of television forms of light entertainment by Dyer (1973). Brunsdon and Morley (1978) is a detailed analysis of *Nationwide*. News and current affairs programming is treated in Davis (1976), which also gives a useful account of early satellite transmissions. For an assessment of the strengths and weaknesses of broadcasting as an educational resource see Bates (1984) and Crisell (1986).

Within a helpful outline of broadcasting during this period, Tunstall (1983) describes the ITV franchise reallocations, as does Potter (1989), who also provides a detailed account of the subsequent difficulties which the service encountered.

The fall and rise of radio

Chapter 7

The fall and rise of radio

The BBC's dwindling audience

Despite maintaining the high quality of its radio programmes, the BBC continued to lose listeners throughout the 1960s. Only the statutory limit which the government had imposed on television's transmission hours prevented radio from being hit even harder. It was in the evenings, TV's peak period, that the older medium suffered most, though its audiences were never negligible.

Yet if TV was the main cause of radio's woes (BBC expenditure on vision began to exceed expenditure on sound in 1958–9), there were also problems within its own network structure – that cultural pyramid with the Light Programme at its base, the Home Service in the middle and the Third Programme at its apex. The reader will recall that in order to give the structure an edifying aim – in Haley's words, to lead the listener 'from good to better' (Smith 1974: 83) – there was a deliberate element of overlap between Light and Home and between Home and Third.

However, the overlap was such that the networks were not sufficiently distinctive to command listener loyalty. This was a particular problem for the Light and the Home. Some serious programming existed even on the Light. On the other hand, the comedy show *ITMA* had been on the Home Service, while some of its other programmes would not have seemed out of place on the Third. In search of a certain kind of output, a listener might find herself scanning the schedules of two or even all three networks. Since programmes on the Third were unwaveringly serious it commanded the strongest loyalty – but of a tiny number. Even before 1951, when television had yet to make its impact, the network never gained more than 2 per cent of the total radio audience.

In order to boost its following, surgery – or more accurately dismemberment – was performed in 1957. Its output was cut from five and a half to three and a half hours a day and confined to the evenings, while the other two hours were devoted to an educational concept, mostly consisting of instructive talks, called Network Three. This attracted even fewer listeners than the Third. On Sundays the daytime service was re-named the Music Programme, which from 1965 was extended to weekdays, and was followed in the early evenings by Study Session (Sport Service on Saturdays) and later by the curtailed Third Programme.

Thus over several years the BBC adopted the extraordinary measure of offering two and then three separate services on a single wavelength, the inevitable effect of which was to blur the identity of the old Third Programme and strain the loyalty of what few adherents it had previously possessed. But it was not simply the case that the Third Programme and its associated services were too serious and demanding for the great majority of radio listeners; for many, so were the Home and even the Light: Radio Luxembourg, which had reopened after the war, was again eating into the BBC's audience.

Despite all this, television remained radio's greatest enemy, and 1964 perhaps marked the nadir of BBC sound broadcasting. This was the year in which it yielded several kinds of programmes to television and in which the latter, confident in its ascendancy, launched a third network. *Children's Hour* had already been axed in 1961, but now *For the Young* was also discontinued, bringing to an end all regular sound broadcasts for children.

The year 1964 also saw the death of the charismatic head of radio features, Laurence Gilliam, who knew that his department would not long outlast him. Back in the 1920s and 1930s features had been radio's programme laboratory, the place in which it had tried to create its own unique genre. Its closure seemed to have dark implications for the medium in general.

Technological developments in radio

However, the melancholy events of the 1960s had been preceded by three developments in radio technology, two of which would help to secure the medium's future.

Perhaps the least important, though rewarding to the suitably equipped listener, was *stereophony*, a system by which sound is split into and reproduced by two separate channels in order to create a spatial effect. The first test transmissions took place in 1958, the first regular broadcasts in 1966.

Stereo meant that despite television, radio was to remain for many years the medium to which people turned when sound quality was paramount. It also prompted the development of 'simulcasts', television programmes, especially music concerts and operas, which were simultaneously carried by radio in order to provide a standard of sound commensurate with what viewers could see. It was only with the arrival of stereo TV sets in the 1980s that simulcasts died out.

Much more important was the development of *very high frequency* or VHF transmissions. The first two VHF transmitters were opened in 1955 at Wrotham in Kent, one of them also providing *frequency modulation* (FM) which gave freedom from interference. There was little public demand for VHF/FM: in 1972 about 60 per cent of radio listeners were still unequipped to receive it. But its long-term significance was considerable. First, it offered much better sound quality than the medium and long waves, and by the 1990s all of the four traditional BBC networks had moved to the VHF waveband.

Second, it greatly increased the number of stations which could broadcast, since its low-power transmissions allowed stations that were a reasonable distance apart to occupy neighbouring or even identical wavelengths. VHF was therefore the technology which facilitated the expansion of local radio during the 1970s and 1980s – something of a return to the very first pattern of sound broadcasting which John Reith had replaced during the late 1920s by a centralized, national service.

However, quite the most important of these technical innovations was the *transistor*, because it ensured that even in a television age radio would continue to be used by significant numbers of people. Developed in the United States in 1947, the transistor was a tiny semi-conductor device which replaced the wireless valve. The latter, somewhat like a light-bulb in appearance, was large, costly and fragile. It also consumed a lot of electricity, which meant that a battery powered wireless was hardly an economical proposition.

The new transistor radios could make use of batteries since they consumed much less power. They were more reliable and cheap enough for almost everyone to buy. And they were so much lighter and smaller than the old wireless sets that they could be easily carried around. They were first marketed in America in 1953, and in 1956 the annual sale of portable sets reached 3.1 million, double that of the previous year. At about this time transistor sets also appeared in Britain, but it was from the beginning of the 1960s that ownership increased dramatically, and for some years radio receivers became generically known, especially among the young, as 'trannies'.

By the end of the 1970s the transistor meant that nearly 70 per cent of radios were either portable or, since it had also stimulated the growth of car radios, 'mobile'. In 1960 radios were fitted in only 4 per cent of cars on the road. By the end of the 1980s they were standard equipment in all new cars and could be found in 85 per cent of cars of any age. But the importance of the transistor was not simply that it enabled more people than ever before to own a radio set: along with television it caused a revolution in the way the medium was used.

As well as sitting and listening to the wireless, audiences had always used their large, immoveable receivers in a secondary way, as a background to other activities. This was especially true during the working day, which was spent by many women in the home and by many men in the factory or workshop. But during leisure periods, and particularly in the evenings, the emphasis was often reversed: instead of using the wireless as an accompaniment to other activities, people would engage only in those activities which allowed them to listen to the wireless.

However from the 1950s onwards, more and more people were devoting their leisure to watching television. This meant that from about this time many of them only *ever* experienced radio as a background medium, as entirely secondary. What the transistor did was to greatly expand the range of situations in which radio could be so used. A receiver was no longer tied by a wire and its own weight to the sitting room or kitchen or workshop: thanks to its cheapness and portability it could be heard anywhere in the house, or in the garage or the countryside, at the beach or in the car. As Frank Gillard pointed out: 'Radio is no longer something to which you necessarily have to go. Radio goes with you' (1964: 8). The sound medium had insinuated itself into the daily routine in a way that television could never do, because aside from the fact that portable TV had not yet arrived, it was in this respect handicapped by its own visuality.

Thus at the very moment when radio seemed to be facing extinction because of its blindness, it discovered, thanks to the transistor, a new and impregnable advantage in that blindness, in the fact that it was 'secondary'. But the advantage was ambiguous: the transistor ensured not only that radio would undergo a revival but that the revival would be limited. The medium would be heard in many more places and situations than before, but for this very reason listened to rather less – treated simply as a background noise and sometimes ignored altogether.

In these circumstances the BBC's cultural pyramid, with its banded varieties of programming, made less and less sense because it assumed devout listeners instead of casual hearers. We noted that even before the arrival of the transistor, the generality of the BBC's output was regarded as too serious and demanding by many people, who were again turning to Radio Luxembourg. By 1955 the latter was once more winning the Sunday ratings battle and claiming that its weekday evening audience outstripped the Home's. In encouraging casual, background listening the likely effect of the transistor was simply to strengthen this drift towards Luxembourg.

Since, like the BBC, Luxembourg had been forced to yield much of its programming to television the range of background listening it could offer was limited. For many years it had combined music programmes consisting of record requests and tunes from the hit parade with quiz shows and talent contests, but in 1955 the latter were lost to ITV, leaving it with nothing but music.

However, although we shall see later that certain kinds of 'spoken word' output were suitable for the new listening habits, it is hardly surprising that music, especially of the kind which Luxembourg broadcast, was ideal for them. Music was essentially non-visual (TV had not yet learned how to exploit it); it was generally easier to assimilate than spoken word; and light or popular music was even better than other kinds since its short and simple tunes were more suited than symphonies or concertos to the intermittent or 'shallow' nature of the new listening. But the other characteristic of this music was that it was almost invariably *recorded*. Why?

Radio, records and rock

We will recall from Chapter 2 that the record companies soon learned to use radio as a source of talent and material, and to appreciate its promotional value to them. But they also felt an anxiety, which lingers to this day, that it would discourage the public from buying records.

The BBC's initial attitude to the use of records on the air typified that of most broadcasting institutions: it was reluctant to play music which the listener could purchase for herself. Since they were already publicly available, records were as far as possible treated on the radio as an 'understudy' to the uniqueness of a live performance – and although this attitude was softened by a necessarily greater dependence on records during the war, it persisted till the end of the 1940s.

The first radio institutions to rely almost totally on gramophone records were in the United States. Why? Until the mid-1940s the great majority of its several hundred local stations were affiliated to one or other of the main broadcasting networks, from which they obtained a substantial amount of programming. But at the end of the Second World War the networks turned their energies to television, and the proportion of radio stations unaffiliated to a network rose from 18 per cent of the total in 1946 to 47 per cent by 1952. Even the affiliated stations were now expected to originate more of their own output. How were they to fill the empty hours?

Given the increasing use of radio as a background medium, thanks first to TV and then to the transistor, music was the obvious answer – and above all *recorded* music, because records were cheap and thus enabled the stations to dispense with their own musicians. But what were at first regarded as a poor dead substitute for live music soon came to seem in certain respects superior to it: records benefited radio in two important ways.

First, the richness and variety of sound that they could provide would have needed a multitude of live bands and orchestras quite beyond the studio space, let alone the budgets, of most radio stations. And, second, each tune represented the best performance that an artist or band was capable of, for in the process of recording mistakes could be eliminated and the best version chosen from a number of 'takes'. Records also meant that listeners' favourites could be played again and again without any variation in musical quality.

This suitability of records to radio perhaps meant that an interesting philosophical question about the purpose of broadcasting was rather too quickly disposed of. Should broadcasting simply act as 'the common carrier' of any material which was of interest to its audiences, including that which they could already obtain by commercial means? Or should it not confine itself to material or performances of material which were not available in any other medium? Broadcasting had never, of course, wholly succeeded in this latter aim, though it had largely done so. Now, however, it was offering popular music which was almost entirely in 'the public domain'. A similar tendency has occurred in television, which often screens as 'a live event' feature films that many viewers have already seen not only in the cinema but on video, and may even own on cassette – a tendency which darkly hints at the potential redundancy of much broadcasting.

But if records benefited radio, it was equally true that radio benefited records. Despite continuing misgivings among record companies and musicians, radio stimulated sales rather than depressed them, the evanescence of the medium tempting millions of listeners to go out and capture their favourite tunes on disc. This was helped by the fact that recent technological developments and the general growth of affluence in America and Britain made the products of the recording industry much more attractive to the public.

By the end of the 1940s the wind-up gramophone, with its huge and heavy pick-up and endless need for needles, was giving way to the electrically powered record-player, with a lightweight pick-up and long-lasting stylus. The old graphite record, which contained one tune on each side and was played at 78 rpm, was heavy, scratchy, soon worn out, and easily broken. Its successor was the 45 rpm disc, which was developed by RCA Victor in 1949, and was usually a 'single' (one tune on each side) but might also be an EP or 'extended play', with two tunes a side. It was small, easily handled, and made of vinylite, which was virtually indestructible. Of the same material was the LP or 'long play' record, which had been developed by Columbia in 1948, and playing at 33⅓ rpm was capable of carrying six or even eight tunes per side.

What cemented the perfect marriage of radio and records was the sudden and explosive popularity of rock'n'roll in the mid-1950s. As Roy Armes points out, rock 'became the first form of popular music for which the record is the key element – the "original" as it were' (1988: 81), for the launching pad of new performers like Elvis Presley and Jerry Lee Lewis was not the ballroom or concert hall but the recording studio. Yet so perfect was the marriage of records and radio that it is difficult to make a claim for the achievements of one without acknowledging the crucial contribution of the other: if records were the key to the success of the new stars and their music, it was radio which enabled them to find their enormous markets.

The sales of records rocketed. Between 1954 and 1957 they more than doubled in the United States, from $213 million to $460 million, and continuing their upward flight, reached $4 billion in 1980. Though recording technology has changed since the 1950s, with vinyl discs yielding first to cassettes and then to CDs, the highly profitable relationship between the record industry and broadcasting has changed little, except in being strengthened since the 1980s by a larger contribution from television.

But to return to Radio Luxembourg during the second half of the 1950s. In addition to their cheapness and popularity the station had a third reason for its heavy reliance on records: it lay outside the reach of Phonographic Performance Limited (PPL), the organization which acted on behalf of the record companies and in league with the Musicians' Union to impose 'needle-time' agreements on broadcasters – limits on the number of records they could play. In fact despite PPL, the major British record companies, Decca and EMI, made extensive use of Luxembourg to promote their latest releases. The station focused increasingly on rock, for rock was young people's music, and it was the young, as we have seen, who had most money to spend on records.

Nevertheless, Luxembourg was not fully able to exploit its lead in this field because its programmes in English were restricted to the evenings, and in many parts of Britain its signal was weak. Still, for many young rock addicts it was the main source of supply for nearly ten years, until the initiative was suddenly snatched from it.

Pirates ahoy!

In 1964 an Irish entrepreneur named Rohan O'Rahilly found a more effective way than Luxembourg's to circumvent the BBC's monopoly of sound broadcasting. He converted a trawler into a radio station which he called Radio Caroline, moored it just off the Essex coast, and on Easter Sunday, 29 March, began beaming all-day pop music onto the mainland. Its success soon attracted rivals. In December a second ship, broadcasting as Radio London, dropped anchor nearby, and by 1967 no fewer than nine stations were broadcasting on pirated wavelengths from ships and offshore forts around Britain.

Of all these pirates, Caroline and London were quite the most professional. Commissioning their own call-signs from a radio station in Texas ('Sounds fine, it's Caroline!', 'Wonderful Big L!') they developed coherent marketing strategies, broadcasting almost round the clock and directing their signals at the Home Counties, and thus at the largest and most affluent segment of the population.

But wherever they could be heard, the impact of the pirates was sensational. In cocking a snook at authority and reflecting the obsession with pop music which had been fuelled by the Beatles and Rolling Stones, they were a perfect expression of the swinging sixties. As early as 1965 their daily audience was estimated at between 10 and 15 million, and by 1966 they were attracting nearly £2 million worth of advertising a year – some of it from government-funded bodies like the Egg Marketing Board!

The pirates were certainly inspired by Radio Luxembourg, but even more by US radio, in that the Top 40 was the nucleus around which their programming revolved. The concept of the hit parade, a ranking of the current most popular songs based on sales figures, was well known in Britain long before rock and modern pop music developed. It had originated in the United States during the war as 'The Lucky Strike Hit Parade', a product of market research, and during the 1950s the two leading British record manufacturers, Decca and EMI, had promoted their own versions of the hit parade on Radio Luxembourg.

However, the pirates' innovation was to use the hit parade not just as an incidental feature of their output but as its focus, an idea which had also come from the United States. In 1949 the owner of the Mid Continent Broadcasting Company, Todd Storz, observed the choices of records which customers made from juke boxes. These coin-operated record players had begun to be mass produced in 1934, and for many years before they appeared in Britain were an important medium for promoting records in the States.

From the fifty or sixty records that the juke box suppliers changed weekly, Storz noticed that the customers selected the same few current favourites. He then adopted a similar selection at his radio station, getting his presenters to play only the most popular (that is, the best selling and fastest rising) records over and over again, right round the clock. As the practice spread to other US stations the sequence of records (and of course, commercials) was gradually enriched with other ear-catching elements – time checks, weather reports, golden oldies, station call-signs, trailers, traffic information, news summaries – to make up what became the standard Top 40 format. Competitions and merchandising were other elements that were added later.

Though pre-dating rock music, the format was ideally suited to it, and quite apart from their stronger signals gave the pirates two significant advantages over Luxembourg. First, their versions of the Top 40 seemed in spite of their minor variations to be more authentic than the hit parades of the latter. On Luxembourg, Decca and EMI continued to offer their own, proprietorial versions of the hit parade, for their shows were basically sales-pitches – extended commercials in which each company tried to pretend that all the hits were entirely from its own labels. Second, the pirates seemed keener to entertain the listener than simply to sell her something, for they played each record in full, whereas the Luxembourg shows often faded them early in order to tease the listener into buying them.

Though the great majority broadcast pop, one or two of the pirates explored the market for other kinds of music. King Radio, later known as Radio 390, specialized in sweet music and offered daytime programming described as 'Eve, the woman's magazine of the air'.

There is no doubt that the pirate phenomenon caught the BBC unawares. Its Audience Research Department quickly discovered that in that part of the country where both could be received, Caroline captured an audience one third the size of the Light Programme's. About 70 per cent of Caroline's listeners were under the age of 30 and treated its output as background listening. Yet the audience thus captured caused no decline in the Light's. This could only mean that the pirates had tapped into a large listenership which the BBC had ignored. Thanks to rock'n'roll, the new popular music, radio suddenly became a young persons' medium, and it has largely remained such even though the audience for rock music has since fragmented.

In the BBC's defence it has to be said that the Corporation could not easily have competed with the pirates, even had it been minded to do so. Its long-standing public service obligations did not allow it the option of sacrificing mixed programming to a continuous output of pop music, and in any case its use of records was severely limited by the expensive needle-time agreement it had made with PPL. Its rivals, on the other hand, were not called pirates just because they usurped their frequencies: they observed no restrictions on their use of records, paid no royalties, acknowledged no copyright or performance laws.

For their part, the pirates at first hoped that the Conservative government, naturally sympathetic to business initiative and enterprise, would bow to the enormous popular demand they had identified and legalize them. But the Conservatives were defeated in the 1964 general election, and the Labour Party was ideologically hostile to what it regarded as their unscrupulous commercial opportunism. It was determined to close them down.

To do so, however, would incur the wrath of that large portion of the electorate whom the pirates had won over, so before acting the new government instructed the BBC to prepare a similar service of continuous pop music. In August 1967 the Marine Broadcasting (Offences) Act was passed, and though it was intermittently defied in subsequent years succeeded in forcing the pirates off the air. Their crumb of comfort was that although they had quickly been scuttled, their impact was permanent. British sound broadcasting would never be the same again.

The Beeb strikes back

A month after the Act was passed the BBC launched its first-ever network to be dedicated not to mixed programming but to a single kind of output. Radio 1, broadcasting nothing but pop music, took over one of the frequencies previously occupied by the Light Programme, which was itself re-named Radio 2. At the same time the Third Programme and its associated services became Radio 3, and the Home Service was henceforth known as Radio 4.

As the result of being handed on a plate several million listeners of whose existence it had scarcely known before the pirates had identified them, the BBC enlarged its audience by 14 per cent. But Radio 1 was not the perfect equivalent of the pirates and in open competition would surely have fared badly against them. It aped their presentational gimmicks and jingles and even recruited many of their presenters, or 'disc jockeys' as they were then known, such as Tony Blackburn, John Peel and Simon Dee. But from the Light Programme it also acquired one or two presenters of incongruous maturity, such as Jimmy Young and Pete Murray, and its start-up budget was only £200,000. Moreover, since it had been able to extract from PPL only two hours of extra needle-time per day, presenters needed to have a 'gift of the gab' in order to eke out the supply of records. These were also supplemented by live cover versions of current hits, in which with sometimes embarrassing results old-fashioned session musicians tried to imitate the quite different idiom of the rock groups.

Even so, Radio 1 could not manage more than about five and a half hours of its own output per day, and for the rest of the time was reabsorbed by Radio 2. Some years would elapse before the network acquired the clear-cut identity and professionalism of a respectable pop music channel. Moreover with regard to its radio operations as a whole, the BBC had still not learned all the lessons. Despite the pirates, television remained the arch-enemy – and as if to confirm this, colour transmissions began in the very year that the pirates were scuppered.

Yet although TV's impact was strongly felt the Corporation still seemed unwilling to shape radio to withstand it. Radios 2, 3 and 4 were new in name only: they continued to offer the same kinds of mixed programming as before. Yet while there were many for whom sound was still a medium to be listened to and not merely overheard, there were not enough to sustain three separate networks of this kind. The fact that radio was no longer the main mass medium would have to be confronted, and in the networks as a whole the old Reithian pattern of varied and self-contained programmes would have to be cut back.

But for its dwindling band of close listeners, there was no decline in the quality of radio during the 1960s, even if its range was eroded somewhat. The most celebrated comedy shows of the era were *Beyond Our Ken* (1958–64) and its successor *Round the Horne* (1965–9), written by Barry Took and Marty Feldman and starring Kenneth Horne, Kenneth Williams, Hugh Paddick, Betty Marsden and Bill Pertwee.

These were radiogenic in the sense that their magazine format, with Kenneth Horne as the compere, mimicked the increasingly popular news and current affairs magazines of radio and television, each with their own anchor-man like Richard Dimbleby or William Hardcastle. Within this format were sketches which also parodied broadcasting genres – plays, movies, documentaries. Moreover the shows aptly expressed the swinging sixties in their exploitation of the *double entendre*, a device which carries a particular resonance in a non-visual medium and which was almost personified in the hilarious camp couple, Julian and Sandy. As Derek Parker (1977) puts it, the shows 'seemed like a string of good dirty jokes that you weren't sure you'd heard'.

Among the hardy survivors from an earlier era were *Desert Island Discs*, in which a celebrity imagined life as a castaway and chose the eight gramophone records she would take with her; the audience-focused programmes *Housewives' Choice*, *Family Favourites* and *Down Your Way*; and panel games like *Round Britain Quiz* and *Twenty Questions*, which were joined in 1967 by *Just a Minute*. In 1962 the soap opera *Mrs Dale's Diary* was re-named *The Dales*, and thus rejuvenated, managed to last until the end of the decade.

The news and current affairs magazine was a significant development in BBC radio during this period because it was among the few programmes which took some account of the intermittent and variable nature of the new listening patterns. Held together by a presenter it typically consisted of a string of items, such as bulletins, interviews, debates, reports, short talks, weather and traffic announcements, each lasting only a few minutes and some of them repeated at intervals.

Though we have seen that music was perhaps ideal for the new listening, these informative 'bites' or segments were also well suited to it. They have subsequently helped to create a sense of news and information as being part of radio's irreducible repertoire or programming 'rump', since unlike the news items of the press or television they can be absorbed by the audience even while it is otherwise occupied. This also helps to explain why news output seems to have assumed a more dominant position on BBC radio since the rise of television.

The earliest notable example of the current affairs magazine was the breakfast programme *Today*, which began on the Home Service in 1957, and became popular under presenter Jack De Manio. At first dealing more in topics of general interest, it subsequently became harder and newsier, and for the last quarter century its interview slots have been much coveted by all politicians who are seeking publicity. It was followed in 1965 by the lunchtime magazine *The World at One*, which with its celebrated presenter William Hardcastle found, as we have seen, a crazy echo in *Round the Horne*.

The launch of local radio

We noted earlier that the arrival of VHF in the 1950s facilitated the development of local radio since it created much more room on the waveband. But two questions remained: was there a public demand for local radio? And if so, what broadcasting institution or institutions should be allowed to run it?

Asa Briggs (1995) observes that there is no evidence that there was a substantial demand for local radio. Nevertheless the pirate phenomenon and contemporary political thinking combined to make the concept fashionable. The pirates were relevant because they were, in a loose sense, local. Few broadcast over an area bigger than the Home Counties, many of them promoted local events, and some appealed to local loyalties by taking names like Radio Essex and Radio Kent. Moreover, although they offered no broadcasting access to the public they broke the BBC's virtual radio monopoly to answer a huge demand which the Corporation had ignored, and so in that sense they assumed a public voice.

It was in this respect that piracy converged with mainstream politics, for among politicians there was a desire to stimulate local democracy and make the mass media not only more responsive to public opinion but a more efficient conduit for it.

Under a Labour government it was almost inevitable that local radio would be run by the BBC, especially as Pilkington had favoured this. After a successful experiment in 1963–4 the Corporation opened its first local station at Leicester in 1967 and followed up with many others during the 1970s and 1980s. Part of their purpose was to replace regional radio, which was discontinued in 1983.

Though some of the stations were also given medium wave frequencies to attract larger audiences, their prime mode of delivery was VHF, and they thus led the network conversion to VHF/FM which began at the end of the 1980s. Moreover part of their 'democratic' achievement was to make radio something of a two-way medium by using the phone-in as a staple of their output.

The phone-in was first heard on BBC Radio Nottingham in 1968 and was a genuinely new broadcasting development in the sense that it enabled the ordinary listener to become a broadcaster, not because she was a guest of the radio station or an expert or an interviewee, but simply because she chose to initiate the broadcast from her own private environment. It could almost be claimed, then, that the phone-in was the first *interactive* form of mass communication. It has also, of course, been adopted on network radio and even television, but is perhaps used to best effect at local level.

The BBC has always seen news gathering as the primary asset of the local radio system, its purpose not just to serve the immediate community but to feed the networks in the way that the old regions had done. Its output typically consists of local news, chat, phone-ins, programmes on local themes, and educative features. However Lewis and Booth (1989) express disappointment in the achievements of BBC local radio, pointing to financial starvation (including a needle-time allowance of only two hours a day) and excessive control from London. As long as it was a BBC monopoly it certainly kept a low profile, most stations managing only between six and twelve hours of output a day before opting into one of the networks, usually Radio 2.

Broadcasting in the Seventies

It was not until the end of the 1960s that the BBC was forced to grasp the nettle of network radio – and as is so often the case, the spur was financial. At the end of the last chapter we mentioned that the Corporation's income was declining in the second half of the decade, yet to its two TV channels and four sound networks had been added the burden of local radio. Nevertheless the government would allow no further increase in the licence fee and so the BBC hired management consultants to investigate its structure and use of resources. Retrenchment was the inevitable cure that they prescribed.

This forced a hard look at radio as the less popular of the two broadcasting media, and the consequence was *Broadcasting in the Seventies*, a BBC policy document published in July 1969 and announcing a radical new plan for network radio. It acknowledged that television had now replaced radio as the primary leisure medium: 'The millions who once listened to "In Town Tonight" and "Itma" now watch television' (BBC 1969a: 2) – and in a lecture given at about the same time the managing director of radio, Ian Trethowan, developed the point:

> few [listeners] today use radio as the staple diet of family entertainment in the evening. Most of them use it as individuals, mostly during the day, often casually, while they're doing something else. We may not like it: we may wish that everyone was listening intently, but these are listening habits we cannot ignore.
>
> (1970: 5)

Radio was now recognized as a personal possession rather than a domestic fixture. It was no longer collectively consumed as a primary source of entertainment, it was individually consumed – mostly as a background to other activities. Consequently, as Trethowan pointed out, 'the old concept of "mixed programming" no longer applies in radio and . . . what listeners seek is the convenience of predictable networks' (1970: 6). This is an echo of *Broadcasting in the Seventies*: 'experience . . . suggests that many listeners now expect radio to be based on a different principle – that of the specialised network, offering a continuous stream of one particular type of programme, meeting one particular interest' (1969a: 3).

Streamed or 'strip' programming, now typical of so much radio output, was an important development. If the output was all of one kind, then programme divisions became less important – indeed virtually non-existent. On the pirate stations, for instance, which had led the way in streaming, they were merely marked by changes of presenter: the music remained much the same throughout the day. But the idea of a 'stream' or 'strip' of output is misleading if it implies an *entire* absence of divisions, something which becomes more obvious if we recall that news and informational content is almost as well suited to it as music.

The real point of such output is that its significant unit is not the *programme*, which listeners have to adjust to, but the *segment* or 'bite' — a pop record, news bulletin, commercial, interview, or whatever; for the segment adjusts to the situation and attention span of the modern listener. Moreover the aggregation of these segments is an indefinite sequence: 'indefinite' because in general it lacks the progression, the internal causal or logical connections, which would characterize the traditional 'built' programme. The sequence can therefore be of any length. The whole point of it is that the listener can 'get into' and 'out' of it at will without feeling that she has missed, or will miss, anything of importance.

This kind of sound broadcasting later became known as 'format' radio — somewhat misleadingly so since it is not the only kind which is as artfully structured as the word suggests. News, talk and various types of music have on different stations all been adapted to the segmented yet streamed character of format. Yet thanks to the relative brevity of its tunes, pop music clearly fits comfortably into it, as does commercial radio since the duration of its advertising breaks can be assimilated to that of the programming segments within which they are interspersed.

With *Broadcasting in the Seventies* the BBC took its first steps in the direction of format radio, and in April 1970 the old Reithian concept of tempting the listener to a diversity of programmes was largely laid to rest, though not without much public debate and fierce opposition within the Corporation. Radio 2 matched Radio 1's pop format with continuous 'middle-of-the-road' music, alternatively known as 'easy listening'. Radio 3 lost many of its speech programmes to Radio 4 and became mostly a classical music network, although it kept a modicum of serious drama and vestiges of other types of programmes such as sport. Radio 4 survived in something like its old form and is still the nearest thing to a traditional mixed programme network that the BBC offers. Yet even here there is some specialization in spoken word and informational output — mostly news and current affairs, with some drama and light entertainment, but very little music.

It should be added that these changes, which brought large financial savings, were forced on the BBC not just by the ascendancy of television but by the new technological sophistication of radio. Thanks to the transistor, radio receivers had now become so numerous and portable that the Post Office, still the collector of the licence fee, could no longer keep track of those who owned them. Acknowledging the millions who avoided payment, the government abolished the radio-only licence in 1971. But this weakened the position of radio with respect to television within the Corporation because there was no longer a sum of money raised specifically for it, and it was therefore parasitic upon its more popular rival.

The largely specialized pattern of BBC network radio has continued ever since. Audiences accept it and are not greatly enthused by attempts to revive mixed programming, as the launch of Radio 5 was to show some twenty years later.

Sources/further reading

On the developing problems within the BBC's tripartite network structure, see Paulu (1956; 1961) and Briggs (1979). These also deal with the general shift from serious to 'lighter' radio listening and with the post-war resurgence of Radio Luxembourg. Silvey (1974) considers the decline of overall radio use between 1948 and 1960, while Snagge and Barsley (1972) lament the end of radio features.

Briggs (1979; 1995) offers the fullest general account of the technological developments in sound broadcasting, though the nature and origins of transistor technology are usefully sketched in Goldhamer (1971), together with its revolutionary impact on the radio receiver. For a contemporary and farsighted view of the new transistor radios and the differences in listening – and hence programming – that they would give rise to, see Gillard (1964).

Probably the best account of the connections between music, records and radio is in Barnard (1989), but Armes (1988) also offers an excellent historical summary of recording technology and its importance to rock music. For the origins of pop music radio Chapman (1992) is also useful, while Fornatale and Mills (1980) stress the closeness of the early relationship between radio and rock music in the United States and outline the development of format radio there.

The phenomenon of the pirates has attracted much attention, since it is seen by many as the most romantic episode in British radio history. Harris (1970), Baron (1975) and Chapman (1992) are among the best-known studies, and there is a summary of the pirates' impact in Paulu (1981). Barnard (1989) also offers some thoughtful analysis of the pirates and their adoption of the Top 40 format, though he takes the view that they had less influence on the history of radio than is commonly supposed. Silvey (1974) recalls the BBC survey of Radio Caroline's audience and explores its implications.

For the launch of Radio 1 see Briggs (1995). The views of its first controller on the new listening demands created by the transistor, and on the inadequacy of the old networks in meeting them, are in Scott (1967). The *BBC Handbook 1968* (1967) explains what the new network is seeking to achieve, while the major radio programmes which the other three networks offered during the 1960s are concisely described by Parker (1977), Donovan (1992) and Briggs (1995).

The standard study of local radio is Lewis and Booth (1989). It includes an account of the genesis of BBC local radio and explains why it has been less successful than was hoped. Briggs (1995) is also enlightening on local radio, especially on its political and technological background. Smith (1974) points out that interest in local radio was largely stimulated by the pirates, since it was they who prompted the BBC to be more responsive to the listeners' voice.

For an exploration of the nature and significance of the phone-in, a new programming element which would be especially important in local radio, and also for an analysis of the segmented output that would characterize so much format radio, see Crisell (1994).

Broadcasting in the Seventies (BBC 1969a) summarizes the reasons for streaming the BBC networks, details of which are also contained in the *BBC Handbook 1970* (1969b). A further rationale of the network changes is in Trethowan (1970), and the way in which they were carried through, as well as the debate and opposition they fomented, are in Briggs (1995).

Television and its social effects

Television and its social effects

Open the box

We can identify 19 January 1972, the day when all restrictions on broadcasting hours were lifted, as the beginning of the era of modern television. It is an era in which not merely every home but almost every individual has come to own a set, and in which the search for broadcastable material has grown so relentless that the medium may be fairly said to have penetrated every aspect of our lives. From 1972 there would be a steady growth in daytime as well as evening viewing, a growth which reflected more flexible patterns of work and an increase in leisure which was not wholly welcome. Unemployment increased during the 1970s with the quickening decline of the old labour-intensive industries such as coal-mining and shipbuilding.

In fact the expansion of transmission hours had the overdue effect of helping people to regard television as something of a utility and not just a source of entertainment, and the period saw a rise in output of an informative, instructive or educational nature which was partly a response to the problems of the unemployed.

Yet despite its economic difficulties the period was also one of rising living standards, which explains the soaring sales of colour TV sets. Even for those who could barely afford one, the volume of spectacle, entertainment and information that television provided gave a value for money absolutely unprecedented in cultural history. Up to 1970 a mere 775,000 colour TVs had been bought: by 1973 the number had leapt to 6 million, and in 1977 there were more homes with a colour set than with a telephone.

Yet as we shall see in a later chapter, the 1970s were a troubled decade. The country was racked by inflation and strikes, and there were civil upheavals in Northern Ireland, acts of terrorism both in Britain and abroad (themselves fuelled by the publicity which television gave them), and an international oil crisis. In all this the cheapness and domestic convenience of a TV set brought great solace – a point well made by Jeremy Potter:

> The average citizen could do little in the face of economic recession, industrial unrest and sometimes capricious public services, but he and she had a comfortable retreat at home where they could amuse themselves inexpensively through ITV or BBC channels. The more dire the state of the economy, the less other amusements could be afforded and the greater the nation's dependence on the box in its sitting room.
>
> (1989: 12)

Between 1961 and 1986 average weekly viewing doubled from 13.5 to 26 hours. By the latter date nearly 80 per cent of people watched television at some point during the day, for it had become the main leisure activity. Mr and Mrs Briton were now Mr and Mrs Viewer.

We have thus reached a stage in our history when it seems appropriate to consider one or two inherent features and tendencies of the television medium and something of its social impact. To do so we shall range back and forth in time, and since this book is a history primarily of broadcasting *media* and only secondarily of broadcasting *institutions*, we will not scruple to forage abroad in order to make a point about the character of television for which we cannot find a domestic example. In exploring its possibilities broadcasters in other countries may not be bound by the same moral or economic or political constraints as their British counterparts: on the other hand broadcasters everywhere are bound by the limitations of the medium.

To speak of limitations is important. Because TV is 'modern', because it provides both sound and moving vision which enter our domestic and private worlds and take relatively little effort to absorb, there is a common assumption that it has rendered all older media obsolete – that it is more truthful, more sophisticated, than print or photography or sound broadcasting.

We thus need to remind ourselves that it has its crudities and limitations just like any other medium, and indeed some that certain other media, notably print, do not have. In this chapter we shall look at its strengths and limitations and try to assess its effects on various social activities and institutions – as well as on its audiences – before moving into the last thirty years or so of its history.

Seeing is believing

It is not surprising that 80 per cent of the population get their news from television and regard it as the most credible news source. As Alvarado, Gutch and Wollen (1987) point out, moving photographic images seem more real than words. Whereas different languages signify a dog differently, an image of a dog is universally recognizable. Hence television's images seem incapable of lying. Moreover, they exist within a frame which serves to intensify them: when we perceive the world through TV, vision seems to dominate over sound to an even greater extent than our faculty of sight dominates over our hearing when we perceive the world directly.

The circumscribed nature of television's images, their brightness and the fact that their movements do not correspond to those which might occur in the vicinity of the set, act as a magnet for even the most reluctant eye. Whenever I meet a friend in a pub we never sit within sight of a TV set, even if its sound is inaudible – conversation would succumb to watching.

What television seems to offer is a kind of hyper-realism. It deals mostly in actuality, however vivid. Even its make-believe, its plays and feature films, usually happens in real locations. This is also true of its forerunner, the cinema: yet television seems more real because it is not attended to for a short spell in a darkened place which is separate from our own environment. It is, or can be, co-extensive with our ordinary existence and closely assimilated to it. It seems an innocuous, neutral medium.

Yet TV pictures are selective – not just in choosing certain events or objects rather than others, but in choosing to present them in certain ways. A simple example will illustrate both these things. Let us imagine a television camera at a soccer match. It could be directed at the pitch, where the match is in progress, or at the terraces, where a fight has broken out. It (or at any rate its operator) decides to focus on the fight, which it could cover in at least two ways – by long shot, which would show the fight as an isolated incident amid a sea of peaceable spectators, or in close-up, so that fighting fills the screen. If the latter shot is televised it would be literally truthful, but as a 'statement' about the general behaviour of the crowd it is seriously misleading.

Because television is perforce limited in its vision we could describe it as a metonymic medium: it deals in parts as representative of the whole. The problem is that TV images can only ever deal in particularities or specifics: unlike words, they cannot generalize. Nevertheless, the effect of television is to make us draw general conclusions, not always accurately. This is partly why the medium is so often accused of stereotyping: every skinhead is a criminal; one televised fight on a terrace means that every soccer stadium is a battlefield; a single bomb in Belfast suggests a province exploding from end to end.

Though we may jump to these conclusions we often recognize their naivety. Yet television's images do determine attitudes and behaviour. The isolated bombings in Northern Ireland have badly affected tourism and foreign investment, and there are countless men who have been deterred by crowd violence from taking their wives and children to soccer matches.

Indeed television is so influential in certain respects that when politicians dismiss its particular images as accurate expressions of a general truth they do so at their peril. Ralph Negrine (1994) recalls events at the end of the 1970s, when television's pictures of picket lines and uncollected refuse in the streets suggested an entire nation ravaged by strikes and social unrest. The prime minister James Callaghan flew back from the Caribbean intending to steady the nation with his knowledge of a larger and less frightening reality. 'Crisis? What crisis?' he is said to have asked waiting journalists. But the millions who had seen the turmoil on television would not be denied the evidence of their own eyes and regarded the prime minister's reaction as unforgivably complacent. His government fell at the next election.

On the other hand the partial evidence of TV can hurry politicians into measures which with hindsight can seem ill-judged. A few years ago television showed pictures of certain ferocious dogs called pit bull terriers and the horribly injured children they had attacked. Parliament promptly required all 10,000 specimens of the breed to be either neutered or destroyed, three consequences of which were that certain quite docile pit bulls faced a death sentence; other breeds which might be just as vicious remained legal; and dogs which might or might not have been cross-bred from pit bulls gave insoluble problems to the courts.

But of course TV consists not just of pictures but of words, and because words are more versatile than pictures they can explain them. They can generalize, qualify and abstract. Whereas photographic images treat the world as object, language treats the world as idea. Where pictures merely represent, words analyse. Indeed as Neil Postman (1986) so acutely points out, language implies *not* accepting the world as we see it: comparisons, explanations, categorizations, generalizations impose a frame or perspective on things which is not objectively there.

Hence in the case of our soccer match the newsreader's words might tell us that the fight occurred at ground X during a match between clubs A and B and was provoked by a controversial incident on the pitch; that this was the third disturbance this season and will render the home club liable to disciplinary action, and so on. We could therefore say that TV's images are metonymic in standing not just for the larger visual picture but for the broader, more abstract or conceptual reality which lies behind them.

However, words on television suffer from a number of handicaps. First, because they are usually spoken and therefore constantly dissolving, they are much less easily assimilated than words on a page – and are in many cases overpowered by the vividness and movement of the images. Even where words actually appear on the screen there is a severe limit to the number that can be shown, and they are hardly less vulnerable to the passage of time than are their spoken counterparts.

Whether the words of television are heard or seen, then, the quantity of information it can carry is much less than that which can be conveyed by the spatial medium of print. John Whale (1969) instances a 25-minute TV programme in the 1960s about the Bank of France, one whose images were unlikely to distract the viewer. Nevertheless Whale argues that a newspaper article on the same theme could have been read in 5 minutes and would have left a clearer impression. As Anthony Davis (1976) points out, to deliver as TV news the total contents of a single edition of *The Times* would take two to four days of broadcasting time. In a brilliant polemic against American TV Robert Hughes ironically laments that in the primitive days before television people had to make do with books – 'those portable, low-energy, high-density information storage and retrieval systems' (1995: 6). This adoption of computer-speak provides a bracing antidote to our infatuation with new technology, especially when we recall that printed books, a form of 'information system' which television and computers do not entirely emulate, have been available for the past five hundred years.

Since sustained and complex reasoning, argument and explanation are possible only in print, newspapers and journals have reacted to the rise of broadcasting by developing their strength of 'news in depth', backgrounding and contextualizing the major stories. Hence because of the inherent character of television and despite the best efforts of certain broadcasting institutions, TV news seems by comparison to be desultory and superficial. Ralph Negrine (1994) observes that although its explanation of events – of their causes and contexts – is sometimes lengthy, it never seems quite adequate. There is a tendency, too, for TV journalists to tailor their words to its images rather than to explain or qualify them – a practice which often results in puns and metaphors which are more colourful than enlightening. A recent report that political extremists in Turkey were resorting to arson accompanied its images of burning shops with the reflection that the liberal future of the country could 'go up in smoke'.

Even a big story will run on television for no more than a few weeks before being superseded by another. (This is also true of newspapers, but at least the extensive backgrounding of the broadsheets affords some reservoir of knowledge to their readers.) The story will not be revived until a fresh crisis breaks, offering the medium something specific and tangible to point its cameras at. Thus news on television is essentially a series of discrete events: the medium hops from the tip of one iceberg to the next. Television news is naive news.

The problem is that because TV is so 'realistic' and is modern and ubiquitous, it has become for many people the yardstick of cultural and intellectual absorption:

they are unaware of the limitations from which it suffers. Robert Hughes remarks that:

> there are many things tv cannot do. Because it knows this . . . tv would like to create a mind-set in which those things no longer matter particularly: skills like the ability to enjoy a complex argument, for instance, or to see nuances, or to look behind the screen of immediate events, or to keep in mind large amounts of significant information.

> (1995: 7)

Above all, I would suggest that because its relatively fitful and superficial coverage of the world is determined by the moving image, it has created a widespread impression – despite the best efforts of many of its practitioners – that appearance and reality are much the same, or at least that reality can be judged in terms of appearances.

It has to be said at once that where there is a fair amount of congruence between the visual and the real, the effects of television have been hugely beneficial. Quite simply, TV enables us to see more things, and to see them better, than we ever could with the naked eye or from natural viewpoints. It has shown us not simply those things which are normally unseeable, such as the moon's surface, the ocean depths, animals inside their burrows at night, or the internal organs of the human body, but seeable things and places which are nevertheless so remote and exotic that few of us are likely to see them with our own eyes.

Yet perhaps most remarkable are the unfamiliar views which TV offers us of *familiar* things – first-class cricket from micro-cameras fixed to the stumps, soccer goals from cameras attached to the tops of the stanchions. Most obviously in its coverage of sport, television's use of angles, close-ups, long views and slow-motion replays has enormously enhanced our understanding of what we are watching – to such an extent that actual attendance at games can seem a paltry experience by comparison. To remedy this, many stadiums and arenas provide giant TV screens to give those present a better view – a timely reminder that it was television and not computers which first taught us the joys of virtual reality! But to describe this as 'vicarious' experience is in a sense unfair, for it is an experience which is *preferable* to the real thing, not an inferior substitute for it.

Yet certain other benefits which television brings are more serious and substantial than these. For years newspaper accounts of famine in Africa had left their readers relatively unmoved. When TV showed pictures of the starving people of Ethiopia in 1984–5 audiences all over the world were galvanized. Characteristically, television was not very effective in explaining the causes of the famine, but the images left nobody in doubt of its horrors: Live Aid and an enormous relief operation rapidly followed.

In this instance the physical fact that people were suffering was what mattered above all, and television was very good at showing it. One can think of other situations in which its focus on the physical and the visible is, or would have been, beneficial. Its 'real time' coverage of wars can, and does, powerfully influence public opinion in ways which might embarrass governments but rightly so. The colossal tragedy of the First World War would surely have been averted, or at least curtailed, if like that of Vietnam it had been seen on television. Where television can observe them, an increasing number of nations must find solutions to their disputes which are more generally acceptable than a use of armed force.

In yet another sense, then, television is a strongly democratizing medium. We have already seen how it acts as a leveller in demystifying expertise, rank and authority; it also, of course, puts politicians under the critical gaze of the voters; and in the broader context, thanks to satellite technology, it now seems to be creating a global pressure towards open government, democracy and fair play. With everyone watching everyone else it is becoming harder for nations to conceal their misdeeds.

Seeing is deceiving

But sometimes the assumption that reality can be judged on appearances can have consequences which are less straightforwardly beneficial. In 1995 television ran a number of news items on the export of British veal calves to the continent. The exporters' case, though almost certainly made, was never heard – drowned by pictures of velvety heads and melting, bovine eyes between the slats of the cattle lorries – and there was an immediate outcry against the trade.

This is a characteristic effect of television. Because its images can overwhelm explanation, discussion or qualification, the response of many of its viewers is likely to be instant and emotional rather than considered and rational. Robert Hughes puts it more strongly: 'tv teaches the people to scorn complexity and to feel, not think' (1995: 7). He is actually describing American commercial TV here, but I would suggest that although the more responsible broadcasters may try to mitigate it, this seems to be an almost inherent tendency of the medium.

On occasions some are willing to exploit it. One evening in the mid-1990s ITN made its lead news item the funeral service of James Bulger, a little boy who had been abducted and killed by two other boys. This was not 'news' at all, for as its association with 'novelty' implies, news is concerned with the unexpected, or with that which materially advances or alters an existing course of events. Whatever its emotive effects it is essentially a factual or intellectual matter. But James's funeral was not news because it did not tell us anything about the Bulger case which we did not already know or could not reasonably infer – and it was passed off as news only because television could present it in a number of poignant images, including that of James's teddy bear sitting in the church. Indeed the medium will often go further, not just attaching a misleading significance to an actual event but creating a 'newsworthy' event virtually out of nothing. For less moving but also for emotive purposes it will stage 'photo-opportunities' and meet-the-people routines for politicians and other public figures.

It could be argued that the coverage for purely emotive purposes of James Bulger's funeral or even of celebrity walkabouts, though in itself misleading, is innocuous. But the coverage of the veal trade illustrates something more. Certain sections of the public were so outraged by it that they immediately began to blockade the ports and chain themselves to the lorries. One protestor was run over, becoming a martyr to the cause, and before long few ports would continue to handle the trade.

For many this was another simple instance of television's power to do good: thanks to its haunting images an evil activity was stopped and the consequent financial losses to exporters, their employees and the port authorities were a price worth paying. But what others found disquieting was that the protestors' actions forestalled all rational consideration of a trade which, given the hard fact that all cattle are bred for slaughter, might conceivably have been less evil than it looked. Whether evil or not, the trade was lawful, and it was perhaps an even bigger cause for concern that the processes of democracy could be so easily supplanted by the actions of an unelected pressure group.

But the assumption that the visual and the real are much the same on television is dangerous not simply because it can encourage instant, emotional and possibly inappropriate responses, but because even when TV's metonymic nature is acknowledged its images can be seriously misleading about the reality they reflect.

In 1995 the BBC showed a film documentary about euthanasia. An elderly, terminally ill man and his wife were visited by their doctor at their quiet, softly lit flat in Amsterdam. Viewers would have been struck by the tact and unhurried kindness of the doctor. At a point entirely determined by the patient the doctor administered an injection, and the former, comforted by his wife, slipped into a final unconsciousness. A momentous event was managed with great dignity and intimacy.

The programme could not fail to mislead us, however, about the number of those who were present: as Bryan Appleyard observes, viewers might have been shocked to recall that the event was also being witnessed by a film crew. Television, he adds, 'is a more effective liar than any other medium precisely because it seems so like the truth' (1995a: 19).

But the deception is, of course, more than a merely numerical one: the event is less 'intimate' than it seems not just because more people are present than we can see, but because those extra people do not have the same humanitarian reasons for being there as the doctor and the patient's wife. They no doubt feel that instinctive, abstract sympathy for the patient that we all feel for any suffering human being, but they lack the *particular* relationship to him – the doctor's professional relationship based on care, the wife's personal relationship based on love – which would justify their presence. They are, in a precise sense, as indifferent as if filming a horse race or a cookery lesson, for as Appleyard remarks, they are checking the camera angles, lighting and sound levels even as the poison is flooding into the patient's veins.

This is a disquieting reminder that in covering famine stories, television crews perforce *film* the sufferings of the starving before or instead of relieving them. Whatever the long-term benefits of this – and they are often considerable – the idea that in such circumstances watching should take precedence over doing, even for a few moments, is somehow repugnant.

But what is particularly disturbing about the euthanasia film is that the TV crew are there *on our behalf*: their essential indifference to the event, their voyeurism – in a word, their lack of a right to be there – is ours. As long as we can forget about them and take the intimacy of the event at its face value, we can, in a sense, forget our own presence: we can overlook the fact that a private occasion is being observed by millions of strangers, including ourselves. We might even be able to persuade ourselves that simply by watching we are proffering a kind of sympathy, though to do so would betray that confusion of seeing and participating which is the hallmark of the voyeur. But when we remember the film crew we are obliged to face the fact that we are there not to sympathize but merely to watch.

Hence in giving us a deceptive impression of the reality they reflect, television's images can mislead us about our moral and emotional relationship to that reality. Yet they may also be deceptive in seeming to promise some *intellectual* insight into reality, whether they accurately reflect it or not. We watch the euthanasia programme in the belief that seeing will in itself bring moral enlightenment, some insight into the ethics of humane killing.

It is here, as elsewhere, that the medium co-operates so neatly with modern liberal politics. 'The public has a right to know' is the slogan of democracy. 'To see is to know' is the promise of television. It therefore follows that 'The public has a right to see'. Yet there is little likelihood that the mere sight of someone being put to death will bring illumination of a moral kind, and we are once more forced to the conclusion that despite its intellectual and moral pretensions and its air of tact and decorum, the euthanasia programme is simply a spectacle. It can offer nothing more than titillation, entertainment, and might therefore tempt us to think that there is something potentially corrupting about television – about the idea that because something is visible we have an absolute right to see it.

But what I am concerned to stress here is that the complex of feelings involved in watching such programmes may fairly be described as voyeuristic: a lack of self-consciousness, a self-oblivion; a measure of sympathy or identification with what is being observed and which is often termed 'vicarious experience'; yet also a detached curiosity, sometimes even a hint of *schadenfreude*; and certainly a pleasure, an excitement, in seeing what we are not normally able or permitted to see.

Television and the dramatic

Though all the above examples were taken from factual television, it would seem that the viewer's experience of them is similar to the satisfactions of being at the theatre. Television's inevitable preoccupation with spectacle and imagery, with the appearance or surface of things rather than with reasoning or abstraction, tends, like the theatre's, to create viewing experiences whose intellectual content, however substantial in itself, is caught up within impressions of a more diffusely emotional nature. In the documentary on euthanasia the complex, voyeuristic relationship which we discerned between the viewer and an actual event is very similar to that which exists between the theatre- or cinema-goer and the fictional events she observes on stage or screen.

The analogy is strengthened by certain physical similarities between television and the conventional theatrical media. The TV frame, which we earlier described as *intensifying* its real-life images, could also be compared to the proscenium arch of the theatre or cinema in serving to *distinguish* those images from the 'real world' of our own experience. In this respect television also differs sharply from those more ambient media, radio and books – and if instead of flats and painted scenery it gives us real locations, their verisimilitude is blunted by the fact that we have long been accustomed to them in cinema feature films. Television's output is certainly domestic and continuous as we claimed earlier, but much of it is divided into distinct programmes whose narrative structure and elements of characterization, conflict and resolution, even in the case of news and documentary, mostly follow those of drama and fiction.

The tendency of television to turn real life into theatre was apparent in the trial, which also took place in 1995, of O. J. Simpson, a famous American football player and film star who was charged with the murder of his estranged wife and her companion. The argument for televised trials seems irresistible: in a democracy the truth should be made public; justice, in an old adage, must be seen to be done.

But in a shrewd newspaper article at the time Bryan Appleyard pointed out that by increasing the audience from a few score in the courtroom to many millions, television wrought a change which was more than merely quantitative. The fact of being a spectacle, combined with TV's cultural baggage of courtroom series, serials and old cinema movies, as well as the viewers' option to switch to another channel, introduced an imperative to entertain, to play it for the cameras. As

Appleyard observes, all the participants, judge, jurors, lawyers and witnesses as well as the accused, betrayed 'the fallen, corrupt consciousness that this show was turning them into stars' (1995b: 19).

The trial also maintained interest by borrowing its trappings from the fictions of *Perry Mason* and *The Defenders*. Though it was, of course, actual it became 'virtual' for an audience conditioned by television not to believe its own experience of real life: that appearances can deceive, that truth is difficult and reality ambiguous.

Appleyard points out that to make things easy for the jurors and the viewers, Simpson's lawyer Johnny Cochrane borrowed a familiar cinema plot: the liberal defence attorney fighting a corrupt racist system (Simpson is black), and his client was duly acquitted. Movies are made about trials; juries expect real trials to be like movies; so lawyers behave like movie actors. Reality imitates make-believe, TV turns fact into fiction. The verdict may or may not have been right, but the trial itself was corrupted by the medium which relayed it. This preference of a theatrical, fictional version of events to reality again illustrates how television has anticipated the virtual world of computers, but we should point to two of its more important consequences.

First, the character of television led several decades ago to a widespread realization that the best chance of attracting its attention was to behave in a theatrical way. Those who opposed the veal exports were well aware that just as the source of their anger was pictures, a spectacle, so that anger, in order to be effective, must itself take the form of a spectacle: to stop the trade they would have to provide something as visual and emotive as the images which had aroused them.

In an era before television they might have attempted argument and persuasion, but these are abstractions and television is uneasy with abstractions: if you cannot see it, it may not exist. The answer was 'direct action', which along with the demonstration (so familiar a ritual of modern socio-political life that it was long ago shortened to 'demo'), depends heavily on the presence of television cameras. Hence in the veal episode real life was shaped into the form of theatre: for many years, as Robert Hughes points out, 'the basic message of network tv has been that human life tends to the condition of drama. Conflict. Goodies and baddies. Moral absolutes' (1995: 7).

The veal episode had it all: confrontations, struggles, pursuits and other physical business; anger, suffering, even tragedy; and the moral simplifications and certainties that theatre, with its need to render most things in physical, visible terms, tends towards. The goodies were of course the demonstrators (and the innocents were the calves): the baddies were the exporters and their minions the police. Moreover, thanks to the metonymic character of television the direct action was meant to suggest a *universal* hostility to the trade. The strategy seems to have worked, though the real extent of the hostility is hard to determine.

Actors and actresses have traditionally been ridiculed for behaving in the exaggerated manner of those who are used to being watched. It is perhaps not too fanciful to suggest that one diffuse effect of the spectacle of television has been to make ordinary social behaviour more demonstrative than it once was, on the basis that if feelings are not apparent their existence will be doubted. Some years ago the mother of a woman who was believed to have been abducted and murdered fell under suspicion because she did not show enough grief before the television cameras.

As will already be clear from much that has been said, its essentially theatrical character means that television is, despite its occasional efforts to the contrary, associated above all with *entertainment*. Thanks to television, then, entertainment has become, in Neil Postman's words, 'the natural format for the representation of all experience' (1986: 87). TV is for most people the main source of culture and general knowledge. Consequently the way in which it imparts these things tends to become the norm for other, more specialized branches of knowledge, and whether through television or some other medium, politics, religion, the law, business and education have in more or less subtle ways sought to pass themselves off as forms of entertainment, as affording the emotional gratifications of a film, play or TV show. Many in the teaching profession will have heard visiting inspectors commend a course of study as 'exciting', on the assumption that students will find it hard to learn unless the experience is enjoyable or diverting. To teachers of quadratic equations or irregular verbs this poses a stern challenge.

Television and genre

Although the ultimate distinction between fact and fiction is absolute and inviolable, I have tried to show that television is characterized by a profound equivocation between real life, even banality, on this side and theatricality on that – a kind of mutual contamination in which each strives for the virtues of the other. Factual television borrows the shape and sequence of drama and sometimes the visual beauty of a feature film. (Some recent news coverage of the horrific tribal warfare in Rwanda prompted a moment's disbelief: this blue-green landscape and the frail, colourful elegance of its people was surely part of a Hollywood movie?) On the other hand, TV dramas and feature films often strive for the verisimilitude and authenticity of news, documentary and current affairs output and for the diffuseness and indeterminacy of real life.

It is hardly surprising, then, that television's most original contributions to cultural genres are those which explore, or attempt to straddle, this indestructible border between truth and fiction, reality and make-believe. Its more recent ones are spawning new and hybrid names like 'infotainment' and 'edutainment', but in a history book we need to concentrate on those which have become established: docudrama and soap opera.

Docudrama, variously known as drama documentary, documentary drama, dramatized documentary, dramadoc and faction (a blend of 'fact' and 'fiction'), attempts imaginative reconstructions of significant social or political events. Before video and film equipment became better and more portable in the early 1960s many conventional TV documentaries contained dramatized elements whose 'fabricated' nature was made clear to the viewers. What docudrama sought to do was to blend fact and fiction much more subtly, to exploit that paradox by which artistic licence can come closer than known fact to an essential moral truth. On the other hand ethical problems arise when, as is often the case, viewers can have no way of distinguishing between literal fact and fictional licence. Not surprisingly many of the best known docudramas have had repercussions in the real world, some of them beneficial but most causing controversy.

The BBC's docudrama *Cathy Come Home* (1966), which explored the problems of the homeless, is credited with a change in government housing policy, but *The War Game*, a 'preconstruction' of nuclear war which it intended to show at about the same time, was considered too frightening and banned until 1985. In the next decade its docudrama *Law and Order* was felt to be so unfairly critical of the penal system that the Prison Officers' Association stopped the BBC from filming inside gaols for a year. Its *Monocled Mutineer* (1986), attempting 'a greater truth' about the First World War, also attracted censure, but perhaps the most controversial docudrama was *Death of a Princess* (ATV, 1980), which dealt with the execution of an actual Saudi princess for alleged adultery and provoked a diplomatic row between Britain and Saudi Arabia.

Docudrama has also, of course, been put to uses which have won general approval: for instance the dramatic reconstructions of *Crimewatch UK* (BBC 1, from 1984) have been successful in prompting the public to assist the police in their fight against crime. But a less controversial, more fertile dramatic genre is the *soap opera* — as we have seen, a child of radio but one which has thrived even more lustily in the newer medium. Among the best known are *Coronation Street*, *Emergency – Ward Ten*, *Crossroads*; the American soaps *Dallas* and *Dynasty*, which were popular during the 1980s; and more recently *EastEnders* and the Australian imports *Neighbours* and *Home and Away*.

The most remarkable, though as we shall see not the only, innovation of the soap opera was its lack of an ending, for unlike all previous narratives it never reaches an ultimate climax, denouement and point of closure or completion. These features were traditionally thought to be essential to a narrative in providing its readers or audience with the motivation to begin it, and in constituting the main characteristic which distinguishes fiction from the endless nature of life itself. But soap opera also differs from traditional stories in being presented from rapidly changing points of view: it has no narrative 'centre'.

The genre is concerned above all to reflect the texture of *domestic* life. Indeed it reflects the domestication of television (and radio) itself because like television its habitat is usually domestic and its content unending. It is a kind of fragmented version of the 'sequence' programming discussed with reference to radio in Chapter 7, in the sense that the viewer can step into or out of it at any stage without feeling that she has missed, or will miss, anything of crucial significance.

In an excellent discussion of soap opera John Fiske (1987) points out some other distinctive features: its huge casts consisting of forty or more characters and as many as twelve protagonists; 'real time' chronology, which implies that the action continues whether we can view it or not; and stars whose celebrity depends not on the usual qualities of distance and mystique but on their familiarity. All of this suggests an art form which is closer to the real world than are traditional art forms – or conversely, an original theatricalization of everyday life.

One small instance of its uncertain status is the dilemma caused by the practice of 'product placement' to which it often gives rise. When a character in a soap eats a 'real life' chocolate bar or buys some real world detergent in a shop, is this merely realism in a basically fictional genre or a direct form of advertising?

But of more interest are those unprecedented aesthetic satisfactions which viewers derive from soap opera and which have never been adequately explained: the lack of distance and 'difference', and above all, the lack of closure. Here we must content ourselves with the observation that soap opera seems to epitomize vicarious living. We suspend our lives in order to watch it, yet so banal is it that it seems merely to give us our own lives back again. Television can be a strangely paralysing and self-enclosed medium.

From hatstand to arbiter

Although an important aim of this chapter is to chart the extraordinary rise in the popularity and significance of television, we must not forget that it has always been part of a much broader media landscape. The word 'media' is used as a singular by many people (among them media studies students, who ought to know better) and often as a synonym for 'television': but television is not the only medium, nor even the only medium of broadcasting.

As with most newcomers its arrival began a process of displacement while its predecessors – radio, cinema and newspapers – made room for it, mostly with an ill grace. The latter were largely obliged to surrender to television what television did best and concentrate on their own unrivalled strengths. Whereas in current affairs, for instance, TV (and still radio) were best equipped to focus on concrete facts and events, provide the very latest news, and deal in certain kinds of actuality, cinema eventually had to quit this field altogether, while the newspapers not only increased news backgrounding but expanded into 'softer' news, features and 'life-style' topics, thus displacing a number of magazines and periodicals. Among the latter, those which cater for special interests have stood the best chance of survival.

But if the other media have been displaced and in some instances diminished by television, they have been able to get their revenge by living off it: television and its content have provided them with a great deal of subject matter. This is especially true of the newspapers, which contain daily reviews and previews of TV programmes, listings, and gossip about TV personalities and even about the characters in the soaps.

Hence as seems always to be the case in media history, the initial period of displacement has given way to a fairly close if often unacknowledged collaboration between all the media, especially in the business of setting the news and cultural agendas. In this respect I have more than once been fooled by some item on BBC Radio 4's *Today* programme, which in dealing with an obscure yet important issue has made me applaud the alertness and diligence of its news staff. It is only when I open my newspaper that I discover the item has been lifted from that day's edition of the *Independent* or the *Guardian*.

A more obvious instance of the way in which the media will perpetuate a story by batting it about among themselves, rather as the flippers and studs of a pinball machine can be used to keep the ball in play, was an episode in the decline of the marriage of Prince Charles and Princess Diana. It began with a *book* – Andrew Morton's biography of Diana which included disclosures about her relationship with her husband. The book was then serialized in a *newspaper*, the *Sunday Times*, but also covered in other papers and on *radio* and *television*, the two latter breathing fresh life into the story by question-begging references to 'the continuing controversy' about the royal marriage. Though doubtless a story that was popular with the public, it was hard to resist the impression that those whom it excited most were the broadcasters and journalists themselves.

Nevertheless while television has undoubtedly had an enormous impact on the media ecology, it is the history of its effects on social institutions with which we are primarily concerned. We will begin with sport because this offers perhaps the most vivid illustration of a progression which if not already familiar to us will soon become so.

After at first being barred from many sports events because of its likely impact on crowd attendances, and then admitted only on the strictest conditions, television has gradually begun to take them over, in some instances adapting them to its own particular requirements by changing the way in which they are played. It has been able to compensate them for the overall drop in their live attendances with huge sums of money in screening rights and with vastly bigger 'home gates'; and although this is of course very much a matter of media economics and the politics of media ownership, we should be clear that its precondition is the nature of television itself.

Some of the changes it has caused are perhaps subconscious, like the theatrical head-clutchings of soccer players when they miss a goal or lose a game, but others are premeditated. Ostensibly superficial, though even more spectacular, are the changes in 'packaging': in sports kit, which has become much more colourful and often includes sponsors' logos, and in the proliferation of stadium and trackside advertising. (In motor racing advertisers prefer television to cover circuits with tight bends because these force the cars to slow down and thus make the track-side hoardings more legible to the viewers.)

Professional boxing provides perhaps the most striking example of the growth of packaging. Before televised title fights there are now prolonged fanfares, the play of spotlights in a darkened arena, pounding music, and colourful processions to the ring. The latter often boasts advertisers' logos on its corner posts and canvas, the boxers wear garishly patterned shorts, and between the rounds scantily clad women circle the ring displaying the number of the next round.

However, some changes have been more fundamental and are likely to increase in the future. Despite the effect on the players, many matches of the 1994 soccer World Cup, which was staged in the United States, were played in the fierce midday heat so that they could capture peak evening viewing in Europe. As I write this, BSkyB has concluded a deal with English rugby league whose provisions include a switch from a winter to a summer season and the broadcaster's right to veto the transfer of players.

But so far it has been on cricket, that most sedate and conservative of games, that television has made its biggest impact. It was in 1977 that the Australian media magnate Kerry Packer launched his 'cricket circus', and with it a new era of flood-lit games, players in coloured pyjamas instead of the traditional all-whites, and stumps with logos. Limited-over cricket was largely a consequence of television, but yet more changes are likely. In order to accommodate its commercial breaks BSkyB wants longer intervals between overs, but much shorter breaks for lunch and tea. There is even talk of one-hour, eight-a-side matches in which each player would both bowl and bat.

We shall shortly see that sport is only one area in which television has graduated from modest onlooker to a mighty arbiter whom the world cannot oppose and whose gaze it often courts. This is how Colin Seymour-Ure reviews its post-war progress:

> As TV poured over the surface of everyday life its programmes made fewer and fewer concessions to pre-existing forms, institutions, media, manners. TV made plays, told the news, taught school, increasingly on its own terms, not as a parasite, imitator, or tolerated intruder concealed as a hat-stand . . . [It]

responded to popular taste, observing new taboos about racism and sexism, just as it helped to demolish old ones of sexual modesty or obscene language. But common to all programming, on any channel, was an eventual confidence in the distinctive value of the TV medium. By 1990, TV did not need to make excuses for itself.

(1991: 143)

Television and politics before 1959

The historical relationship between television and politics typifies that which has existed between television and most institutions of public life. Television begins as a loftily patronized messenger boy or barely tolerated guest, and ends up largely dictating how these institutions should present and even conduct their business.

For the genesis of its relationship with politics we have to go back to the days of sound broadcasting. At first it was the politicians who determined what issues radio and television would cover, and they retained the initiative until the end of the 1950s. The broadcasting of politics was shaped by two notable principles.

The first was that the coverage of the views of the different political parties should be 'balanced', a principle which was in any case implicit in the BBC's public service tenet that it should not identify itself with sectional interests. It was later applied to BBC television and to ITV and is still sometimes invoked. When, as often happens, one or other institution is accused of bias by *all* of the main parties it will take this as a comforting sign that it is managing a fair measure of balance.

In practice balance has always been an impossible concept and therefore a constant bone of contention. How can balance be defined or quantified? Is 2 minutes of soaring eloquence by the politician of one party 'balanced' by 2 minutes of stumbling prevarication by the politician of another? Should the party spokespersons be chosen by the programme producers or by the parties themselves? – an important question since it is often wayward politicians who make the best or most interesting broadcasters. Does balance mean affording equal coverage to all shades of political opinion or coverage which is proportionate to the numbers of seats which the parties occupy in parliament?

In the day-to-day coverage of politics balance has generally meant an even-handedness between the three main parties, but it has not extended to views which do not have significant parliamentary representation – views which would be, almost by definition, eccentric or 'extreme'. Moreover there have certainly been times when even this degree of even-handedness has been sacrificed to a practical need (usually the BBC's) to appease the party in power.

However, with reference to party political and party election broadcasts, 'balance' has meant coverage proportionate to the parliamentary strength of the main parties. The principle might equally be used to justify coverage which was *inversely* proportionate to it: that is, one could argue that if a party has few seats, it should be entitled to more coverage in order to bring its views before a wider public – but this notion of balance has only logic, not *realpolitik*, in its favour.

Ministerial broadcasts have always been especially contentious. Ministers could not demand air-time since this would make nonsense of the BBC's independence. They might therefore seek an invitation. But if they did, could the BBC withhold it? And if not, should it extend a similar invitation to the opposition?

In 1947 an agreement between the government and the BBC established four categories of political broadcast. The first was the straight ministerial broadcast to be given usually at times of emergency and always 'in the national interest'. Since there could be no dispute about the national interest this broadcast was uncontroversial and allowed the opposition no right of reply. The second was the controversial ministerial broadcast, to which the opposition was entitled to reply. The third was the party political broadcast, the numbers of which were allocated on the basis of parliamentary strength. These broadcasts were produced by the political parties themselves. And the fourth category was the controversial discussion.

Apart from placing the BBC in an invidious position between government and opposition the 1947 agreement achieved little. The opposition claimed, not unreasonably, that the definition of an 'uncontroversial' ministerial broadcast was itself controversial, and so the distinction between the first two categories all but collapsed. Moreover there were constant squabbles between the parties about the number of broadcasts to which each was entitled under the third category, with the Corporation used as a common whipping-boy.

However acrimonious, these squabbles were usually settled informally and away from the public view, but a judicial element was introduced as recently as 1995 when opposition MPs sought an injunction against the BBC to prevent it from showing in Scotland an interview with the prime minister just before that country's local elections. Their action was successful because the opposition was to be denied equal coverage.

Before the arrival of ITV political television mostly consisted of party election broadcasts. In the broader field of politics the BBC and ITV have seldom been so naive as to believe that the principle of balance or even-handedness has applied to conflicts between Britain and her external enemies, though during the Falklands and Gulf Wars there were complaints among certain sections of the public that the Argentinian and Iraqi cases had been insufficiently explained.

167

However the question of balance between the unionist and republican positions on Northern Ireland, both of which have sometimes been expressed through acts of terrorism, has always been a peculiarly thorny one and tackled by the broadcasters with varying temerity. The BBC's attempt to express the republican point of view in *Real Lives: At the Edge of the Union* (1985) caused predictable outrage, while a *This Week* documentary called *Death on the Rock* (1988), which investigated the killing of certain IRA activists by the SAS in Gibraltar, was shown by ITV despite government pressure.

Though balance may be difficult to define or achieve, broadcasting institutions are still required to be 'neutral'. Unlike the newspapers, they may not take an editorial line on political issues or urge their audiences to vote for a particular party. Since radio and TV have differed from newspapers in being limited by the shortage of frequencies, it has always seemed proper that each broadcasting institution should reflect the widest range of opinions and attitudes rather than one narrow and partisan point of view. But since digital broadcasting will shortly provide an almost limitless number of channels the obligations to be balanced or neutral could conceivably be ended.

The second principle which shaped the early broadcasting of politics was that a broadcasting institution should not pre-empt or prejudice discussions which were due to be conducted in parliament by the country's elected representatives. This was somewhat analogous to the *sub judice* rule in courts of law, which forbids public pronouncements about innocence or guilt before the conclusion of a trial so that the verdict shall not be improperly influenced. The principle was enshrined in an informal understanding reached in 1944 between the BBC and the political parties and became known as the 'fourteen-day rule': there could be no broadcast coverage of any issue which was due to be debated in parliament within the next fortnight.

Though it was the BBC which had proposed the rule, it soon formed the view that parliamentary discussion was likely to be informed and stimulated rather than prejudiced by any preceding broadcast coverage. In 1955 it therefore asked the government to revoke the rule, but the government's response was to make it formal and binding on BBC and ITV alike.

Nevertheless by this time the tide was beginning to turn in the relationship between broadcasters and politicians. The latter could deal confidently with radio, having been used to it since the early 1930s, but the new medium of television was less easy to handle. It could show politicians in pitiless close-up, exposing not only physical blemishes but idiosyncrasies of character.

Broadcasters, too, were growing more aware of their power, particularly with the arrival of ITV, whose commercial source of income meant that it was not beholden to politicians in the way that the BBC was. Its new generation of interviewers like Robin Day were more journalistic, less deferential. But in this respect competition strengthened the BBC too, because if its political broadcasting grew more incisive so as to match ITV's, the politicians could complain only by admitting that in the old days the BBC had been partly under their thumb.

It was the Suez crisis of 1956 which marked the beginning of the end of the old relationship between politicians and broadcasters. In July of that year President Nasser of Egypt nationalized the Anglo-French-controlled Suez Canal Company, as a consequence of which British, French and Israeli forces bombed and occupied the canal zone. This colonialist adventure split the country from top to bottom as well as incurring the displeasure not only of the Soviet Union but of Britain's main ally, the United States.

Paddy Scannell (1979) points out that before 1956 the BBC's political broadcasts focused on foreign affairs because it was here, in the twilight of empire and with the Soviet Union as everybody's *bête noire*, that controversy could be avoided and party consensus lay. But consensus collapsed with Suez, and as Asa Briggs (1995) observes, Suez threatened the BBC because for the first time in the history of broadcasting the Corporation was obliged to reflect a deep rift over foreign policy and report a large body of domestic opinion which was strongly critical of the government on a matter of great national importance.

One consequence was that the BBC incurred the deep hostility of the prime minister, Sir Anthony Eden. When Eden or one of his ministers broadcast, the opposition demanded a right of reply. But Eden's view was that this was a national crisis which transcended party politics, and therefore that the BBC should not attempt to be even-handed between government and opposition but support the government. This was in accordance with the 1947 agreement between the government and the Corporation, but as the Labour politician Clement Attlee had remarked in 1934:

> The control of the BBC by the State in an emergency is obviously necessary, but there is a point where it is difficult to decide whether the emergency is really that of the State or of the Government as representing the political party in power.

> (McDonnell 1991: 17)

Was Suez a crisis for the nation — or merely for the government? The BBC certainly saw it as the government's and its popularity with the latter sank to a new depth.

Nevertheless broadcasting in general, and the BBC in particular, ended the year 1956 with its power enhanced rather than diminished. First of all, under the pressure of events in the Middle East and elsewhere, the government indefinitely suspended the fourteen-day rule in return for assurances from the broadcasters which were as insincerely given as they were unrealistically demanded. The rule could hardly survive because ITV was much less vulnerable to government threats and pressures than was the BBC, and if the independence of its editorial line on Suez could be praised, as it was by many people, to criticize the BBC's would involve the admission, unthinkable in a democracy, that the latter was a creature of the government.

The BBC was also able to maintain its independence precisely because there was no general agreement, even within the ruling Conservative Party, as to where 'the national interest' lay. But finally, and only a few months after the Suez crisis began, a mass uprising broke out in Hungary against the Soviet Union. In Britain (as elsewhere in the west) there was almost unanimous support for Hungary and a general agreement, endorsed by many Hungarians themselves, that the BBC's coverage of the uprising was excellent. The Corporation was thus able to restore its fair standing with the government.

Thenceforward both ITV and the BBC took steps to raise the quality of their political broadcasting, though as we noted in Chapter 5 the former had already taken the lead with the launch of ITN. It is perhaps not surprising, then, that an ITV contractor, Granada, was the first to offer in-depth TV coverage of a by-election campaign. This took place at Rochdale in February and March of 1958, and programmes included a live discussion of the election issues between all the candidates and interviews of the latter by three experienced journalists.

Television and politics since 1959

The general election of 1959 was the first in which television could be said to have played a major role in the electoral process and the point at which the broadcasters seized the initiative from the politicians. Sir Hugh Greene, the overall head of BBC news and soon to be director general, announced that the Corporation would cover the election on 'news values' rather than according to literalistic notions of balance: in effect that broadcasters rather than politicians would set the agenda. The sheer scale of the BBC's coverage was unprecedented, with fifty-seven cameras in the field, some of them moving on election night from one constituency to another.

Since 1959 television has increasingly dictated the terms on which election campaigns have been conducted – and, indeed, on which politics in general can be publicized. From 1985 it was allowed into the House of Lords (radio had been relaying the proceedings of both Houses since 1976) and from 1989 into the Commons. It is for the individual to decide whether TV has altered the behaviour of politicians for better or for worse, or had no discernible effect.

But of equal interest is the way in which thanks largely to the medium itself, the general understanding of what 'politics' consists of has broadened beyond the traditional and well-defined realms of cabinet, parliament and party warfare. The year 1958 marked television's importance in terms of the conventional political processes: it covered the Rochdale by-election and for the first time the state opening of parliament. But it also covered politics of an unconventional but no less significant kind: the first of the Aldermaston marches organized by the Campaign for Nuclear Disarmament (CND) and an example *par excellence* of pressure-group publicity.

On the nation's screens appeared an astonishing, motley procession of people: bearded students in duffel coats; young couples with placard-bearing infants in push chairs; leading public figures – radical clergymen, aquiline intellectuals like Bertrand Russell, and personalities from theatre and the arts; and accompanying the spectacle the sounds of skiffle groups, jazz bands and oratory. This was a new kind of 'visual politics' which television had largely brought into being and which would reach its apotheosis in the great Vietnam and civil rights marches of the 1960s and 1970s. But it is still with us in the publicity coups of Greenpeace and the anti-motorway protestors.

As Ralph Negrine (1994) points out and as we noted earlier in this chapter, such campaigners and protestors have always made an emotive and moralistic appeal on single issues, which are represented as straightforward clashes between good and evil. And they have always attracted TV coverage not only because of their deliberate theatricality, but because in cutting across the lines of conventional party politics they could be seen as in a sense non-political. The broadcasting institutions could therefore televise them without having to worry about 'balance' or accusations of being politically partisan.

But television has had a theatrical effect on politics *in general* (indeed, we saw earlier that it is liable to theatricalize almost every sphere of activity). It often replaces thoughtful discussions of abstract issues with 'personalities' and confrontations, and concocts phoney news items like photo-opportunities and walkabouts. Yet thanks to TV some news items have managed the sinister feat of being both 'concocted' and genuine: the IRA set its bombs to explode in the late afternoon so that the effects could appear on the early evening news bulletins.

Where we once thought of politics simply as a business which was conducted by politicians in designated arenas such as Downing Street, the Houses of Parliament and the election hustings, television has made us see it as a broader, more inclusive matter of social issues and problems – of campaigns, direct action and demonstrations. Yet during the 1960s TV extended even the traditional political arenas by luring the politicians more and more often into its own habitat: the studio. As the tribune of the people it felt justified in devising its own political programmes – not only *Panorama* and *News at Ten* but *Question Time* and *World in Action*.

Whether they wished to or not, the politicians were obliged to adjust their demeanour to the needs of the small screen. Harold Macmillan, who was prime minister from 1957 to 1963, was quite adept at this, combining a reassuring patrician image with a hint of self-parody. Before he submitted to a television interview by the American Ed Murrow, only 37 per cent of the electorate thought that Macmillan was doing a good job: afterwards the number rose to 50 per cent. The leader of the opposition, Hugh Gaitskell, was thought dull by many viewers, as was Macmillan's successor, Sir Alec Douglas-Home, but Harold Wilson, who was prime minister from 1964 to 1970 and from 1974 to 1976, was the first to make a careful study of television, and with his pipe and mackintosh projected the image of a canny man of the people.

Despite this Wilson was discomfited by the BBC in much the same way as Sir Anthony Eden had been many years before. In 1966 he used television to explain his National Plan for Britain's economic recovery. But despite this rhetoric the BBC declined to regard it as other than a matter of party politics and allowed the opposition a right of reply. It thus incurred Wilson's undying hostility, the episode proving that dealing with the media, and with television especially, is like riding a tiger: woe betide the person who thinks it will serve only the purposes that she or he wants it to serve!

But the adjustment of politics to television has been much more fundamental than this. It is not just appearances but political events and whole election campaigns which have had to be tailored to the medium and its news schedules. Indeed television is itself a part of politics in the sense that almost every political decision will include some calculation as to the effect it will have on the viewing electorate.

Moreover the medium is even more pervasive than I have so far suggested. I mentioned above that it has enticed politicians out of their traditional habitats and into its own: but the world, not just the studio, is television's oyster and politicians may find themselves being accosted on airport runways, answering questions in a shopping precinct, giving in-flight or on-train interviews. For many years there have been permanent TV studios at Heathrow as well as at Westminster. In sum it could be said that the relationship between television and politics, though punctuated by rows and crises over Suez, the Falklands, Northern Ireland and so on, is so close that they can scarcely be disentangled from each other.

Colin Seymour-Ure (1991) has discerned three main effects that the media, with television pre-eminent among them, have had upon the role of the premiership. First, the prime minister must give more time and thought to dealing with the media. Second she or he is more often drawn away from the power bases of the office: Downing Street and the House of Commons. Third, and predictably in view of television's requirements, the prime minister must be more of a 'personality', an opinion leader or mobilizer – in a word, more like an American president.

We must conclude with some brief remarks about the government's formal policy on broadcasting. In the paradoxical impression it gives of not being subject to special legislation yet being closely monitored by a number of public agencies, television (and radio) reflects the ambivalence which society feels towards it. In a democracy we believe it should be both free to tell the truth and report the news as much as it can, yet carefully restrained so that it does not exert too much power or influence over people.

This helps to explain why governments traditionally have had a 'non-policy' towards broadcasting. There is no 'Department of Communication' (the Postmaster-General's regulatory reponsibility for the electronic media disappeared in 1969), and such statutory provisions as exist are piecemeal and of makeshift origins – intended, as Seymour-Ure (1991) points out, to serve broad objectives like 'freedom of speech', 'freedom of information', 'public service' and 'balance'. Legislation affects aspects of broadcasting and its audiences (for example, the TV licence), but in other respects, television and radio are regarded as 'nothing special' – subject to those ordinary laws of obscenity, blasphemy, copyright, defamation and official secrets which affect many other spheres than broadcasting.

Nevertheless we are aware that both the BBC and the commercial sector are carefully if discreetly policed by publicly appointed boards. Moreover certain government departments such as the Treasury and the Foreign Office take an oblique interest in broadcasting (by fixing the TV licence, financing the World Service and so on); and media legislation has established various self-regulatory bodies such as the Broadcasting Complaints Commission and the Advertising Standards Authority. It has been calculated that at the end of the 1970s some thirty organizations were involved in controlling or in some way shaping British television and radio output.

Television and the royal family

The history of television's dealings with royalty is very similar to the history of its dealings with politics and sport. At the 1937 coronation it was a mere spectator in the crowd. At the 1953 coronation it was a humble supplicant, knocking at the door of Westminster Abbey and being allowed in to watch discreetly from the loft, though there was a part of the ceremony from which it was excluded. By the 1990s it was a monstrous dictator before whom a prince and princess would come to justify their private lives.

Until the 1970s the royal family retained a fair degree of mystique and was held in some reverence. It is true that there had been a scandal and a constitutional crisis back in 1936, when after the death of George V it gradually emerged that his son and successor, Edward VIII, intended to marry the twice-divorced Mrs Wallis Simpson. But the crisis was well managed. Television scarcely existed, and the BBC and the Newspaper Proprietors' Association, with their instinctive respect for rank and authority, joined in a conspiracy to keep the news from the wider public. When the king decided that he would rather renounce the throne than Mrs Simpson he explained the decision in a radio broadcast which ensured both sympathy for himself and support for his successor and younger brother, George VI.

It was not until 1969 that royalty decided to make some concession to the democratizing effects of the new medium of television by allowing itself to be seen in a more intimate and less formal light. The result was Richard Cawston's documentary *The Royal Family* (both BBC and ITV), in which the Queen appeared in a happy domestic setting and thus inaugurated a honeymoon period in royalty's relations with television. The royal family still maintained much of its dignity and detachment through televised events like the investiture of Charles as Prince of Wales in the same year, and his marriage to Lady Diana Spencer in 1981; but the images of family picnics and bustling corgis lingered in the nation's mind. The royals were likeably human – at bottom, 'just like the rest of us'.

However the three decades since the screening of Cawston's programme have shown that television is always a dangerous guest to admit since it ends up hosting the party. As members of the royal family were seen more and more often on TV, their magic began to wane and popular reverence to diminish. They came to seem unremarkable, even a little dull. An attempt by its younger members to show that they could laugh at themselves by taking part in a gameshow, *It's a Royal Knockout* (BBC 1, 1987), seriously dented their dignity: the nation was not amused. And finally, with the revelations of matrimonial breakdowns and sexual adventures, notably those of Prince Charles and Princess Diana, royalty began to acquire a negative, more tawdry kind of glamour.

It has to be said that television was not the only, perhaps not even the primary, cause of this change. Its news programmes simply echoed stories which had invariably originated in the tabloids – and even then, only when they had become so sensational that they could no longer be ignored. But television clearly gave them a wider currency, and its pictures fleshed out and made us all too familiar with those about whom they were written. Yet instead of shunning TV on the reasonable assumption that a measure of retirement, an interval of oblivion, might restore their standing, each seemed to solicit the medium to put their case, seeking yet another dose of publicity – and this time a favourable one – to counter the damaging effects of the last.

These interviews of Charles and Diana – the former on ITV in the summer of 1995, the latter on BBC in November of the same year – were an extraordinary instance of the power of television. Each broadcast was a curious mixture of intimacy and exhibitionism, a series of confidences which implied the acceptance of millions of prurient viewers as confessors and even judges. But while prince and princess were seeking to justify themselves and restore their reputations, what television revealed above all was their ordinariness, their merely average weaknesses – that at close quarters, royals, like everybody else, are anything but royal.

We are of course used to this inherently debunking tendency of television. Either by interviews and documentaries or by naturalistic forms of drama, it has often revealed the ordinariness and fallibility of figures in authority: teachers, police, clergy, judges. Indeed television has constantly been blamed for the decline of respect for the very concept of authority. If this decline is real, not everyone will see it as unhealthy. In a democracy it may well be a good thing that the future king and his wife should regard themselves as accountable to the people via the people's medium of television.

But it could be argued that royalty's loss of status has a more significant consequence, for however quaintly anachronistic it may seem, however politically moribund, it remains the keystone of the British constitution and the ultimate legitimation of all other forms of authority, even in the democracy that ours is. For the first time in many years republicanism is back on the political agenda, and that may be no bad thing: the royals have only themselves to blame for this. But the situation prompts two contrasting thoughts.

The first is that authority and rank or status are arbitrary and intrinsically absurd, since television has taught us that they are a mantle which no one is good enough or big enough to assume. How, then, can they be maintained and justified? But the second is that however arbitrary authority and status may be, they are absolutely essential for our common survival and self-betterment, for our efficient function as members of society. What sanction for them could we find which would *not* be discredited under the pitiless gaze of television?

Some readers may think that I have carried this argument too far. What is not likely to be in dispute is that television has contributed to a decline in the popularity of the royal family by exposing lapses and weaknesses which were more easily concealed in a former age: there is a growing feeling that such ordinary, fallible people should no longer hold extraordinary privileges. Even the Queen herself, to whom no wisp of scandal attaches, has suffered. In 1984 her Christmas message was heard by 28 million; by 1994 the number had dropped to 14.5 million.

It is of course true that as well as destroying mystique and exposing the ordinariness of those in power and authority, television is capable of taking people who are already 'ordinary' and elevating or idealizing them. But these tend to be pop or film stars, who are generally allowed to use the medium on *their* terms precisely because they deal in fantasy and entertainment rather than in 'real world' matters. The bulk of their TV appearances consists of soft-focus movies and videos, and the few close interviews they give are carefully stage-managed.

Television and audiences

As the number of TV channels has increased, and with it the kinds of content that they offer, the television audience has divided along class lines just as it did with the proliferation of radio networks after the war. Since ITV was launched with a need to deliver the biggest possible audience to its advertisers, we noticed that it attracted a large number of working-class viewers, while most of the middle class stayed with the BBC.

With the arrival of BBC 2 in 1964 and the first move towards narrowcasting, further divisions became apparent: the working class stayed with ITV and BBC 1; the middle class divided its viewing between BBC 1 and BBC 2 and later extended its interest to Channel 4. With similar motivation to ITV, satellite and cable television are seeking and capturing a strong working-class audience.

A knowledge of this sort is clearly vital to broadcasting researchers, who need to keep advertisers and programme planners well informed as to who is watching what and in what numbers. But the answers to certain other questions they ask, though just as desirable, are much more elusive. What effect do programmes have on people? What do they think of them? And how far do programmes influence their views and behaviour? As the reader will appreciate, our earlier discussion of the characteristics of television was in many respects inseparable from a discussion of its likely effects on the viewer, but we must now try to take a more systematic and empirical look at audience effects and influences.

For the first twenty-five years of competition the BBC and ITV were incapable of co-ordinating their audience researches. While the BBC depended on its own broadcasting research department, the individual ITV contractors engaged companies like Television Audience Measurement and A. C. Nielsen to do theirs. The BBC had one system of measurement, ITV had another: they were incompatible, and not surprisingly each system tended to favour the organization which used it.

In the early years of television it was assumed by virtually everyone that the social and moral effects and influences of the medium were considerable – a view fervently espoused by the Pilkington Committee, which penalized the ITA for being among the few who doubted it. After Pilkington there was a flowering of interest in this field which we may broadly divide into industry based, audience based and academic.

ITV was quick to atone for the heresy it had uttered. In 1964 it co-ordinated its research efforts under the Joint Industry Committee for Television Advertising Research (JICTAR), though it was another seventeen years before BBC and ITV set up at the behest of the Annan Committee a joint company, the Broadcasters' Audience Research Board (BARB), with a single system of audience research.

Among audiences themselves the interest in television's effects took the form of campaigning rather than investigation, since they were already convinced that they knew what those effects were – or should be. Most audience groups were interested in television as either a moral or an educational force. The most publicized because of its opposition to 'permissiveness' was Mrs Mary Whitehouse's National Viewers' and Listeners' Association. Others included the more libertarian Television and Radio Committee, under the leadership of Professor Richard Hoggart, and a group with a special interest in educational broadcasting, the Television Viewers' Council.

But British television (and to a much lesser extent, radio) was also beginning to attract the attention of academics. The key date is 1959, when Joseph Trenaman left the BBC's Further Education Unit to become the first holder of the Granada Research Fellowship in Television at Leeds University. Soon after, the Centre for Mass Communication Research was founded at Leicester University, and degree programmes in media studies began to sprout at polytechnics and at other universities during the 1970s and 1980s.

Since then, theories of audience effects have been developed which are increasingly complex and problematical, but based on solid empirical work by researchers like David Morley and Roger Silverstone. Morley (1992) observes that since the home is primarily a place of relaxation and leisure for men, but a sphere of work for women, even those who have jobs outside it, the former watch television in an attentive and wholehearted way while the latter's viewing is mostly intermittent and perhaps informed by a sense of guilt. It is thus a fair generalization that women's use of the medium is more fitful and *ad hoc* than men's, and that because it is less premeditated women make much less of the VCR to pre-record television output.

But use is one thing and effects are another, and despite the early optimism of academics, those questions of audience research which are more than merely quantitative have proved impossibly difficult, yielding few certain answers. For this reason I do not intend to offer a historical account of a field which Colin Seymour-Ure (1991) with his usual metaphorical flair describes as 'too much like an ancient map of the world: large wastes of conjecture punctuated by occasional islands of knowledge'. I shall merely sketch some of the problems involved in the study of effects and influences and offer one or two reflections about probabilities.

One obvious difficulty is that of separating the effects of television from those of the other media, or indeed from those of other social phenomena such as personal relationships, education and general life experiences. Another difficulty is to determine how far television is an influence or an effect – and even if we could isolate it from all the other social and cultural phenomena, its identifiable influences are likely to be much more complex than we might suppose. An individual programme such as a play or political debate might be highly influential, yet have different influences on different viewers because it embraces different, even conflicting, values.

Even if we could assume that viewers were able to describe the way in which a programme had affected them, how could their differing subjective judgements be measured and compared? Their viewing needs and motives are in any case likely to be multi-layered. Beneath the wish for news and entertainment lie deeper needs – for companionship, escape, excitement, romantic or erotic pleasure. It is impossible to know whether scenes of sex or violence desensitize, repel, gratify or incite their viewers. A sensible answer might be that they do all these things, but that they do different things to different viewers. Yet this merely moves the question somewhere else: why should these scenes have such *varying* effects?

And so to reflections. Our concern is with television, but though it is surely a dominating influence we need to remember that it acts in concert with several other media: radio, books, newspapers, magazines, cinema films, CDs and tapes, videos. In some ways the media seem hugely influential, in others wholly ineffectual. Despite the recent resurgence of nationalism in the world, and the renewed emphasis on local differences and distinctions, we are everywhere watching the same programmes, and thanks largely to the lifestyles promoted by such programmes and by TV commercials, eating the same food, singing the same songs, and wearing the same clothes.

Though we must always remember that the media follow as well as set trends, it is clear that we are highly susceptible to those messages we like – to new fashions in clothes, to the fantasies offered or implied by much advertising, to new slang and speech patterns (invariably American), to pop music, and changes in sexual mores. But we may also be highly susceptible to messages we do *not* like. We are easily incensed by veal exports or new motorways, and the metonymic character of television can quickly implant in us 'moral panics' about violence, public order, education, diet or disease. Nevertheless, these often seem as fleeting as they are intense, for the restless, roving eye of TV is constantly throwing up fresh concerns, relatively few of which effect a permanent change in behaviour.

In many other respects television seems unable to influence us even temporarily. It may teach us a great deal about politicians but unless we are already inclined to, it is unlikely to make us vote for them. However it may seem to be unable to influence us only because its influences are long-term rather than immediately apparent, or because they are not what the broadcasters intended. Most individual programmes seem to have negligible effects, not least because they are rapidly superseded by others, day after day and over umpteen channels. But if we take a longer view, say over one or two decades, we can see a veritable sea change in certain social attitudes, to which television has surely contributed – attitudes to the environment, to women and sexual issues, to race and ethnicity. We might describe this as the 'drip, drip' effect of television and the other mass media.

On the other hand its influences may also be overlooked because they were not intended or anticipated. If a politician uses television to solicit our vote, his failure to do so may not simply be a 'lack' of influence but a negative one: that is, instead of merely failing to win our vote he may actually persuade us to vote for his opponent. As I suggested above, there is some evidence that despite its largely good intentions constant TV publicity has demystified the royal family and others who occupy positions of status or authority, making us hold them in rather less respect than before.

Something else which has been demystified through familiarization is television itself. The way in which it is 'consumed' has probably changed from the early years of rapt viewing to varying degrees of passivity and fitfulness – a tendency which was strengthened by the arrival of the remote controller, since this allows the easy 'zapping' of uninteresting material and the practice of 'channel surfing'. These newer viewing patterns must surely make television less influential than it was, or at least less influential than it might be.

As we have also seen, much television consists of entertainment – in effect if not in intention – and one important consequence of this has been an extension of the 'entertainment imperative' into other spheres of activity, such as news, education, even religious worship. In this context, the early fears that television viewing would encroach on children's study-time and result in them reading fewer books – part of the rationale behind the 'toddlers' truce' – were probably well-founded. Some teachers are certainly worried that even for older pupils reading is a difficult and by no means habitual or congenial activity. If television could supply all the benefits of the print medium as well as its deficiencies, this would matter little. But as I have tried to show, print can perform certain vital intellectual tasks much better than TV can.

Television has seen birth, death and copulation. It has been into churches, courts of law and prisons; above the clouds and under the seas; on the moon and down microscopes; inside vaginas, brains and scrotums. It has revealed everything. How far has it increased our wisdom or changed our behaviour? No one can be sure. We are convinced of the medium's importance, yet unable to define it in an entirely satisfying way.

Sources/further reading

For an excellent survey of the social and political background to the growth of television viewing during the 1970s see Potter (1989). The realism and domesticity of the TV medium are neatly described in Alvarado, Gutch and Wollen (1987), while Negrine (1994) points out the desultory, deracinated way in which television seems to present the news.

There are many thoughtful and extensive studies of television's social effects, some general and some specific, but all affording insights which greatly extend, and in several cases contrast with, my own. For a wide-ranging and highly intellectualized account of the place of TV in daily life, which deals at length with the domestication of the medium and proposes a theory of its audience, see Silverstone (1994). In an analysis of viewers' attitudes to the miners' strike of 1984–5, Philo (1990) found that a significant number believed the medium distorts and exaggerates by focusing on violence, while others felt that such violence represented the everyday reality of picketing.

To Postman (1986) I owe a general debt for his excellent critique of TV and for his insight into the contrasting functions of imagery and language. Whale (1969) argues that television is a crude medium for the presentation of news and politics, since pictures cannot be used to 'explain'. He and Davis (1976) also stress its quantitative limitations.

For a brief yet scintillating polemic on television see Hughes (1995). In two newspaper articles, the first dealing with the programme on euthanasia, the second with the coverage of the O. J. Simpson trial, Appleyard (1995a; 1995b) demonstrates the way in which television tends to colour and falsify what it presents. Postman (1986) argues persuasively that the medium has made entertainment the model for almost all other kinds of discourse, and in his impressive analysis of television form Corner (1995) acknowledges the medium's 'overall dramatic character' in relation to both fictional and non-fictional output. There are some interesting remarks on television aesthetics in Mulgan (1990).

Corner (1995) provides a fascinating account of the historical development of the documentary genre in cinema, radio and TV, together with analysis of the conventions of both documentary and docudrama which recognizes some of the inherent problems discussed in this chapter. Kerr (1990) also has useful information on the historical development of docudrama, while Geraghty (1996), Fiske (1987) and Mepham (1990) are excellent on the general characteristics of soap opera. Three specialized studies of the genre are Hobson (1982) on *Crossroads*, Ang (1985) on *Dallas*, and Buckingham (1996) on *EastEnders*. The traditional view that narrative structures are informed by the sense of an ending is set out in Kermode (1967). Tunstall (1993) presents a range of television genres from the viewpoint of the producers.

For much material in this chapter I must acknowledge a substantial debt to Seymour-Ure (1991; 1996). He is illuminating on the interrelationship of the mass media, even more so on the comprehensive way in which television has invaded many areas of modern life and often modified them to suit its own requirements. See Whannel (1990) for some helpful remarks on the way in which television modifies sport.

There is a thoughtful account of the first forty years of broadcasting and politics in Goldie (1977), and Scannell (1979) is enlightening on TV and politics before 1956. A comprehensive account of the relationship between the mass media and the political process is in Golding, Murdock and Schlesinger (1986). Among the many other works on the media and politics Tunstall (1983) is brightly written and perceptive, and Negrine (1994) is also useful – particularly on the question of balance and on the nature and behaviour of political pressure groups.

For an account of the fourteen-day rule and of TV's role in the Rochdale by-election see Sendall (1982). A full discussion of the Suez crisis and the other events of 1956 can be found in Briggs (1995). Schlesinger (1978) is still the authoritative work on the BBC's news production and particularly illuminating on its coverage of the conflict in Northern Ireland. I must again cite Seymour-Ure (1991; 1996) for a concise and lucid perspective on the more recent relationship between television and politics – an account which manages to be balanced, yet colourful and witty.

McQuail (1987) is helpful on the nature and behaviour of media audiences and the possible range of influences on them. By contrast, Cumberbatch and Howitt (1989) and Lewis (1990) indicate some of the difficulties of measuring media influences and effects. An informative account of BBC radio and TV audience research up to the end of the 1960s can be found in Silvey (1974). Potter (1989) discusses the historical development of audience research, and for an account of audience campaign groups see Sendall (1983) and Briggs (1995). Morley (1992) is a highly sophisticated discussion of television audiences which includes a critical history of audience research, an examination of theoretical frameworks, and an exploration of the nature and impact of influences. In another stimulating discussion of influences Corner (1995) outlines some of the problems in analysing them and takes a more cautious, subtle and contingent approach than mine.

A growth of sights and sounds

A growth of sights and sounds

'A peevish decade'

During the 1970s the mood which had characterized the 1960s seemed to darken. There remained that scepticism of authority and of traditional values and institutions which television had almost certainly helped to create. But it was now less genial and relaxed, more serious and militant – a change which was doubtless both a cause and a consequence of the economic and political crises that were developing in many parts of the world.

There were new variations on, and additions to, the long-standing antagonism between commmunist East and capitalist West. Politics became more radical, resulting in a leftward shift of the entire spectrum of opinion, and there seemed to be a much greater preoccupation with class conflict and the rights of minorities than with social cohesiveness and interdependence.

The horrific drama of Vietnam continued to play before the TV cameras, but there were many other wars. There was also an upsurge in political assassinations, kidnappings and terrorist attacks. For the first time in living memory there seemed to be a widespread acceptance that the rightfulness of a cause was directly proportionate to the extremity or violence of the methods used to pursue it.

Britain had its own generous share of strikes, sit-ins, lock-outs, occupations, demonstrations, pressure and splinter groups, and acts of terrorism – most of the latter emanating from a conflict in Northern Ireland whose roots went down through centuries. But on top of all this, the country experienced deep economic difficulties in the late 1960s and throughout the 1970s: industrial stoppages were so commonplace and inflation so rampant that Britain became known as 'the sick man of Europe'.

In October 1973 Egypt and Syria suddenly made war on Israel and were just as suddenly defeated. The Arab oil-producing states took revenge on the world economy, and by the end of 1974 the price of oil had quadrupled. As Britain struggled to cope with this crisis, the National Union of Mineworkers called a strike. In February 1974 the Conservative government introduced public expenditure cuts, together with a three-day week to save electricity and a 50-mile-an-hour speed limit to save petrol.

To escape being held to ransom, it called an election for the end of that month on the issue 'Who governs Britain?'. But the public was less sure of the answer than the government had hoped, especially when that magisterial renegade Enoch Powell attacked Britain's membership of the EEC (it had joined on 1 January 1973), condemned its policy on Northern Ireland and exhorted the electorate to vote Labour.

The broadcasting organizations, and the BBC especially, were in an invidious position between the government and its many opponents and critics. Labour won the election, but by a whisker, scarcely consolidating its position when it held another in October of the same year. Nor were its answers to the problems of the time much better than the Tories'. Prices continued to rise: on average they trebled during the 1970s. In 1977 alone, 1 million working days were lost in strikes. In 1979 a 'dirty jobs' dispute disrupted schools, hospitals and ambulances, closed mortuaries and put a stop to refuse collection.

Although as we shall see shortly, both broadcasters produced surprisingly good programmes in such a troubled era, they were inevitably afflicted by the same difficulties as everybody else. The BBC's economic state was a microcosm of the nation's. Inflation devoured its licence fee, necessitating cuts in transmission hours and new programme projects.

In reflecting contemporary issues it was always more vulnerable to the main political parties than ITV was, and managed to fall foul of both opposition and government. In June 1971 its current affairs magazine *Twenty-Four Hours* broadcast a special feature entitled *Yesterday's Men*, which explored what it had been like for members of the Labour government to lose high office so unexpectedly in the 1970 general election. By using music and cartoons the feature injudiciously blended documentary with satire; but the following evening insult was added to injury in the form of a programme called *Mr Heath's Quiet Revolution*, a sober and entirely respectful assessment of the Conservative government's first year in office. The Labour opposition was incensed. However in January 1972 the government was offended when the BBC ignored its advice to withhold a documentary on *The Question of Ulster*. The programme reached, and mostly impressed, 7.5 million viewers.

On the other hand, the Corporation was much less vulnerable to internal labour disputes because strikes saved it money. Not so the ITV contractors, who were confronted by strong trade unions. For ITV, stoppages were instantly damaging. In dealing with disputes the contractors were unable to play a long game because their franchises were scheduled to last for only a few years, with no guarantee of a renewal. Indeed a renewal was unlikely if strikes took them off air for long spells during their existing franchise period.

The worst strike in ITV's history blacked out the entire network for eleven weeks, from 10 August to 19 October 1979. As was usually the case, the cause was a rejected wage claim, but the strike itself cost the contractors £100 million and the huge pay rise which settled it was a victory for the unions. Yet the golden goose was already looking sickly, for by slimming the contractors' workforces and creating more freelance and casual labour, the arrival of new technologies and the growth of independent production houses would soon help to loosen the unions' hold.

The launch of independent local radio

To the surprise of the opinion pollsters the Conservatives regained power in the 1970 general election, and the new government was keen to give commercial interests the opportunity to exploit radio just as they had been able to exploit television since 1955. It saw three main merits in a system of commercial radio: first it would enlarge audience choice; second it would be 'free' to the listener; third it would provide an economic stimulus by allowing business to run stations, and advertisers a new medium through which to promote their products.

Hence in 1972 the Sound Broadcasting Act established a system of independent local radio (ILR) which would run pretty much in parallel with that of ITV. In fact the ITA was renamed the Independent Broadcasting Authority (IBA) and appointed to regulate both. But why was it a system of *local* radio?

Although some medium wave frequencies were allocated to help launch ILR, the modern technology of VHF/FM would allow a large number of stations onto the spectrum, every one of them offering good reception. Thus not only was the system a bow towards the political fashion for 'localism'; it maximized the broadcasting opportunities for aspiring station operators and advertisers. Moreover it provided direct competition against BBC local radio, which had already opened about twenty stations.

The ILR stations operated under similar statutory controls to the ITV contractors. The IBA selected the companies (which could be part-owned by newspapers, but not by the ITV contractors within their respective areas); it owned the transmitters, for which the companies paid a rent; and it enforced acceptable standards of content and balance. As with ITV it drew an absolute distinction between programme content and advertising: sponsorship was not allowed.

The first two ILR stations opened in London in October 1973: Capital Radio, which has always been among the most successful, and LBC, which adopted a news-and-talk format. LBC also provided a news service, Independent Radio News, to the other ILR stations.

The ILR system spread through the United Kingdom fairly rapidly. By 1977 there were nineteen stations; by 1983 forty-three stations covering more than 80 per cent of the population. It was anticipated that they would be very profitable, but for the first two decades of their existence they were not. There were even some mergers and closures. Why? Three main reasons suggest themselves.

First their launch coincided with a major economic recession which lasted until the early 1980s, thus depressing advertising revenues. Second, it coincided with stiffening competition from other media. Even the growing market in audio-cassettes was something of a threat because many receivers were now radio-cassette players, making it just as easy for the aspiring listener to turn on a tape as to switch on the radio. News updates had long been one of radio's strengths, but from 1974 the audience could get these when it required them and not when radio was ready to provide them – by turning on teletext. Breakfast was always one of radio's peak listening times, but from 1983 breakfast television could be watched instead.

The third reason was the most serious. The ILR stations were too tightly regulated by the IBA, which was itself constrained by a government that had still not grasped the fact that radio was no longer used in the way it had been before the arrival of television and transistors. Only a tiny number of listeners now expected the medium to provide the varied range of programmes that characterized TV: most merely sought music and news as secondary listening.

However, under the Sound Broadcasting Act the IBA required from each station a 'balance of programming' (including the provision of substantial – and inevitably costly – news bulletins) which was a vestige of the old public service ideal. If there was not to be old fashioned mixed programming, there must at any rate be 'cross-community appeal' – if appropriate, access, or at least output, for ethnic minorities.

Thus as Stephen Barnard observes: 'In effect, each of the ILR stations outside London had to provide the full range of BBC services within a smaller, localized framework, and entirely from commercial resources' (1989: 75). Moreover, with the arguable exception of Radio 4, none of the full BBC networks attempted to provide such a range of services.

As a result of the duties which were placed on it, ILR acquired an assortment of listeners of different backgrounds and tastes, but no individual group of sufficent size to attract much advertising interest. As Barnard (1989) again points out, the very terms of the IBA franchise precluded the ILR stations from targeting those groups most sought by advertisers.

To try to get round this problem the stations couched their public service material in the form of interviews, announcements, bulletins and short features which were sprinkled within the overall music-and-entertainment format of the sequence programme, but the strategy was not wholly successful. Barnard also observes that the IBA's regulatory zeal tended to vary with the government in office. Under the Labour regime of 1974-9 it got tough with stations who put profit before public service, and in 1979 awarded franchises to two community based consortia, Cardiff Broadcasting and Midlands Community Radio (Coventry). Neither survived in that form.

Programme pageant

The de-restriction of television broadcasting hours in 1972 took both ITV and the BBC by surprise, and they proceeded cautiously. Yet despite – perhaps even because of – the economic and political gloom of the decade, they produced some excellent programmes of all types. According to Jeremy Potter (1989), serious programming on ITV increased both absolutely and relatively during the 1970s.

One form of serious programming which was vitally important to both broadcasters was, of course, news – and for foreign news the decade was a particularly eventful and turbulent one. There were wars in the Middle East, Bangladesh, Cyprus, Vietnam (culminating in the US withdrawal); there was the American presidential scandal of Watergate; there were hijackings and political kidnappings, the overthrow of the Shah of Iran and the resurgence of Islam; a peripatetic papacy; conflict between Iran and Iraq, and between the Soviet Union and Afghanistan.

Fortunately new technology arrived to cover these events more effectively, and the 1973 Yom Kippur War marked the point when television could end the press's lingering dominance in foreign news by providing up-to-date pictures. ITN obtained film of the earliest fighting and beamed it to London via the satellite station at Tel Aviv so that it could be shown on the same day's edition of *News at Ten*.

In the second half of the decade electronic newsgathering (ENG) made TV's news coverage even quicker and more flexible. ENG units were small cameras which used magnetic tape instead of conventional film. No processing was needed, editing was simple and the technical quality better than film's.

In the equally serious categories of arts programmes and documentaries the BBC maintained a steady output, but ITV could boast some great achievements too. *The World at War*, a major series on the Second World War, was launched by Thames in 1973, and in that year Yorkshire TV showed *Too Long a Winter*, a moving documentary about Hannah Hauxwell, a lone subsistence farmer living high in the Pennines. From 1978 LWT's *The South Bank Show*, which was fronted by Melvyn Bragg, consistently achieved the difficult feat of presenting the arts in a way which was both serious and 'accessible'.

Drama and comedy seem to be a good measure of the health of broadcasting, because although less 'serious' than news and current affairs they are often less ephemeral too. In this respect, the 1970s bear comparison with any other decade in the history of television, and from a historical perspective series and serials are always more conspicuous than single plays or shows.

Period dramas opened the decade. The BBC gave us *The Six Wives of Henry VIII*, while Granada portrayed *A Family at War*, and from 1971 to 1977 *Upstairs Downstairs* (LWT) explored life among the servants of an aristocratic Edwardian household. A little later in the decade *When the Boat Comes In* (BBC) showed scenes of Geordie hardship during the inter-war years, and Yorkshire TV launched its first soap opera, *Emmerdale Farm*. Not long after, some tough battles were fought by the hard-nosed cops and robbers of *The Sweeney* (ATV).

There was also an abundance of excellent comic drama, notably *The Good Life*, *Fawlty Towers* and *Porridge* (all BBC) and *Rising Damp* (Yorkshire TV). In mid-decade three serials were marked by high ambitions, albeit of very different kinds. The first was Yorkshire TV's *South Riding* (1974), a sensitive and highly praised adaptation of Winifred Holtby's novel of Yorkshire life. The second was *A Bouquet of Barbed Wire* (LWT, 1976) by Andrea Newman – as Sean Day-Lewis puts it, 'the first of her televisual explorations of sexuality that gave the pleasures as much space as the tears that follow' (1992: 35). And the third was the BBC's dramatization of Robert Graves's historical novel *I, Claudius* (1976), which included a phenomenal performance by Derek Jacobi as the eponymous Roman emperor.

A very different yet even more popular adaptation was *All Creatures Great and Small* (BBC, 1977) – from James Herriot's stories of a veterinary surgeon working in the Yorkshire Dales. High standards were maintained to the end of the decade with *Edward and Mrs Simpson*, starring James Fox, John Mortimer's *Rumpole of the Bailey* (both Thames, 1978), and an extraordinary serial, *Pennies from Heaven* (BBC, 1978), which was set in the 1930s and written by Dennis Potter. This was a popular and highly original blend of allegory, parable, autobiography and musical sequences mimed to the popular songs of the period – a rare and successful attempt to break out of what is sometimes the claustrophobic naturalism of the television medium.

The year 1979 marked the beginning of outstanding comedy series on both BBC and ITV. *Minder* (Thames) was about the relationship between Arthur Daley, a lovable spiv played by George Cole, and his gullible bodyguard, Terry McCann (Dennis Waterman). Critics might now look back on it as an ironic prologue to the frenziedly entrepreneurial Thatcher years. *Yes, Minister* (BBC), by Anthony Jay and Jonathan Lynn, concerned the manipulation of cabinet ministers by self-serving civil servants, and was enriched by the viewers' deep suspicion that what they were watching was unhealthily close to the truth.

We should note two important trends which occurred in TV drama during the 1970s. The first was the development of co-productions between one or other of the British broadcasting organizations and a foreign partner. Their obvious advantages were that they could be more ambitious and lavish because they could raise more funding and find bigger audiences. The international television market was now growing rapidly, creating an unprecedented demand for quality programmes.

Within the BBC co-productions provoked an interesting debate. Aubrey Singer, the Controller of BBC 2, thought them a straightforwardly beneficial way of cutting costs and expanding markets, whereas the Managing Director of Television, Huw Wheldon, believed that they compromised the integrity and editorial independence of a non-commercial organization which continued to regard itself as the only genuine public service broadcaster.

The second and more disquieting trend was the decline of the single play. For obvious reasons drama is one of the most expensive forms of television program- ming, and as we noted in Chapter 5 new recording technologies and the cinematic mode of production they allowed could offset costs by enabling several episodes of a series or serial to be shot together. During the 1970s, an era of high inflation, the cost of a single play became almost prohibitive. It was also a high-risk venture because many viewers were now unused to the conventional theatre and therefore to the need to absorb plot, situation and character fairly rapidly. Finally, and a consideration of increasing importance at this time, the single play was difficult to package and sell in the export market.

The single play posed a problem for both broadcasters, but as one might expect it was greater for ITV, whose need to win a large audience and keep costs down was more acute. One compromise it tried was to 'anthologize' the single play – to make it part of a themed series such as 'Love Story' or 'Tales of the Unexpected'. One triumphant example of a play which was *not* part of a series was Philip Mackie's *The Naked Civil Servant* (Thames, 1975), a brilliantly witty portrait of the famous homosexual, Quentin Crisp. But there was no disguising its growing rarity. In 1969–70 ITV screened 112 single plays; in 1979–80 it showed thirteen.

The BBC fought a stronger rearguard action against the trend, featuring works by Alan Bennett, Trevor Griffiths, John Mortimer, Peter Nichols, Dennis Potter and William Trevor – a small yet striking instance of what could be regarded as a public service. Why? What was so important about the single play? Thanks to television with its series and serials, vast numbers of people were seeing more drama than ever before. Where, then, was the loss?

There were two strong reasons why the single play could not be allowed to disappear from television. The first was that it was a form which made intellectual demands on the audience and created aesthetic satisfactions that could not be derived from the series or serial. Though many of the latter were undoubtedly serious and ambitious in nature, their forms, in allowing the audience rather longer to assimilate plot, situation and character, were potentially less disciplined and liable to admit what were at certain levels less challenging kinds of drama. The single play, however, was a concentrated form of expression in which the dramatist was obliged to make his artistic statement within a single 'sitting' – a statement which the audience took a special pleasure in seeking to understand.

The second reason for preserving the single play was that it was the only form which drama took in the traditional theatre, where the series and serial were unknown. To abandon it would therefore be to deny the television audience access to all the major dramatists of the past – Euripides, Shakespeare, Ibsen, Chekhov and so on – not to mention those of the present, like Alan Ayckbourn, Alan Bennett and Tom Stoppard, who also wished to write single plays. Hence even though the series and the serial were much more cost-effective, and even though they had in certain respects enlarged and enriched the traditional perception of drama, the loss of the single play would have meant a real impoverishment of television content.

We looked earlier at comic drama, but there was also much good comedy which was not dramatic in form. On BBC, *The Two Ronnies* – Barker and Corbett – delighted audiences from 1971, while from 1973 *That's Life*, presented by Esther Rantzen, offered an original mixture of serious consumerism and comic features. ATV scored a huge success with *The Muppet Show* (1976), and two years later Mel Smith, Rowan Atkinson and Griff Rhys Jones brought broadened graduate humour to a large BBC audience in *Not the Nine O'Clock News*. During the long ITV strike of 1979 the BBC was able to use its two quiz shows *The Generation Game* and *Blankety Blank* to secure especially large audiences.

The Annan Committee

Ever since the BBC had been awarded the third channel, there had been a general understanding that the government would soon allocate a fourth – and a further assumption, most consistently made by the Conservatives, that once it had put its house in order after the strictures of Pilkington, the ITA would run the channel in symmetrical continuance of the duopoly.

That assumption was much less common on the parliamentary Left, where there was talk of giving the channel to the BBC to transmit programmes for the proposed Open University; and it was Labour who came to power in 1964. However in 1966 the government announced that because of other priorities it would defer the allocation of a fourth channel until 1969. In 1969 the allocation was again deferred because of the financial difficulties of ITV, which had to be regarded as at least a contender for such a channel. But in 1970, retaining its natural suspicion of commercial television, the Labour government decided that the whole future of broadcasting in the United Kingdom merited a committee of inquiry and appointed Lord Annan as its head.

Annan was certainly not predisposed to give the channel to ITV, believing that this would simply intensify competition for the mass audience and result in a neglect of minorities. However 1970 was also the year of a general election and before his committee could be appointed the Conservatives returned to power. Seeing no need of Annan and his committee they adjourned it indefinitely, resolving to open up sound broadcasting to commercial competition before settling the question of the fourth channel. But before they could do so, the country was once more in crisis, there was another election, and Labour resumed office in 1974. The Annan Committee was promptly reconvened by the Home Secretary Roy Jenkins and began work in March of that year. While its report was awaited and then debated, the life of the IBA and its contractors was prolonged to 1976 – and then it and the BBC's Charter were extended to 1979, and finally to 1981.

However, the climate had changed since 1970. To Labour's distrust of ITV was added, after the affair of *Yesterday's Men*, a distrust of the BBC. And outside parliament there were strident attacks on both broadcasters, mostly though not entirely from the political Left. ITV was a predictable target of ideologues, whether students, academic media theorists or trade unionists, not so much for the quality of its programmes as for its connections with big business, the size of its profits, its preoccupation with ratings, the evils of its advertising, and for the concentration of media ownership into the hands of a few large companies. But the BBC also came under fire for its arrogance and its social and cultural elitism.

The mood of the 1970s was typified by the various radical pressure groups – the Free Communications Group, the 76 Group (some disaffected BBC and ITV producers), and the Standing Conference on Broadcasting – all with ostensibly democratic aims: to widen public access to the production side of broadcasting (in an astute public relations move the BBC formed its Community Programmes Unit in 1972) and/or to increase the public accountability of broadcasters.

In the latter aim they were joined by an unlikely ally from the Right: Mrs Whitehouse's National Viewers' and Listeners' Association, which attacked both broadcasters, but especially the BBC for its 'permissive' programming and contempt for the moral majority. Despite their differing perspectives, then, the one thing on which all these groups were agreed was that the broadcasters were out of control, answerable neither to the people nor even to those who were elected to express the people's will, the politicians – and therefore that the fourth channel should go neither to ITV nor the BBC. The duopoly should be broken, especially as the imminent technologies of cable and satellite could provide a range of choice and specialization which would bring broadcasting somewhat closer to the less restricted world of newspaper and magazine publishing.

With these views Annan was largely in sympathy. The extent and vehemence of the broadcasting debate made it clear that from now on only one model of public service broadcasting would be sustainable. The aim of the old Reithian paternalism was to expose the entire audience to the best of everything, with the broadcasters deciding what constituted 'the best'. We will recall that one early dilemma was whether the best meant 'highbrow' as opposed to 'popular' or whether qualitative differences were discernible within both categories.

It was many years since anyone at the BBC had formally or publicly committed themselves on the matter, but with respect to television at least, there was an enduring belief that public service broadcasting consisted in exposing the audience to the full range of programming. After the compromises of the cultural pyramid at the end of the war and the impact of the pirates in the 1960s this belief could no longer hold for radio, with its largely specialized networks. But it was still tenable for what was now the main medium of television, as is clear from the equivocations concerning BBC 2 – the insistence that it would offer a *range* of programming, some of which would be populist.

The problem was that as television channels began to proliferate, even this insistence seemed unnecessary and patronizing. Annan himself was of the view that public service was best expressed in the pluralist concept of serving minorities or special interests, a concept which was well suited to the 1970s world of radicalized and dissonant pressure groups.

> Our society's culture is now multi-racial and pluralist: that is to say, people adhere to different views of the nature and purpose of life and expect their own view to be expressed in some form or other. The structure of broadcasting should reflect this variety.
>
> (1977: 30)

It was not for broadcasters to say which of these views were valid and which were worthless (as Reith believed they should); it was not even for them to make the judgement that it was good for the audience to be exposed to the whole range of output. The broadcasters' duty was simply to cater for as many tastes and interests as possible: how far the viewer chose to indulge her particular interests to the exclusion of others (and the aim of the newer channels was to make this easier), and how far she chose to lay herself open to the full range of programming, was entirely a matter for her.

This conclusion was a momentous one because it was the first explicit renunciation of the Reithian idea of broadcasters as moral or cultural leaders. 'We do not accept that it is part of the broadcasters' function to act as arbiters of morals or manners, or set themselves up as social engineers.' (quoted in McDonnell 1991: 68).

The Committee sat for three years, presenting its report in March 1977. There was a widespread feeling that its deliberations were better than its recommendations, all 174 of them. *The Times* described the report as 'a fair audit but a weak blueprint'. Part of the problem was that the Committee seems to have reflected the spirit of the time in being riven by internal disagreements: consequently its recommendations bore the marks of compromise and were not always consistent with its findings or conclusions.

The heart of its difficulty was that its two main aims – to extend and diversify broadcasting services and to provide for greater public control and access – were ultimately conflicting: in order to liberate broadcasting from the straitjacket of duopoly it merely proposed an increase in the number of bureaucracies which would control it. These were its main recommendations:

The existing ITV system should not be awarded a second channel and its governing body, the IBA, should be renamed the Regional Television Authority. The new fourth channel should be a network catering for interests and minorities presently ill served by television. It should be supervised by an Open Broadcasting Authority which would be modelled along lines suggested by Anthony Smith, an academic and former BBC producer. It would not make programmes but be a publisher and commissioner of programmes made by others, and its funding would come from a variety of sources: the Open University, the Arts Council, charities, the Trades Union Congress, the Confederation of British Industry, advertising.

The duopoly of the BBC and the IBA would also be broken at local level. A Local Broadcasting Authority, also partly financed by advertising, would control all local radio, together with the new field of cable TV.

The third major recommendation was that there should be further regulatory bodies: a Public Enquiry Board, a Broadcasting Complaints Commission, a Telecommunications Advisory Committee.

To 'open up' broadcasting the Annan Report was thus proposing a veritable thicket of authorities, commissions and committees. It nevertheless met with the broad approval of those who had called for it. In 1978 the government announced its intention to allocate a fourth channel, and in the following year that the channel would begin broadcasting in November 1982 and be administered by an Open Broadcasting Authority.

Nevertheless it lost the 1979 election to the Conservatives, and as so often happens with public committees, the recommendations of Annan, so lengthily and laboriously arrived at, were lightly set aside by the politicians. The Tories simply placed the fourth channel in the hands of the IBA, though as we shall see, under an arrangement which reflected Annan's general concern to diversify both the sources of programme production and the kinds of programmes viewers could hope to watch.

New ITV franchises and the arrival of breakfast television

After the Annan Report had been published and discussed, the ITV franchises fell due for renewal in 1980. The previous period, which had quite unexpectedly run for an unprecedented thirteen and a half years, had been one of very mixed fortunes for the contractors. The lack of contractual upheavals, which was partly thanks to the delay in appointing Annan's committee, gave ITV a healthy continuity that was expressed in many programmes of high quality. On the other hand, it suffered recurrent and often damaging industrial disputes and from a chronic inflation which was only partly offset when in 1974 the government switched its levy from ITV's income to its profits.

The new contracts would run until the end of 1989 (in 1981 the BBC's Charter was renewed for another ten years) and the changes which were made in 1980 were as much determined by the technicalities of sharcholding and the contractors' sources of investment as by programme quality, which would remain fairly consistent during the next ten years or so. In the Midlands ATV disappeared into a new contractor, Central Television, while TV South replaced Southern Television and Television South West replaced Westward. Tyne Tees and Yorkshire TV were once again split into two strictly separate companies.

However the 1980 franchise round contained one novelty. Ever since 1972, when restrictions on transmission hours were lifted, breakfast television had been blocked by the broadcasting unions' demand for 'golden payments'. The IBA now decided to offer a separate contract for a national service, 'primarily of news, information and current affairs' (Potter 1990: 328), to be transmitted between 6 and 9.15 every morning of the week. It attracted no less than eight different bids, and in an extraordinary re-run of events which had occurred in the previous franchise round, the contract went to a group named TV-AM.

Like LWT back in 1968, TV-AM was a consortium of stars which included David Frost. Its others were Peter Jay, Robert Kee, Angela Rippon, Michael Parkinson and Anna Ford. As LWT had, it bewitched the Authority not only with the calibre of its personnel but with the seriousness of its programming ambitions. It believed that programme-makers, not financial institutions, should drive the new service, and it brought to news and current affairs 'a mission to explain'. Like LWT, it was quickly damaged by populist competition from the BBC – and again like LWT, it had to be rescued by an Australian businessman whose programming instincts were surer than those of the 'professionals'.

Jeremy Potter asserts that the IBA should have seen the danger signs in TV-AM: an over-intellectual approach to breakfast programming, no named chief executive, and too many stars with a say in company policy. It was two years before the company went to air – on 1 February 1983 – and even then it was trumped by the BBC, which launched its own much lighter breakfast service a fortnight earlier. TV-AM's failure to win an audience brought it by way of the usual sequence of dismissals, recriminations and resignations to the brink of bankruptcy, at which point it was bailed out not by Rupert Murdoch this time but by his compatriot Kerry Packer.

It was in fact a rat who saved the sinking ship, for as his chief executive Packer installed Bruce Gyngell, and as his major star Gyngell installed Roland Rat, a puppet. The new company was hugely successful, but as Potter (1990) ruefully remarks, one to which the IBA in its search for a serious and informative service would never have awarded a contract in 1980. The re-launch resulted in an enduring impression of breakfast television as a blend of the bland and the trite, its central symbol the sofa on which the presenters sat simpering at the cameras, their guests and at each other.

However breakfast TV was significant for two reasons. First it marked a further assimilation of television to the daily routines of the public, and thus contributed to that weakening of the distinction between work and leisure which, thanks to new technologies and their impact on the nature and patterns of employment, has become an important feature of modern life. Whether watched by those preparing to go to work or by those who were unemployed or on part-time or shift work, breakfast TV was an acknowledgement that leisure was no longer a clearly demarcated period in the evening but a state which might occupy any part of the day.

Second, the new service ate into radio audiences at what was traditionally a peak listening time. It was estimated that in 1983–4 radio's early morning audience declined by 10 per cent.

The launch of Channel 4

In different ways Channel 4 marked the end of an old broadcasting era and the beginning of a new one. As Brian Wenham (1982) points out, it was the last terrestrial channel to be established before the arrival of cable and satellite during the 1980s. Stephen Lambert (1982) observes that it was also the first terrestrial channel whose birth did not require new viewing hardware, because the facility to receive it had been included in all TV sets made since the late 1960s. When it went to air on 2 November 1982 it was already within reach of 87 per cent of the population.

This meant that the debate on how the channel would be used could focus entirely on programming philosophy, and to this end a radically new structure was devised for the channel which would open another era of television broadcasting.

We saw earlier that the incoming Conservative government ignored the idea of an Open Broadcasting Authority and simply handed the new channel to the IBA. Nevertheless Channel 4 was to embody much of the Annan Committee's philosophy.

In recommending the Open Broadcasting Authority Annan had itself been influenced by the idea of a 'National Television Foundation' which had been proposed by Anthony Smith, a former member of the *Tonight* team and now a research fellow at St Antony's College, Oxford. This would not in itself make programmes but *commission* them – act as a publishing house for independent programme-makers. But where, under the existing duopoly, would the independent programme-makers come from? In fact the independent sector had begun to flourish earlier in the 1970s thanks to an expanding overseas market, a growth in demand for industrial training films, and an increased need for TV commercials to fill the extra broadcasting hours.

For its part, the IBA had always argued that the fourth channel should be integrated with the existing ITV network, and in 1979 it neatly adapted Annan's recommendations to its own purposes by proposing that it rather than the OBA should run the fourth channel, commissioning 35 to 50 per cent of its programmes from the existing ITV contractors; 15 to 35 per cent from the independents; 15 per cent from ITN; and 5 to 14 per cent from foreign sources.

Two-thirds of the channel's output would consist of programmes of special interest, one-third would have a broader appeal – a strategy similar to that of BBC 2. The channel would sell no advertising of its own, but be funded by subscriptions from the ITV contractors commensurate with their rental payments. However each contractor would sell Channel 4's advertising within its own region and keep the proceeds.

This IBA version of Annan (and Smith) was broadly the model which the government adopted in its parliamentary bill of February 1980. With the establishment of a broadcasting institution not as a producer of programmes but as the mere publisher or disseminator of them, the history of television recalled that of print, where a somewhat similar division of labour had developed several centuries before between the publishers and those physical producers of books and journals, the printers and binders.

However an unforeseen difficulty was raised by pressure groups who campaigned for a separate channel for Wales, threatening civil disobedience and hunger strikes if they failed to get their own way. The government capitulated, setting up a separate Welsh authority, S4C – Sianel Pedwar Cymru – which the IBA would supply with programmes, but so, if the authority wished, would the BBC.

Through Channel 4 the IBA intended to show that public service broadcasting in its newer sense of serving special interests and minorities was compatible with commercial broadcasting. The Authority's obligations were fourfold. First it had to ensure that the programming contained a suitable proportion of matter to meet 'the special interests and concerns for which television has until now lacked adequate time' (McDonnell 1991: 71). Even though there would be some populist dilution, this was a much more open declaration of narrowcast intentions than had been made for BBC 2.

The minorities whom the channel served would fall into three broad categories: cultural – lovers of opera, ballet, classical music and drama, 'art films', jazz and other kinds of music, serious talks and discussions; special interest – enthusiasts of certain sports and hobbies like canoeing or fly-fishing; and ethnic – those mostly of West Indian and Asian origin, who since the 1950s had become a significant cultural and political presence in Britain. Though in some respects disparate, these audiences were well worth targeting by advertisers.

The IBA's other three obligations were to ensure that a suitable proportion of the channel's programmes were educational; to encourage innovation in form and content; and to commission 'a substantial proportion' of programmes from independent producers. In the event Channel 4 commissioned over 50 per cent of its first year's output from the independents, who in carrying fewer overheads than the ITV contractors were able to offer quality programmes much more cheaply. This was to have important consequences for all the networks, for ITV came under financial and the BBC under political pressure (in radio as well as TV) to make fewer programmes 'in-house' and buy a significant proportion of them from independents.

The rise of the independent houses was made possible not only by the growth of creative talent in a competitive industry which was now almost thirty years old, but by the development of lighter, more compact, more sophisticated, and in real terms cheaper, hardware. This in turn transformed television from a labour-intensive to something approaching a cottage industry. Yet there have also been countervailing economies of scale. The independent sector has certainly flourished since the launch of Channel 4, but as is often the case in a competitive business there have been fatalities, mergers and takeovers, leaving fewer and larger survivors.

Another potential problem with a broadcasting system which relies substantially on independents is that in order to secure commissions from the networks the latter may be tempted to avoid making programmes on controversial or challenging subjects – a particular problem for Channel 4 since it makes no programmes of its own. However its hard-hitting current affairs series *Dispatches* suggests that this has not been a problem in practice.

Channel 4's first Chief Executive was Jeremy Isaacs, who had gained extensive experience as a producer with both BBC and ITV. Since the channel was launched nearly half a century after the establishment of the first British television service, it would perhaps have been unreasonable to expect it to offer many kinds of programming which were genuinely original. But it has certainly fulfilled its duty to give expression to new themes and otherwise unheard minority views and values, and as a summary of its early achievements shows, it has presented the traditional genres of television in distinctive and interesting ways.

It attempted to push against the limits of the TV medium by broadcasting in the early evenings a specially extended news programme which was resourced by ITN. This was partly a response to some thoughtful criticisms of the superficial and fitful character of television news which had been expressed by John Birt and Peter Jay in a letter to *The Times* in 1975. Under its young and highly able editor Derrik Mercer, who had been recruited from the *Sunday Times*, *Channel Four News* sought to get nearer than any other programme on the networks to TV's Holy Grail: 'news in depth'. As well as events it covered causes and contexts, and did not shrink from exploring issues of broad contemporary significance, even if these had not been marked by events which were individually 'newsworthy'.

The channel also ran a half-hour weekly review programme, *Friday Alternative*, which gave various groups a chance to offer their own perspectives on the week's news coverage. A third innovation came from Isaacs himself, who established the first commissioning editor for film animation, seeing this as a neglected form of minority viewing which the channel could encourage.

In fact it was in the field of 'cinematic' film that the greatest early achievements of the channel probably lay. It made a number of co-production deals with the cinema industry, commissioning full-length feature films which involved both TV premieres, in a series called *Film on Four*, and cinema screenings. The channel also bought important 'art house' movies by such directors as Kurosawa, Satyajit Ray, Buñuel and Fassbinder.

But through another of its innovations it signalled the maturity and self-belief of television by re-running programmes from the medium's own canon, among them vintage series like *The Munsters* and *I Love Lucy*, which were quite unknown to the younger generation. It thus made the point that TV was not simply a museum for old movies but had a rich and growing heritage of its own.

Finally, Channel 4 continued BBC 2's earlier initiative of popularizing minority sports such as American football, something we glanced at in an earlier chapter.

Sources/further reading

For the social, political and institutional background to independent television during the 1970s see Potter (1989). Briggs (1995) provides similar backgrounding, primarily for the BBC and up to the mid-1970s. For the launch of independent local radio see Baron (1975) and Barnard (1989). The latter also offers an excellent analysis of its early problems, which are further explored in Crisell (1994).

Potter (1990), Briggs (1995) and Day-Lewis (1992) all provide useful details of television programmes during the 1970s. Potter (1989) is illuminating on the background to the Annan Committee, and there is a good summary description of its recommendations in Hood and O'Leary (1990). For the full details, however, see the Annan Report (1977).

Curran and Seaton (1991) observe that Annan radically altered public service broadcasting from a cohesive to a pluralistic concept – a view which is broadly endorsed in an interesting discussion of the concept's historical evolution by Scannell (1990). This evolution can be handily traced in the extracts from Annan quoted in McDonnell (1991).

A useful summary of the ITV contract allocations of 1980 may be found in Tunstall (1983), while Potter (1990) gives helpful details on all the ITV contractors during the 1970s and also provides a fascinating account of the background to, and launch of, breakfast television.

For the background to Channel 4 see Potter (1989). Smith (1976) outlines his idea of the broadcaster as publisher, though he partly attributes it to the Labour politician, Tony Benn. There are some sapient remarks on Channel 4 in Wenham (1982). However the classic account of the background to the channel and its genesis and philosophy are in Lambert (1982). Hood and O'Leary (1990) are also useful on how the channel was set up, and Curran and Seaton (1991) offer some acute remarks on the values which informed it.

Part II

The rise
of the active
audience

From as early as the second half of the 1950s the history of broadcasting must be seen in the context of momentous developments which were taking place in the economics and technology of reception. Audiences were increasingly able to decide not only *where* they would receive broadcast messages and *how* they would treat them, but even *whether* they would receive them at all – or put their radio and TV sets to other uses.

Since about 1960 the real cost of receivers has fallen to such an extent that radio and television have become not simply *domestic* but *personal* media. The individual can afford a set of her own, and technological advances allow her to use it not just in her own home but almost anywhere she chooses.

In Part I we noted a progression from the mass or collective to the private or individual consumption of cultural messages – a process which we termed *atomization*. We saw that it is a recurrent feature of the history of communications, just as it seems to have characterized the general development of modern industrial society. However individuality of consumption does not always imply individuality of ownership: when they are still fairly new, media and their messages are often so expensive that many of their consumers must resort to devices of corporate purchase. In Chapter 1 we noted the establishment of the relay exchanges for those who were unable to afford their own wireless receivers, and there are still people who rent their television sets.

But perhaps the most striking parallel in media history is between books and video-cassettes. In the eighteenth century books were too expensive for most people to buy, a fact which explains the contemporary success of the non-proprietary or circulating libraries. The novel was the most 'popular' literary form, as it still is today, yet when the first edition of *Tom Jones* was published in 1749 it cost more than a labourer's average weekly wage.

In the late 1970s video was in a similar position: the first commercially pre-recorded cassettes cost between £80 and £100. Consequently the vast majority of video films which have been viewed over the past two decades have been borrowed from video rental outlets. But during that time, as the price of video-cassettes has tumbled, increasing numbers have been bought outright. Most commercial videos now retail for £10 to £15, and it is not unknown for them to be given away to promote the sales of other products. As I write this, the *Independent* is running a promotional offer of 'classic films' including *When Harry Met Sally* and *Educating Rita*. When a copy of the paper is purchased from the newsagent, a video of each film may also be had for just £3.

The development of the 'utility' wireless set in 1944 meant that the great majority of British households could afford a radio by the end of the Second World War, and thanks to rising affluence during the 1950s and 1960s, television sets were acquired much more quickly. Robert Rowland (1982) calculates that whereas it took a hundred years for the telephone to reach 75 per cent of British homes, it took only twenty-six years for radio, and seventeen years for television. With the arrival of transistor sets in the 1960s and the subsequent growth of 'in-car entertainment', radio ownership and listening became not simply domestic but *individual* – and even, with the launch of the Sony Walkman personal radio/cassette player in 1979, positively solipsistic.

Much the same thing has happened with television. Even when television sets are not miniaturized or portable, they are often individually owned and watched – the latter process helped, in Britain at least, by that other great technological aid to atomization, central heating, which was installed in an increasing number of homes during the 1970s. Where formerly the family huddled round the sitting room fire to watch the one television set it owned, its members have now become centrifugal, retreating to their own warm rooms to tune in to personal radio and TV sets. By 1990 25 per cent of the population owned four or more radios and three homes out of five had at least two televisions.

This individualism of consumption and ownership has had considerable implications for media content and effects and for audience judgement. For instance, the increase in the sexually explicit content of TV plays and films and of commercial videos must have been facilitated by the fact that private or solitary viewing is less embarrassing than public or collective viewing. On the other hand, the solitary viewing of horror or crime movies may well be an even more frightening experience than watching in a cinema.

But what is perhaps more significant is that cultural and artistic judgement has become an unprecedentedly singular and subjective business. The viewer of a feature film or television programme may no longer be guided by the instantaneous reactions of others sitting around her, and it is probably no coincidence that the rise of that arbiter of 'correct' artistic judgement, the professional critic, dates roughly from the development of the first of the 'atomizing' media, print, which transformed poems and plays into private experiences and spawned a 'private' art form of its own, the novel.

The trend towards individualism of ownership and consumption preceded another development which began during the 1970s: the growth of audience *autonomy*. Technology increasingly enabled the audience to put the television (and less importantly, radio) set to uses other than that which was designated by the broadcasters.

The first opportunity to do this was provided by the *remote controller*, which had appeared in the 1960s as a device attached to the TV set by a cord, but which grew much more popular when cordless versions became available. Though offering the viewer of live television little more than an easy muting and channel-changing facility, it has had consequences for programme scheduling and content which, as we shall see in a later chapter, are becoming particularly important in an era of multi-channel TV.

Yet even in the old days of three or four channels, the viewer could use the remote controller to 'refuse' the programmes which were offered to her by the broadcasters and make her own 'programme' out of the elements they provided. As John Fiske explains:

> Zapping allows the viewer to construct a viewing experience of fragments, a post-modern collage of images whose pleasures lie in their discontinuity, their juxtapositions and their contradictions . . . The television text, then, is composed of a rapid succession of compressed, vivid segments where the principle of logic and cause and effect is subordinated to that of association and consequence to sequence.

> (1987: 105)

The next important technology was *teletext*, a secondary broadcasting system introduced in 1974 which delivered to the TV screen continuously updated news and information in the form of print and graphics. The ITV version was called ORACLE (Optical Reception of Announcements by Coded Line Electronics), the BBC's more banally known as CEEFAX (See Facts).

The Annan Committee viewed teletext as a blend of broadcasting and telecommunications, since it was delivered to a mass audience yet allowed an interactive role to the viewer. It was thus an early instance of media convergence which is now becoming much more familiar to us, and meant that for the first time the viewer could opt out of live output and use her television set for news, information and on-screen entertainment – at times which suited *her*. By 1990 a quarter of all viewers had access to teletext.

However it was the arrival of the *video-cassette recorder* (VCR) which provided the television audience with the most exciting opportunity to opt out of live transmission. We have already looked at the role of video technology in broadcast production – a role which dates back to 1958 – but its impact on viewing has been even more important. The first video recorder for the domestic market, one which allowed the off-air recording of TV programmes for time-shift viewing, was a half-inch cassette machine launched by Philips in 1972.

The next eight or ten years saw an international struggle for market dominance which involved not only several manufacturers but several systems or 'formats', discs as well as tapes. Since no single manufacturer could win a significant market share at this time, unit costs remained high. In 1976, for instance, VCRs cost between £450 and £1000, with 60-minute blank tapes retailing at around £20, and Annan calculated that no more than about 40,000 VCRs were in use throughout the United Kingdom.

The market was finally shared by two incompatible Japanese systems: Sony Betamax, and the eventual outright winner, the VHS format, introduced in Britain in 1978 by JVC, the aptly named Japanese Victor Company. By the 1980s VCRs carried a whole range of features: digital timing, fast forward and rewind, frame-freeze and remote control. They also created a vast new market for the hire and sale of pre-recorded cassettes, and a sturdy demand for video cameras so that viewers could use the TV screen to watch their own filmic endeavours.

By the end of 1985, 8.5 million VCRs had been sold in Britain, where the market was especially strong, occupying a place in 40 per cent of the nation's households. A year later virtually half of all households boasted a VCR, and by 1989–90 the figure had risen to 60 per cent.

The appearance of the VCR was a significant moment in the history of television because for the first time the viewer could choose what *she* wanted to see instead of what was being presently provided for her by the broadcasting institutions – perhaps recordings of live output, but perhaps other material too, such as cinema feature films or home movies she might have created for herself.

But just as important as the unprecedented diversity of material that video offered was the fact that such material could be watched in the *viewer's own time*, thus further strengthening individualism of consumption: for video tipped the balance from a situation in which the viewer was obliged to adjust her day's routine to the timing of a programe she wanted to watch, to one in which watching could be adjusted to her day's routine. In this respect video has enabled television to become much more like print, whose messages can also be absorbed in the receiver's rather than the sender's time.

Video recording has also reduced what from the viewer's standpoint is the negative effect of broadcasting competition, since she can simultaneously watch one channel while recording a programme on another. If the viewer is not necessarily watching a programme at the time of its transmission, broadcasters can take a slightly more flexible approach to scheduling. Open University programmes, for instance, are usually transmitted at times when most people, including students, are likely to be asleep. BBC 2's *The Learning Zone* is a series of programmes transmitted between 12.30 and 6.30 in the morning.

But if the VCR has made programme scheduling in some respects less crucial for broadcasters, it has shifted from broadcasters to audience rather more of the responsibility for what children and young people are able to view. Formerly many children would have been unable to view unsuitable programming simply because it was shown after they had been sent to bed. Though most of it continues to be broadcast at late hours, video-cassettes mean that it is now viewable at any time of the day.

Video technology has had another major social consequence. We have noted that the overall effect of radio and television has been to move messages first into the domestic and then into a personal or individual sphere (something which print achieved from the outset); and we have seen that video and audio recording has increased audience autonomy yet further by allowing its members to watch and listen in their own time. But as well as this, the purchase of commercial videos and the practice of off-air recording have introduced the virtual ownership of media *messages* as well as of the media *receivers*, the radio and TV sets. Just as several centuries ago books began to move the poetry of Homer or Virgil or the plays of Shakespeare from the public domain not simply into private consumption but private ownership, so video recording is doing the same to the Hollywood movie and the live theatre. Moreover, it has not only turned spectator sports such as soccer matches and athletics meetings into private experiences; it has *fixed* them – transformed them into artefacts which may also be possessed.

That a cinema film or TV programme costing millions of pounds to make – a BBC costume drama, for instance – can be cheaply bought as a video cassette, or recorded off-air and 'owned' for next to nothing, is a fact so remarkable that it is worth dwelling on for a few moments. In the first place we should remind ourselves that from a time well before the arrival of video, broadcasting has both increased the scope and quality of entertainment and cultural provision beyond all previous imagining and simultaneously reduced its cost to the consumer. (In this respect we may be dwelling in a golden age because as we shall see, it is not impossible that we shall move to a rather more expensive regime of 'pay-per-view' TV in the near future.)

On top of this, and at only small cost, video has expanded the material which broadcasting has already provided, afforded absolute flexibility as to when we will view it and given us the opportunity to 'own' it if we so wish. With respect to broadcast output we might almost say that thanks to the VCR, the TV licence, which was originally a licence to receive media artefacts, has now become a licence both to receive and to *own* them.

Second, video technology (to say nothing of information technology, which has expanded so rapidly in the 1990s) has meant that the enforcement of copyright law and royalty payments has become so problematical as in many cases to be all but abandoned. Audio-cassette recorders and VCRs, many of which now boast twin decks for the easy copying of tapes, could almost be said to have an illegality of purpose built into them.

The magnitude of the change which has taken place in the relationship between the consumer and certain media products can be appreciated only by those who were alive in the years before video arrived; for they can recall the excitement, the sense of occasion, of being able merely to see a major Hollywood movie in a crowded cinema, and reflect that such movies are now reducible to a collection of cassettes on a shelf – as commonplace as a row of books, privately owned and casually viewable, continuously or discontinuously, at any hour of the day or night.

Nowadays it is certainly cheaper to hire a video than to go to the cinema, and it may soon become cheaper to buy one. Like books, cars and even central heating, then, video technology embodies that tendency of modern civilization towards a sense of individual privacy and personal empowerment.

During the 1980s computers followed VCRs in making use of domestic television screens, thus affording audiences another kind of opportunity to opt out of live broadcasts. By 1990 10 per cent of viewers could couple their sets to computers, mostly to play games or solve puzzles, but this meant that the reception of television broadcasts was now only one of *four* functions which the TV set could perform. Such versatility was an early and vivid hint of the multimedia systems which will probably transcend both TV sets and computers in the near future.

Sources/further reading

For the cost of books, the social composition of audiences, and the rise of the circulating libraries in the eighteenth century see Watt (1963). The statistics on the quickening pace of new media penetration are in Rowland (1982). The effects of 'zapping' or 'channel surfing', an activity facilitated by the remote controller, are explored in Fiske (1987).

The discussion of teletext is in the Annan Report (1977), as are the statistics on the early cost of VCRs and tapes and on the number of VCRs in use in the United Kingdom during the mid-1970s.

Armes (1988) provides the best historical account of the development of video technology and of its social implications and applications. The social and political importance of video and of other new media technologies is considered in Hughes (1990) and in Curran and Seaton (1991).

Seymour-Ure (1991) provides data on the ownership and uses of TV sets up to 1990, and the more recent statistic on VCR ownership is in O'Sullivan, Dutton and Rayner (1994).

Cables, dishes and deregulation

Chapter 10

Cables, dishes and deregulation

Broadcasting technology, economics and politics in the 1980s

As we might expect, it was technology which determined the somewhat contrasting tendencies of broadcasting during the 1980s and prompted the new political framework which was devised for it at the end of the decade.

Before looking at these tendencies we need to distinguish two aspects of broadcasting: *production*, or the making of programmes, and *distribution*, the transmission or dissemination of them. Thanks primarily to the microchip and to video technology, programme-making became easier and cheaper than ever before, a fact attested by the rise of the small production companies which we noted in the last chapter.

It was even more sharply attested in 1987–8 by events at TV-AM, the holder of the ITV breakfast-time franchise. The company's attempt to introduce new working practices was resisted by the production staff, all members of the Association of Cinematographic and Television Technicians (ACTT). It therefore locked them out, yet managed to stay on air by using non-technical employees such as secretaries to operate cameras and other equipment.

The 'deprofessionalization' of broadcasting inevitably brought with it a weakening of the once invincible broadcasting unions. Indeed by this time, almost anyone could obtain simple sound recording and video hardware to make media products in her own private sphere. The lucky few might even reach a conventional media audience, for with programmes like *Video Diaries* (BBC, early 1990s) home shot camcorder material began to enter the national broadcasters' repertoire. In radio, with its simpler technology and more localized audiences, the distribution of media products became not a great deal harder or more costly than the creation of them, as we shall see.

But on the distribution of TV programmes, technology, most obviously in the form of satellites, had the effect of a scaling up rather than a scaling down, for it was during the 1980s that television broadcasting ceased to be a merely regional and national activity and started to become a global one. The satellite links between different national broadcasters and the international co-productions which had developed during the 1960s and 1970s had been but straws in the wind: henceforth technology would enable a single organization to transmit its programmes all the way round the world.

These contrasting tendencies of technology – the localization, even domestication, of production on the one hand and the internationalization, even globalization, of distribution on the other – were quickly noted by media analysts. Writing in 1987 Alvarado, Gutch and Wollen observed that 'video technology offers Western societies the possibility of the production, circulation and consumption of low-cost media products designed for highly specific groups but no way of locking in to large-scale audiences' (1987: 254). A year later Roy Armes (1988) made the similar point that the unprecedented individual access to media production coincided with diminishing access to media distribution, since the latter would be increasingly monopolized by a few large organizations operating on a world-wide basis. Why?

The global audience which satellite technology could deliver meant that media organizations could greatly improve their efficiency and profitability. But only large organizations – or consortia thereof – would be able to bear the enormous start-up costs, including that of hurling a satellite into geostationary orbit some 22,000 miles above the earth's surface. We noted that the original ITV contractors were themselves groups of companies. Now even bigger groupings would be needed to play the global game, and two ITV contractors formed part of the consortium which was to make up British Satellite Broadcasting (BSB).

Another and larger member of the consortium, and one which would continue its involvement in broadcasting and multimedia after the early demise of BSB, was the Pearson Group, whose interests outside the media embraced banking, property, the Royal Doulton china company, and even the Château Latour vineyard in France. But there were two other, more disquieting consequences of this necessary enlargement of organizations with ambitions to play a major part in the new age of broadcasting.

The first was the growth of cross-media ownership, a process which such bodies as the IBA and the Monopolies Commission could delay yet never wholly prevent. In addition to its involvement in television, Pearson owned two book publishing companies, Penguin and Longman, and a newspaper, the *Financial Times*. A much more conspicuous example was the most successful organization of them all, Rupert Murdoch's News International, whose interests were largely confined to the media but which included newspapers, book publishing, TV broadcasting and film distribution.

However disquieting, cross-media ownership was a problem which could at least be addressed when the parent company had a specific national identity. But the second consequence of corporate expansion was that the companies perforce raised money and supplied markets on an international scale and were to a large extent outside individual state control. Murdoch himself typified the problem: he was – is – a veritable citizen of the world. Though Australian in origin, he acquired the *News of the World*, the *Sun* and *The Times* in Britain and built another newspaper empire in the United States. He also bought control of Metromedia and Twentieth Century Fox in order to obtain fodder for his satellite channels and readily adopted American citizenship in order to retain control of what he had gained there. His media empire thus spanned three continents.

But quite apart from the unavoidably international character of the satellite broadcasters, the very nature of the technology has made individual state control extremely difficult since the 'footprints' of the satellites – their transmission areas on the earth's surface – mostly transcend national boundaries, causing not just cultural homogenization but problems of regulation and accountability. In the early 1990s the British government had difficulty in preventing the reception in this country of a pornographic satellite channel broadcasting quite legally from the northern European mainland, where the obscenity laws are less stringent.

Indeed as Eric Hobsbawm (1994) has observed, the increasing powerlessness of individual states against the globalizing tendencies of both technology and economics is perhaps the most striking characteristic of the end of the twentieth century, affecting not just the broadcasting media but general trade and the move-ment of capital, physical travel, scientific activity, the traffic in information, and even aspects of private life.

In the Britain of the 1980s there was in any case not much political appetite for state regulation. Sensing that the country was tired of dilatory, inefficient public services, strikes, ubiquitous state intervention and the chronic ravages of inflation, the Conservative administration under Margaret Thatcher determined to roll back state involvement and state provision: the aim was to 'set business free' from bureaucratic, essentially government, controls.

Private enterprise was rediscovered as the engine of the economy, and the old fashioned, labour-intensive industries which the state had directly or indirectly supported – shipbuilding, steel-making, heavy engineering, coal mining – were allowed to go to the wall and were replaced by jobs in financial and specialist services, light industry, leisure, tourism and catering, and information technology. On the supply side the aim was leanness and competitiveness, on the demand side consumer sovereignty – and together these qualities created 'the disciplines of the market', the economic panacea for which poverty, deprivation and unemployment seemed to everyone except the growing number of their victims to be a price worth paying.

Like every other publicly funded organization the BBC would soon find itself under scrutiny with the object of determining whether it could be run more efficiently, and there were some who believed that the government's appetite for this task was whetted by the Corporation's independently minded coverage of the Falklands War and of certain events in Northern Ireland. The options might include requiring the Corporation to support itself wholly or partly through advertising or sponsorship, and even transferring all or portions of it to private ownership: in the Thatcherite era 'privatization' was the great new buzzword.

The Peacock Committee

It was to consider the first of these options – whether the BBC might accept advertising or sponsorship as an alternative or supplement to the licence fee – that in 1985 the government appointed a committee under the chairmanship of Professor Sir Alan Peacock, an apostle of the new economics. As Paddy Scannell (1990) observes, it was the first parliamentary committee to treat public service in broadcasting as a merely secondary consideration. In its report, which was published a year later, it expressed some uncertainty as to what the concept meant, claiming that the broadcasters themselves were hard put to supply a definition.

In view of the changes which had taken place in broadcasting over the previous thirty years this was not altogether surprising: the pristine and most meaningful sense of public service – a provision of the widest range of programming for the audience as a whole – was not sustainable beyond an era of monopoly, which itself could endure only as long as the shortage of frequencies made broadcasting a rare commodity.

Peacock's own idea of public service was essentially that which focused upon otherwise neglected minorities, an idea which since the 1960s had proved more viable than any other. He defined it as 'any major modification of purely commercial provision resulting from public policy' (1986: 130), which might mean programmes that viewers were willing to support as taxpayers and voters but not as consumers. This was, at least, a significant admission that markets could be driven by something other than direct consumer demand.

On the whole, however, the committee expressed the philosophy of the government. It argued that consumers were the best judges of their own welfare and that they, and not the producers, should determine the character of broadcasting. It deplored two monopolies, one enjoyed by each of the main broadcasters: ITV could charge what it liked for advertising, and the BBC collected the licence fee irrespective of what the audience thought of its programmes.

213

Bearing in mind that public service in broadcasting could not be supported by the conventional laws of the market, the Peacock Committee rejected advertising for BBC television but proposed privatizing Radios 1 and 2, whose output, it felt, did not differ materially from that of the commercial stations. In the short term it recommended the retention of the licence fee for the remaining BBC services, but in order to subject them to a greater financial discipline proposed that it should be pegged to the retail price index, which was not rising as fast as programme costs at that time.

One consequence of Peacock, which the government approved, was that to keep costs down the BBC made fewer programmes in-house and followed the lead of Channel 4 in commissioning material from independent sources. But Peacock also recommended that in the longer term, when multichannel TV and radio had arrived and the BBC's audience share had significantly fallen, the licence fee should be abolished and the Corporation thereafter be funded by subscription.

The privatization proposal came to nothing because Radios 1 and 2 were not physically detachable from the rest of the BBC's operations, but as we shall see, Peacock's thinking on how broadcasting should develop underlay many of the provisions of the 1990 Broadcasting Act.

Developments in radio

Though sound broadcasting was no longer a preoccupation of the majority, there was by the early 1980s some dissatisfaction in various quarters with what was being offered by local radio.

Despite its vestigial public service obligations, ILR, which consisted of forty-eight stations by 1984, was largely characterized by a diet of pop music. As Radio 1 demonstrated this was just as easily provided by the networks: there was little that was 'local' about it. And even within that vast section of the public who preferred pop music to any other kind of output, there were many who felt excluded. Why?

Most ILR stations based their playlist on the Top 40 because these songs appealed to the greatest number of listeners. But pop and rock had by now fragmented into various sub-genres – reggae, country and folk, heavy metal, soul and dance music, golden oldies from the 1950s, 1960s and early 1970s. Songs of these kinds featured only rarely in the Top 40 but they were favoured by significant ethnic and social minorities, who thus felt that the ILR stations had little to offer them.

Despite continuing to open new stations during the 1970s and early 1980s BBC local radio was even less healthy than its rival. If in terms of the interest and resources it attracted network radio was the poor cousin of BBC TV, then BBC local radio stood in the same relation to network radio. Chronically underfunded, it offered a thin diet of news, information and light music and opted into one of the networks, usually Radio 2, for those parts of the day when it could no longer afford to provide a service of its own. Despite the many disclaimers at official level, local radio was regarded within the Corporation as existing primarily to feed the networks with new talent and new programme ideas.

But public dissatisfaction with local radio was not restricted to *content*: in neither the BBC nor the independent stations had the dream of wider *access* been realized. Both were largely a professionals' closed shop: even the much vaunted phone-ins were mediated by professional presenters, albeit for unavoidable legal reasons. Whether as members of an ethnic group, or devotees of a particular interest, or even as part of one of the more close-knit geographical communities, many people felt that their needs as listeners and potential broadcasters were not being met by local radio as it was presently constituted.

Their feelings were sharpened by an awareness that modern technology made sound broadcasting an unprecedentedly cheap and simple matter and afforded room for many more stations on the spectrum. If broadcasting was no longer a scarce commodity, why the need for such tight regulation? Why could the airwaves not be opened up to all tastes and all shades of opinion?

An unprecedented growth of interest in 'do it yourself' radio found expression in the launch of the Community Radio Association in 1983, and closed-circuit or in-house stations began to broadcast on college and hospital campuses and even in small communities, such as Radio Thamesmead in south east London. The government, in the form of the Home Office, was happy to license these because they were piped to closed communities, but in the wider world of the airwaves pirate stations could once more be heard.

Most of these were based in London and were of ethnic origin. By the mid-1980s as many as fifty were broadcasting, often relocating and reopening as fast as the Home Office investigators could trace them, raid them and impound their equipment. But neither of the main political parties were unsympathetic to the idea of community radio. The Labour opposition saw it as a forum for local democracy while the Conservative government regarded it as a way of enriching listener choice and fostering business enterprise, and a new framework for sound broadcasting was needed which would allow many more stations on to the air. In 1985 the government decided to license a national spread of twenty-one community radio stations on an experimental basis, but then abandoned the plan in order to consider the broader future of radio (and television) – a measure which would culminate in the Broadcasting Act of 1990.

However in 1989 the IBA seized the initiative by licensing twenty-one 'incremental' stations, so called because under existing legislation they had to be located in areas which were already served by ILR. About a quarter of them were former pirates and most subscribed to the 'community' ideal by appealing, like

Spectrum Radio in London, to ethnic groups; or by offering specialist music such as Jazz FM and Melody FM, also in London; or by broadcasting to people in small geographical areas, like Wear FM in Sunderland.

However the launch of the incrementals coincided with yet another slump in advertising, and those that pinned their faith on 'access' and community-originated programming soon learned the hard lesson that what the public wants to broadcast is not necessarily what it wants to hear. Within a year over half the stations had been refinanced, lost their original management or become part of bigger ILR groups transmitting the predictable diet of chart-based pop. What had begun as an exciting attempt to free up the airwaves, to enable them to carry the full range of values, tastes and opinions that shape our society, ended in an increase of stations sounding virtually indistinguishable from one another.

Meanwhile even the conventional ILR stations had not been thriving, as we saw in the last chapter. They were over-regulated by the IBA, and from the mid-1980s further hit by the pirates who, free from public service obligations, could attract advertisers by targeting their audiences as closely as they wished. The IBA finally moved to ease the sufferings of its licensees. Their public service obligations were lightened: they were allowed to adopt a simple Top 40 and capsule news format. Sponsorship was permitted, transmitter rentals were reduced, and companies with holdings in other media were allowed to run radio stations too. Clusters of ownership soon developed, such as Crown Communications, the Capital Radio Group and the East Midlands Allied Press (EMAP).

Later the IBA also allowed the stations to split their frequencies – that is, to offer different kinds of music on different wavebands so that they could target audiences more narrowly – and the great majority of stations which did so (eighteen of them in 1988–9 alone) broadcast Top 40 music on FM and golden oldies on the medium wave.

National radio enjoyed a more tranquil existence. For most of the 1980s it was still the preserve of the BBC, though there were occasional hints of a more competitive future. Since Radio 4 was the only network which continued to offer anything like the traditional Reithian diet of separately constructed and varied programmes, it was mostly here that the old favourites continued and new creations appeared. Among the latter were *In the Psychiatrist's Chair* (1981 onwards), in which Professor Anthony Clare cleverly exploited the confessional blindness and intimacy of the medium to probe the psyches of his famous 'patients'; and from 1985 *Loose Ends*, a somewhat anarchic chat show presided over by Ned Sherrin. Two years later Radio 4 unveiled its first soap opera since *The Archers*, but despite being provided with a long runway *Citizens* never quite took off and slithered to a halt in 1991.

However, from 1989 Radio 1 suspended pop music once a week and late at night to present a much acclaimed comedy show, *The Mary Whitehouse Experience*, named in ironic honour of the famous 'Clean Up TV' campaigner. And to crown a fairly satisfactory decade, all four of the networks acquired FM frequencies between 1988 and 1991, thus affording a quality of reception which matched their high production standards.

Nevertheless it was clear that the BBC's near monopoly of national radio could not last much longer. For a brief period in the mid-1980s an offshore pop pirate, Laser 558, had dented Radio 1's audience by minimizing disc jockey chat, promising that 'music is never more than a minute away', and in its green paper of 1987 the government signalled its intention to expose the BBC to competition at network as well as local level.

This happened sooner than either the government or the Corporation anticipated with the launch in September 1989 of Atlantic 252, a long-wave pop and rock station offering big prizes and little chat. Although it provoked protests from ILR, it was the first legal national daytime commercial station to be heard in this country – legal because it was beamed in from the Irish Republic and thus escaped British jurisdiction.

The 1990 Broadcasting Act contained important provisions for radio which embodied the government's guiding principle that deregulation would stimulate competition, increase efficiency and widen consumer choice. In essence this meant leaving BBC radio pretty much as it was while greatly increasing the number of its commercial rivals. These would be licensed at national and regional as well as at local level by a new Radio Authority whose control would, however, be lighter than the IBA's had been. None of the independent stations would henceforth incur the public service obligation to provide 'range' and 'balance', and they would be allowed to own their transmitting facilities instead of having to rent them from the Authority.

Three independent stations would present the BBC with competition at national level: one on FM, the others on medium wave frequencies which the BBC networks would be obliged to vacate now that they had acquired frequencies on the FM band. The Radio Authority was empowered to prescribe the kind of programming that the new frequencies would carry before it invited bids for them. In the event it decided that at least one of the stations would offer speech-based output and at least one other carry music which was not pop.

The early 1990s were marked by two other events in the world of radio. In their different ways these contrasted with the Broadcasting Act by recalling the past rather than looking to the future. The first was the BBC's launch in August 1990 of Radio 5, an old-fashioned mixed programme network which was born of expediency rather than any vision of the modern role of radio. The move to FM by the four existing BBC networks had left two spare medium wave frequencies which the Corporation realized might be assigned to yet other competitors if it failed to improvise a way of filling them. The result, if you were a critic of

Radio 5, was a 'ragbag', 'mish-mash' or 'dumping ground' of programmes that did not fit into any of the other networks. But if you were a supporter, it was a 'treasure chest' of adult education and schools broadcasts, sports commentaries, stories and magazine programmes.

The second event was the death of the once hugely popular Radio Luxembourg, weakened by waves of competition at, or nearer, home (first the pirates, then Radio 1, then ILR), and now expiring at the prospect of independent national stations. It disappeared from the medium wave in December 1991, but persisted for a few months more as a satellite channel.

Brief mention must be made of a technological development which has enhanced the autonomy of the listener: the Radio Data System (RDS). First incorporated into car radios by Volvo in 1988, RDS transmitted inaudible data alongside the audible radio signal. This data would automatically re-tune the radio to the strongest signal of the station that the listener wished to hear, irrespective of its frequency. People in cars have for many years been an important sector of the listening public and a device which would spare them the need to constantly re-tune to low-power FM transmitters was a real boon. RDS would also, if they wished, interrupt the signal with information about traffic and travel conditions.

While RDS could strengthen station loyalty (always strong on radio since listeners re-tune much less than viewers) another facility could weaken it by replacing it with loyalty to a particular kind of output. The listener could preselect a certain type of programming, such as jazz, news or drama, and the system would search for it among all the stations on the spectrum. RDS was clearly attractive to those who did most of their listening in cars: what was less clear was whether it would appeal to others, since it could more than double the cost of a cheap radio set.

Cable TV

The development of cable TV in Britain has been partly interwoven with that of satellite TV, from which many people cannot clearly distinguish it. Satellite television has so far had a more exciting history and gained a larger share of the audience, but as we shall see, cable television, though it largely depends on satellite feeds, may well have a bigger future than direct reception from satellite.

We need to begin by reviewing the differences between cable technology on the one hand and the more conventional kinds of broadcasting (including satellite) on the other. Earlier in this book we observed that conventional broadcasting, whether in the form of radio or television, was a 'wire-less' process: messages were transmitted from sender to receivers 'over the air' or through the atmosphere. Satellite technology is simply an extension of this process: messages or signals are transmitted from the sender up to the satellite and thence beamed down to the receivers, who are usually located on some other part of the globe.

The meaning and origins of 'broadcast' are important in this context. An ancient word which had been used to describe the sowing or scattering of seed, it usefully evoked the aerial nature of this new form of communication together with the indefinite plurality of its reception. Its messages would certainly be seen and/or heard by more than one person, but the precise number would be unknown: with the right equipment anyone within a given area could receive them.

'Cable', on the other hand, is a fixed, physical link and implies a rather more specific, less random relationship between sender and receivers. To describe the cable transmission of TV and radio programmes as 'broadcasting' is thus a significant modification of that word, though perhaps acceptable given the widespread nature of their reception.

Still, it is clear that cable transmission is at a certain disadvantage when compared to conventional broadcasting, and especially to satellite, its main competitor. Satellite transmissions can be received almost anywhere by means of a 'dish', whereas cable is available only in those areas which are sufficiently populous to justify the huge cost of laying it.

Nevertheless its reception of the satellite channels is (unlike that of the domestic dishes) invariably excellent, and it has two crucial advantages which, as we shall see, emerged with the development of fibre optic or 'broad band' cable at the end of the 1970s. First, its channel-carrying capacity is vast, and second it can serve as a medium of two-way communication. As well as relaying the conventional radio and television stations, then, cable has enormous potential in the fields of 'informatics' or information technology, telephony ('telecommunications' or 'telecoms', to give it its grander modern name) and interactive television, on which such services as home shopping, home banking and teleconferencing will soon become commonplace. It is therefore an early instance of that phenomenon of *media convergence* which many analysts believe will characterize the future, when a single item of equipment may combine the functions of computer, radio, TV, telephone, VCR and others besides.

This ability of cable not only to carry all the broadcasting channels but to offer a range of other services means that the cable companies cannot simply be equated with the conventional broadcasting organizations like the BBC or Channel 4. They are also telecoms operators in direct competition with the likes of British Telecom (BT): indeed telecoms are likely to form the most profitable part of their business. The BBC, ITV and Channel 4 may make and/or commission programmes and use their own means to disseminate or distribute them, but the cable companies are the providers merely of channels, they are the carriers or distributors of material originated or commissioned by others.

If, to take an analogy from the literary world, the conventional broadcasters could be compared to the creators of books in both the artistic and material senses, and also to the publishers, the cable companies could be compared to bookshops, selling a range of wares including those of the BBC, ITV and Channel 4. (Moreover, if one recalls their ability to offer other services than broadcasting, they could be compared to those bookshops which sell a range of products in addition to books, such as newspapers and confectionery.) Like the bookshops, they have a broad legal responsibility for what they carry, but they take no direct editorial role in the shaping of programme content: that is the province of the individual broadcasting organizations.

Cable television has existed in Britain since the early 1950s, but the first systems were to be found in places where the reception of conventional broadcasts was likely to be difficult, such as large blocks of flats. The first city-wide cable system opened in Gloucester in 1951, yet until recently cable development in Britain has lagged behind that of certain other countries such as the United States, and for a good reason. In the latter the size and terrain of the transmission areas mean that the conventional broadcasting signal is often so inferior that cable offers a better alternative, whereas with its relative compactness Britain has always enjoyed excellent TV reception.

Nevertheless in the 1970s British cable systems were developed which were similar to the old radio relay system, although they were allowed to carry only the three national networks. They were also an early form of pay TV, the first experiments in which had taken place in London and Sheffield in 1966 – an experience which was quite foreign to most British viewers until the present decade.

Cable received a boost at the end of the 1970s, when new fibre optic technology produced cables with vastly increased capacity – 250,000 times that of ordinary telephone wire – and the potential for *interactivity* (another grand word meaning 'two-way-ness'). Glimpsing its informatic potential, the government appointed an information technology advisory panel and conceived the idea that the establishment of a national cable infrastructure would be entertainment-led and privately funded. It also set up the Hunt Committee to consider how this idea could be given institutional shape.

In its 1982 report the committee recommended that cable TV should be seen as supplementary to what it regarded as the public service duopoly of the BBC and ITV, not as an alternative or rival to them. It therefore proposed that the cable companies be required to carry the ordinary BBC and ITV channels as part of the basic programme package they would offer to the viewer in return for a subscription. This proposal, which the government accepted, has become known as the 'must carry' rule. Most of the other programming would be delivered to the companies by the satellite operators: few if any channels would be originated by the companies themselves.

When cable was launched in 1983, eleven regional franchises were offered by the Department of Trade and Industry, whose responsibility for it was taken over in the following year, and in accordance with Hunt's recommendations, by a Cable Authority. By the end of 1985 companies were operating in eight different regions. Only one operator was licensed in each region, but for both the system and the programming, and each offered about twenty channels. Most of the operators, like US West and Videotron, were from the United States or Canada, where cable was already well-established.

The expansion of the cable infrastructure was bound to be slow, but was made slower by the operators' failure to attract many subscribers in the areas already cabled – a failure which deterred some potential investors. On average, the new service was taken up by fewer than 20 per cent of those whose homes the cable passed. For this there were three obvious reasons. First, most viewers were quite happy with the four, ostensibly free, channels offered by the BBC and ITV, which between them continued to give fairly good programming range and quality and excellent reception. Second, those viewers who were not happy with them could shortly subscribe to what seemed to be the more flexible technology of a satellite dish. And third, what was by now the wide ownership of VCRs already gave access to alternative sources of viewing.

However the economics of cable somewhat improved in 1990, when the Broadcasting Act at last allowed the operators to offer telecoms to their customers as well as a wide range of TV and radio channels. This gave them the possibility of doubling their revenue for about a 21 per cent increase in the installation cost.

Satellite TV

The history of satellite TV in Britain has been marked by three overlapping developments. During its first phase, which was outlined in Chapter 6, the BBC and ITV used satellite links as an element within their own earth-based or 'terrestrial' broadcasting. In 1968, for instance, they took pictures from the Mexico Olympics via satellite and then relayed them to the domestic viewers in the conventional way. This use of satellite pictures within terrestrial broadcasts has become increasingly common since its inception in 1962.

In the second development, which dates from 1984, whole programmes were originated by satellite broadcasters which by-passed the BBC/ITV duopoly and were relayed to the viewing public via the cable operators. Satellite continues to provide the greatest part of cable TV programming. And in the third development, which began in 1989, programmes were originated by satellite broadcasters which by-passed *both* the BBC/ITV duopoly *and* the cable operators and (in return for a subscription) were beamed direct to viewers via a circular aerial, or 'dish', and a decoder. This was known as direct broadcasting by satellite (DBS).

As a cable supplier, satellite TV began a trial service in mainland Europe in October 1981. In the following year it was officially launched as the Sky Channel, transmitting general entertainment programmes for a mere two hours a day to the cable systems there. In 1983 Rupert Murdoch's News International gained control of it and a year later began a service to cable operators in Britain, where the two media fledglings were covered by the Cable and Broadcasting Act of 1984.

However plans for the third development in satellite technology were already under way, for in 1982 the government had granted the BBC a licence to provide DBS in the United Kingdom. The plan was that the Corporation would use a British satellite built by Marconi, GEC and British Aerospace. But the costs proved even more astronomical than the project itself, and although the IBA was later brought in so that they could be more widely shared, it had to be abandoned in 1985.

In 1986 the government then asked the IBA to advertise for a contractor to provide a DBS service of three (later five) channels. This would carry certain public service responsibilities and would be expected to go to air before 1990. In due course the franchise was awarded to British Satellite Broadcasting (BSB), a consortium of companies including Virgin (which later dropped out), Pearson, Reed International, and two terrestrial contractors, Granada and Anglia TV. However, the technology required by the IBA was unproven and the start of the new service was repeatedly delayed until suddenly 'scooped' in February 1989 by Rupert Murdoch's Sky Channel, which had re-launched as a DBS service using the Astra satellite.

Since Sky was based abroad it fell outside the IBA's control. It was a subscription service which was also supported by advertising and at first offered just four channels: Sky One, Sky News, Sky Movies and Eurosport. In the meantime BSB was spending £30 million on a pre-launch promotional campaign, marketing its own square receiving dish, which was called a 'squarial', with the tag-line 'It's smart to be square'. It finally went to air in April 1990 but had lost the game almost before it began. Whereas BSB's headquarters and its launch parties smacked of extravagance, Sky TV was a lean outfit with an aggressive sales team who were eager to get dishes on to walls and roofs.

Neither company would easily recoup its huge start-up costs in what was now another economic recession, but Sky had pre-empted BSB by securing rights to all the available major Hollywood movies. Whereas the programmes on Sky One were almost entirely American in origin, BSB was obliged to originate its own programming on all channels, and in November 1990 it collapsed. By this time the companies had spent between them some £1.25 billion to persuade a mere one in fifteen households to buy their dishes. As in the case of cable TV, most viewers felt too happy with the abundance afforded by four terrestrial channels and the video suppliers to be tempted to subscribe to an infant DBS service.

Sky immediately absorbed BSB in what was wittily described as a merge-over, and the result was British Sky Broadcasting (BSkyB), a five-channel service which began in April 1991 and consisted of the original Sky package plus a second movie channel. A sixth channel, the Comedy Channel, was added in October.

The IBA was, of course, quite unable to prevent or influence the union of Sky and BSB. Because its permission had not been sought, it revoked BSB's licence and ordered it to stop broadcasting by the end of 1992. Had the new company been naive enough to obey, Britain would have been left without a satellite TV service, and as things stand, the service is run by a company which is entirely outside the regulator's control.

We might conclude this account of the early years of satellite TV with one or two broader observations. The first is that whether it wished to or not, the government was prevented from subjecting satellite to tight control by the knowledge that this would discourage potential operators from incurring the enormous start-up costs that were involved. One consequence of their relative freedom was that like the cable operators, the satellite companies sought to follow the lead of radio and maximize their audiences not simply by *narrowcasting* – that is, by offering a range of programmes to a specialized audience as BBC 2 and Channel 4 do – but by *formatting*, providing the specialized audience with only one kind of programme on each of its channels: comedy or sport or movies. We shall have more to say later about the aims and implications of TV formatting.

But we have also seen that whatever the attitude of governments to the ownership and programming of the companies, satellite TV is essentially a transnational business and therefore harder to bring under political control. Its 'footprints' transcend national borders and its operators can ignore the restrictions imposed by some of those countries to which they broadcast. But in Britain this has had consequences for terrestrial broadcasting, for the ITV contractors have cited the freedom of the satellite operators, with whom they compete for the same audience, to support their own demands for fewer restrictions on ownership and programming. One portent of a more liberal future occurred in 1988, when the IBA allowed the sponsorship of all TV programmes except those relating to news, religion or current affairs.

These TV times: the rise of pop music

Like every other decade the 1980s produced television programmes of merit. Granada's adaptation of Evelyn Waugh's melancholy masterpiece *Brideshead Revisited* (1981), starring Jeremy Irons, John Gielgud and Laurence Olivier, was so lovingly done that to the mingled pride and exasperation of ITV executives it was mistaken in the United States for the handiwork of the BBC.

In 1984 Granada began another adaptation which was highly lauded: *Jewel in the Crown*, based on Paul Scott's *The Raj Quartet*. On BBC Dennis Potter capitalized on the success of *Pennies from Heaven* with *The Singing Detective*, and comedy remained a prolific genre, and moreover one which was keen to reflect the contemporary world: the BBC launched *Only Fools and Horses*, starring David Jason, another series about shady entrepreneurs, while Central offered *Auf Wiedersehen, Pet*, tales of British labourers seeking high wages in Germany.

From 1984 Central also staged a welcome revival of television satire, though in an original form; for *Spitting Image* attacked its victims not by using comedians to ridicule or mimic them but by caricaturing them in the guise of gruesome latex puppets. Endued with that bilious vitality we expect from all good satire, the series made a particular target of an institution whose stature television had already done much to reduce: the royal family.

It is hardly surprising that the banality of television which had resulted from the constant extension of broadcasting hours should spawn new soap operas alongside those American diehards *Dallas* and *Dynasty*. Reacting to the gritty new world of *Brookside* on Channel 4, the BBC launched *EastEnders* in 1985, only to incur the wrath of Mrs Mary Whitehouse, who declared that the series put the nation 'in moral peril'.

The middle of the decade saw an interesting development in the broad genre of 'talk' television. Before the 1960s most studio discussion programmes had been the rather stilted preserve of authorities and experts, but *Late Night Line-Up* (BBC 2) gave us the less formal 'talk show', where conversation ranged more widely and was leavened with wit and vivacity. The 1970s were marked by the celebrity 'chat show', in which the likes of David Frost and Michael Parkinson, panders rather than interviewers, allowed their guests to dilate on cherished subjects: themselves and their careers.

But the discussion programme of the 1980s, though still located in a studio, took the *audience* as its focus, placing them on a discursive par with its guests, who were typically experts rather than celebrities. The audience sat on a sort of studio grandstand, with the experts identified in the front row or else seated on a stage and confronting them. Each programme would focus on one issue, and its host would roam through the assembly, selecting or responding to speakers with a hand held or boom microphone. It was, of course, cheap to produce and invariably screened outside prime time, so that its preoccupation with economic, political or sexual matters could assume a serious and 'relevant' air for that growing sector of viewers who had the leisure to watch off-peak television but scrupled to devote it entirely to 'pure' entertainment programmes.

The genre originated in the United States in the late 1960s, and one of its best-known exports was *The Oprah Winfrey Show* (Channel 4, later BBC 2), which in Britain alone commanded off-peak audiences of over 1.5 million. Of home-grown versions the most popular were *Kilroy* (BBC 1), hosted by the former MP Robert Kilroy Silk; *The Time, the Place* (ITV) with Mike Scott; and *Question Time* (BBC 1), then chaired by Peter Sissons and sometimes watched by a late night audience of more than 4 million.

The audience based talk show was a logical development of 'access' programming, which as we saw became fashionable during the 1970s, notably with the phone-in, a genre that gave audiences a 'voice' on both radio and TV, though not yet a 'presence'. The talk show now gave the wider public a chance to question and argue with authority on equal terms, to pit first-hand experience against specialist knowledge, common sense against expertise, and was thus an apt expression of that characteristic of television which we have frequently alluded to in this book: its tendency to impugn rank and professional status. In the words of Livingstone and Lunt, it was original because it challenged 'traditional oppositions of programme and audience, producer and subject, expert and laity' (1994: 36). Nevertheless it is a matter of some dispute whether the audience based talk show has been a genuine occasion for democratic debate or merely a cheap and insignificant way of filling air time.

It seems inappropriate to attempt a comprehensive account of the programmes of the 1980s. Most of them are in recent memory, some are still running. Moreover, and with the exception of the genre we have just discussed, there were few, even among those that were of undoubted quality, which threw new light on the medium itself, for it seems fair to say that the pioneering genres and formats were mostly in place by the beginning of the decade. Third, it is important to stress that during this time the significance of TV broadcasting was diminished, however slightly, by the video alternative. For at least part of the week the growing number of those who had VCRs (nearly half the viewing public by the middle of the decade) would opt out of live output and watch videotapes, many of which had not even originated on television: commercial videos, rented cinema films, home movies.

We should, however, note one kind of content which was becoming much more conspicuous on television and sometimes able to exert an influence beyond its own essentially frivolous nature: pop music. Television's problem with pop was always how to render in visual terms something which was essentially acoustic. Shots of musicians singing or playing, or of people listening (as in *Juke Box Jury*), were of limited potential. The best images came from dancing, though these seemed to detract somewhat from what was felt to be the centrality of the music. They certainly played an important part in the BBC's *Top of the Pops*, whose popularity had never faltered since its debut in 1963.

Later and cultish shows like *The Old Grey Whistle Test* (BBC 2) included in-depth interviews with rock musicians, for by the 1970s rock was old enough to take itself seriously – to develop that critical introspection which had long been a characteristic of jazz. Meanwhile the visual interest of mainstream pop shows was gradually enhanced by the growing sophistication of production techniques and the resources of the medium itself – flashing lights, fancy zooms and camera angles, video film and graphics – not to mention a greater showmanship among performers like Elton John, Queen and Pink Floyd.

It was not altogether surprising that the biggest media event of the decade should involve pop music, though perhaps remarkable that pop music and television should combine to raise awareness of a distant political problem and provide a remedy for it. In November 1984 the BBC journalist Michael Buerk presented a TV report on a famine in Ethiopia. Its pictures of the dead and dying horrified the millions who saw it, among them the Irish rock musician Bob Geldof. After making a fund-raising record at Christmas, Geldof went on to organize two televised rock concerts which were held in sequence on 7 July 1985 – one at Wembley Stadium, London, the other at JFK Stadium in Philadelphia.

Known collectively as Live Aid, their aim was to raise enough money from around the world to feed Africa's starving and to prevent a recurrence of famine. Featuring rock music's elite – Mick Jagger, David Bowie, Queen, Dire Straits and many more – Live Aid was the biggest media event since the first moon landings. It was watched by 59 per cent of the population of the United Kingdom and by one and a half billion people in over 160 countries round the globe. The sum raised was £40 million.

In a number of ways the episode of Ethiopia and Live Aid seemed to express the essence of modern television. First there was that shrinkage of the world that the medium both causes and reflects. In covering events in an obscure part of eastern Africa it galvanized first Britain and soon the world. Then during Live Aid itself, TV made use of satellite technology to link two concerts many thousands of miles apart and both concerts with a global audience. It also demonstrated another kind of technological shrinkage, for viewers saw Phil Collins perform at both. After singing at Wembley he flew to the States on Concorde, and just a few hours later sang again in Philadelphia.

Second there were the bizarre juxtapositions in which television almost inevitably deals. In Chapter 8 we noted the desultory way in which a visual and live medium tends to cover news and current events, one consequence of which is that its momentary and disjointed images, within adjacent items or even within a single item, will often 'comment on' one another in unintended ways. This explains the medium's incipient tendency towards irony – in this instance generated by the contrasting yet related pictures of a desperate, naked, starving people and the glitzy world of pop stars, lavish concerts and supersonic gallivantings.

Live Aid also illustrated that merging of fantasy and reality which we have asserted to be another characteristic tendency of television. Here rock music

– the stuff of dreams, wishes and make-believe – became an instrument of practical politics, part of the fight to provide millions with the physical necessities of life; and it was television, above all, which had brought the two together.

This was nicely symbolized by the Live Aid concert logo. It featured a silhouette of Africa which was treated as the body of a guitar, with a fretboard emerging from the top. Hence in the flippant style of pop culture, a vast geographical and political entity was pressed into the service of rock music; yet at the same time rock music was proposed as a cure for what in essence were the political ills of a continent – a kind of visual pun which was, of course, perfectly suited to the medium of television.

Finally the episode of Ethiopia and Live Aid typified the often huge yet ephemeral effects of television. Its images of suffering caused instant and global revulsion: there followed a deluge of generosity: then the TV crews looked for a new story and Ethiopia sank back into oblivion.

But in terms of pop music itself, Live Aid coincided with that third phase of its development which had in fact begun several years before. We noted in Chapter 2 that in its initial phase popular music acted mainly as the accompaniment to dance. Thanks to the 'domesticating' effect of records and radio, it then became something which was listened to much more than danced to. Finally, from about the 1970s television managed to transform it into something *visual*.

Just two years after Live Aid, in August 1987, the MTV (Music Television) satellite channel was launched in Britain, at first via cable, later on DBS, and ensured that music could be 'watched' round the clock. MTV was the television counterpart of pop music radio, for whereas the latter broadcast a sequence of pop singles the former broadcast a sequence of video versions of them. Henceforth no singer or band with serious ambitions to be successful could afford to make a record without also providing a video to accompany it.

Some of the videos merely show the artists performing their songs in studios or at concerts, but many use the medium to try to express the music more directly and less literally – perhaps by placing the artists in evocative settings where they could not actually be performing even though they might seem to be; or by filming other, sometimes more abstract, subjects; or by intercutting the two. In different ways MTV seems to offer as near a synthesis of pop music and the visual media as is presently conceivable.

The 1990 Broadcasting Act

In the late 1980s the government proposed a new dispensation for broadcasting which would accommodate the proliferation of channels made possible by technology (FM in the case of radio, cable and DBS in the case of television) and would liberalize the provision of services in a way that reflected its own faith in a deregulated market. In so doing it aimed to destroy two virtual monopolies: the BBC's of national or network radio and ITV's of television advertising.

The future shape of British radio and TV was enshrined in the Broadcasting Act of 1990. With effect from January 1991 the IBA was split into two separate organizations, the Radio Authority and the Independent Television Commission (ITC). We have already seen that the Radio Authority would ensure more commercial stations at local and regional level, and for the first time up to three national stations. The ITC absorbed the old Cable Authority and was also given responsibility for satellite TV, but its control over independent television was to be lighter than its predecessor's. Whereas the IBA had been for legal purposes both the broadcaster and regulator, in that it transmitted the programmes which the contractors provided as well as prescribing their nature and standards, the ITC was merely a regulator: it was the contractors and not the Commission which had to meet the requirements of the new Act.

The procedure of tendering for the franchises was also radically altered: henceforth these would simply be auctioned to the highest cash bids, which the successful contractors would be obliged to pay in instalments over the ten years that the franchises lasted. As an afterthought the government introduced a 'quality threshold' which the bidders would also have to meet. This was to embrace a range and diversity of output including news, a substantial amount of regional material, and religious and children's programming. Furthermore, the ITC could 'exceptionally' award a franchise to a lower bidder if its quality promise seemed better than that of the highest bidder.

However, after 1993 the contractors who collectively made up the ITV network on the third of the four national channels would no longer enjoy their near monopoly of advertising. In the short term they would have to compete not only with the fledgling cable and satellite channels, as at present, but with Channel 4, which from that year would be established as a separate corporation and be obliged to sell its own advertising. Thus the ITV network and Channel 4, which had originally been envisaged as mainly complementary, would now compete with each other to a much greater extent than before – and from 1994 there were criticisms that the content of Channel 4 was becoming excessively populist.

But in the longer term the ITV contractors would also have to compete with a network franchise which the ITC was empowered to auction for a new fifth channel. The fact that this would be national and not regional reflected the larger scale on which television broadcasting was now obliged to operate. Indeed it was unclear whether even a national franchise would be attractive to bidders at a time when broadcasting was an increasingly transnational, global activity.

ITN was another bastion of the ITV system which would be exposed to greater competition, for it was obliged under the Act to change from a supported service to a profit-making business. It would remain the sole supplier of news to the ITV network for a further ten years, though its position was to be reviewed after five; but its contract with Channel 4 would be at risk after 1993, when the latter became self-financing and free to shop around for its news provider. A predictable consequence of ITN's need to become more competitive was that during the 1990s its approach to the news became rather more populist, more concerned with 'human interest' stories.

The BBC was left relatively untouched by the 1990 Broadcasting Act but its Charter was renewed until 1996, and to free up the system yet further (and achieve something of a 'scaling down') the BBC, the ITV contractors and the future operator of Channel 5 were all required to move slightly in the direction of Channel 4 and S4C by ensuring that not less than 25 per cent of their total programme output was obtained from independent producers.

The Act set out restrictions on the number and nature of the radio and TV franchises that could be held by any one company, and as we have just seen, it also contained some belated and nebulous attempts to make 'programme quality' and 'public service' something more than merely synonymous with 'that which captures the largest audience'. But its main concern was to usher in a new era of multichannel broadcasting. Nevertheless we shall see that subsequent technological and economic developments in the field have been so rapid that within a year or two of its passage the Act would already be in need of revision.

Sources/further reading

For a general discussion of the political and policy issues surrounding broadcasting in the 1980s, see Curran and Seaton (1991). The contrasting tendencies in the production and distribution of media products – towards localization or democratization in the former and globalization in the latter – are outlined in Alvarado, Gutch and Wollen (1987) and Armes (1988), while the contemporaneous decline in the power of the broadcasting unions is charted by Sparks (1994). The trend towards conglomeration and globalization in media ownership is also described in Seymour-Ure (1991; 1996), while Hobsbawm (1994) stresses the powerlessness of individual states against the globalizing pressures of technology and economics.

Though Hood and O'Leary (1990) provide a good summary of it the Peacock Report (1986) can easily be read in its entirety, and it is also quoted and glossed by McDonnell (1991). Scannell (1990) includes a discussion of Peacock's particular approach to public service broadcasting.

For a general account of developments in radio during the 1980s see Crisell (1994). Barnard (1989) is excellent on the difficulties and dilemmas of ILR, and Lewis and Booth (1989) helpfully distinguish community radio from the public service and commercial models, looking at developments in all three. For the network radio programmes of the time Donovan (1992) is a useful source of reference.

The authoritative account of the background and establishment of cable TV in Britain is Negrine (1985). The huge capacity of broad band cable is described by Bowen (1994) and for the deliberations of the Hunt Committee see McDonnell (1991). The economic consequences of allowing the cable companies to offer telecoms are outlined in Bulkley (1992).

Negrine (1994) gives a useful general account of the development of cable and satellite broadcasting, but for more detailed accounts of the latter see Goodfriend (1988) and Negrine (1988).

Day-Lewis (1992) offers lively descriptions of the terrestrial TV programmes of the 1980s, and Livingstone and Lunt (1994) provide an exhaustive analysis of the audience based talk show. On the background to the 1990 Broadcasting Act see Hood and O'Leary (1990) and Negrine (1994). The main provisions of the Act and its consequences for the ITV franchises are outlined in O'Sullivan, Dutton and Rayner (1994), but for the changes to ITN see McNair (1994).

Chapter 11

And now
the nineties

And now the nineties

Contrasting signals: radio

Since the 1990 Broadcasting Act scores of new radio stations, nearly all of them commercial, have come on air at national, regional and local level. Yet the growth of the medium has masked its uncertain health. The choice of listening is huge and there is a boom in radio advertising, but the audience is spreading ever more thinly – the popularity of the medium is static or even slightly in decline. Moreover only Radio 4 survives as a reminder of the range and plenitude that individual networks once offered, a fine relic of the old Reithian values yet one which, because it is not television, seldom figures in the debate about the BBC and public service broadcasting.

In accordance with the 1990 Act the Radio Authority invited cash bids from aspiring commercial operators for three national wavelengths, and these were duly awarded, though only after one or two initially successful bidders were later deemed unsuitable or failed to meet their undertakings. Classic FM, Britain's first home-based, legal, national, commercial radio station finally went to air in September 1992, no less than seventy years after organized radio broadcasting began in this country! It has been a very successful attempt to shape classical music to the format of a pop station and has meant keen competition for BBC Radios 2 and 3.

It was followed in April 1993 by Virgin 1215, broadcasting music for the older rock fan, and in February 1995 by the self-explanatory Talk Radio UK (TRUK), both stations occupying medium wavelengths which the BBC had been forced to give up. Each of the national commercial licences lasts for eight years.

After trying to raise ratings by using 'shock jocks' – presenters who declaim outrageously reactionary views on all the usual intellectual chestnuts: crime and capital punishment, race, the role of women – Talk Radio sought to usher in a new post-literary age of stimulating conversation and debate. Neither approach was greatly successful, and a year and a half later the station was in poor health.

Virgin 1215 scooped up those older rock fans whom Radio 1 abandoned in its attempt to target the devotees of contemporary pop music, but it was strongly challenged by Atlantic 252 and the ILR stations. The Radio Authority has licensed yet more of the latter, along with several regional stations mostly offering light or popular music.

During its first four years BBC Radio 5 was a failure, for the diverse and unpredictable nature of its content, however good in itself, flew in the face of modern listener requirements. In March 1994 it relaunched as Five Live, a populist news and sport network whose evident appeal to a hearty and mainly male section of the public earned it the affectionate soubriquet 'Radio Bloke'. It was certainly more successful than its predecessor.

BBC radio was at first hit hard by the burgeoning competition from the commercial sector. While Classic FM and Virgin made steady progress through 1994, Radio 1 suffered a spectacular fall in listening figures, its popularity plunging below Radio 2's for the first time in their history. It subsequently rallied somewhat, largely by ceding older pop music lovers to Radio 2 and the commercial stations and concentrating on younger listeners.

In early 1995 independent radio's audience share overtook the BBC's for the first time. Advertising revenue rose from £141 million in 1992 to £270 million in 1995, and in the three years up to 1996 was showing an annual increase of 23 per cent. The boom was created by aggressive marketing and distinguished by a slight improvement in the quality of the commercials.

Until the arrival of the national stations the creation of radio commercials lacked a strong tradition. Most advertising agencies employed creatives with a background in graphic design, and since they honed their skills on billboards and TV screens, their early efforts in the medium of sound were often amateurish. But since the launch of the independent national stations radio copywriting has become rather more imaginative and persuasive, and with revenue soaring and greater cross-media ownership having been allowed by the 1996 Broadcasting Act, prospects for the commercial sector seem bright.

Radio is thriving not only institutionally but in technological terms. Following the vast number of stations which have already gone to air, satellite pay radio is imminent, and digital audio broadcasting, which eliminates transmission noise and can thus make the music of any station sound as good as that of a CD player, has already arrived. The BBC began a digital radio service, carrying all its networks, in September 1995, but geographical coverage is limited and its listeners require special receivers.

Despite all the recent and current developments there is some darkness on radio's horizon. Total listening is fairly stagnant, for the new stations have not so much created a new audience as filched the BBC's old one. What is most worrying is that 30 per cent of young people *never* listen to what has, in the forty or so years since the upsurge of pop music, been regarded as a mainly young persons' medium. The youthful obsession with pop continues unabated, but whereas it was first satisfied by trannies, then by car radios, and latterly by ghetto blasters and Walkmans, many youngsters now get their fix from bedroom television sets offering frequent rock shows on the terrestrial channels and an endless stream of MTV on satellite and cable.

With digitization imminent, BBC radio faces some particularly hard decisions. It is conceivable that its local stations, along with the formatted networks, Radios 1, 2, 3 and 5, may become commercial operations. Another possibility is that the mixed programme Radio 4, and perhaps with it the highbrow Radio 3, could be offered as part of a subscription package with the BBC's two terrestrial television networks and several formatted TV channels.

Outlook unsettled: BBC television

Ever since the publication of the Peacock Report the BBC has sought to placate a government eager to subject it to the financial discipline of a commercial organization. Only thus could it win the renewal of its Charter and the retention of the licence fee. Having shed 7,000 staff between 1986 and 1990 the Corporation has continued to make tough economies. Under Director General John Birt it has also introduced the policy of 'producer choice', by which every programme production becomes an autonomous entity bidding for funding against other productions and buying its resources according to the best deal available, whether within the BBC or from external suppliers. Its reward for this policy has been an extension of its Charter and Licence to the year 2001.

Yet the Corporation's future is cloudy. We have seen that once the BBC's television monopoly was broken and as channels multiplied, the original Reithian notion of public service – the exposure of the audience to a variety of programming on each channel – became harder to sustain. If viewers craved variety they could introduce their own by switching between channels, something which became even easier in the 1980s and 1990s with the arrival of cable and satellite.

In other words, a great deal of the old public service rationale rested on the *specialness* of broadcasting – and that in turn depended on its scarcity, the shortage of wavelengths. Reith had taken the view that broadcasting was too precious a resource to be limited to one kind of programming – least of all to be 'prostituted' to non-stop populist entertainment. But no one demands 'public service' from a plentiful medium such as the press, and as the problem of scarcity in broadcasting has disappeared the public service imperative has disappeared with it.

Nowadays television, let alone radio, is 'nothing special'. It serves us twenty-four hours a day on scores of channels, with hordes more to come. The paradox is that the more pervasive and commonplace the medium, the less influential and significant it seems to be, a situation which weakens the need for political balance, and even, perhaps, for political control, except over the extremes of violence and pornography. For the first time in broadcasting history the number of channels appears almost equal to the range of content it seems possible to broadcast.

As its share of the audience shrinks the BBC will thus find it harder and harder to make the case for a universal licence fee. Nicholas Garnham (1994) has shown that despite the government's wishful thinking, broadcasting is not crudely reducible to the laws of free market economics; that even in the United States, with a multitude of channels to choose from, many of them formatted, viewers watch only six with any regularity; and that the classic over-air 'generalist' networks still capture 60 per cent of the audience. Garnham argues that even if under a similar system licence funded broadcasting were to fall to a 30 per cent audience share, there would still be a strong case for it. Provided most households avail themselves of BBC output at some time or other, they would continue to get a good bargain for their licence fee. Nevertheless, the prospect of digitization throws even a 30 per cent audience share into grave doubt.

What, then, is the BBC's survival plan? In the past it has been the licence fee which in freeing the Corporation from narrowly commercial considerations has allowed it to pursue high standards over the widest range of programmes. Its aim must now be to find alternative sources of revenue which will allow it to maintain those standards — revenue not from direct advertising, which could so easily compromise them, but from pay per view and subscription services, and also from the sale of programmes to other broadcasters.

Nevertheless this revenue will prove an adequate replacement of licence income only if the BBC moves simultaneously in opposite directions. It must slim down as an organization and thus cut costs; yet it must also 'go global' — maximize its earnings by reaching a vast international audience.

During the first half of the 1990s the BBC did both these things. It reduced its overheads by selling off many of its production and transmission facilities and becoming more of a commissioner or publisher of programmes in the style of Channel 4. But it also formed partnerships with commercial organizations in order to distribute its programmes and services more widely. Its commercial partners provide the financial investment and the access to new audiences while the BBC provides the programming, the ideal role for an institution which not only has a long-standing and international reputation for high programme standards but – a trump card this – possesses a huge library of old material with which to feed the burgeoning number of channels at home and abroad.

In 1995 the BBC joined with Pearson and the American-owned cable and satellite company, Flextech, to create the nostalgia pay TV channel, UK Gold, which is carried by BSkyB. A year later it made a further deal with Flextech to launch in 1997 eight pay TV channels on cable, but which are also likely to be offered on satellite by BSkyB. The channels will carry highbrow arts and culture, documentaries, lifestyle programmes, sport and entertainment. In 1996 the BBC also made a deal with Flextech's American associate, Discovery, to launch channels in the United States. Hence it may fairly be said that despite the BBC's reluctance to carry advertising, there is for the first time in broadcasting history an unavoidable convergence of the licence funded and commercial sectors.

In addition the Corporation announced plans in 1996 to launch a subscription service of digital television in Britain which would consist of its two traditional networks together with a number of formatted channels. This service was probably planned as a test-run for life after 2001, when it is quite likely that the government will take a momentous step and abolish the licence fee. The aim will then be to see whether BBCs 1 and 2, with their old fashioned diet of mixed programming, will be able to survive as subscription services. If not, it is conceivable that the BBC would move to an entirely formatted service whose many channels would be funded by subscription or pay per view.

Whatever its future two things seem certain: the BBC will face ferocious competition from hundreds of other channels, many of them delivered by satellite and cable, and it will no longer occupy its traditional, vaunted place at the centre of our national culture.

ITV: a changing landscape

The renewal of the ITV regional franchises on the third channel, which had been delayed until the 1990 Broadcasting Act became law, now took place in 1992. Thanks to the latter, it assumed the unprecedented form of an auction in which, barring special circumstances, the franchises would go to the highest cash bidder – an aleatory affair with an element of farce.

The highest successful bid – £43 million for the London weekday franchise – came from Carlton TV, exceeding by £10 million the bid made by the incumbent, Thames Television. At the other extreme was Central Television in the Midlands, which in the absence of a rival was able to renew its franchise with a contemptuous £2,000. Yorkshire TV extended its tenure with a £37 million bid, while Meridian and Westcountry (£7.75 million) replaced TV South and Television South West respectively, neither of whose business plans impressed the ITC even though TV South outbid Meridian's £36.5 million.

Finally GMTV gained the breakfast television franchise with an offer of £34.5 million – over £20 million more than the then holders TV-AM. It was TV-AM whose lock-out had largely destroyed the power of the broadcasting unions some four years previously, and its defeat now prompted a letter of sympathy from Mrs Thatcher deploring the result of a franchising system which her own government had introduced.

For the ITV contractors life since 1992 has been tough and is getting tougher. Their advertising revenue was immediately hit by the cable and satellite channels, and soon after by Channel 4, which from 1993 was no longer funded by a subscription levied on the contractors but obliged by the Broadcasting Act to sell its own advertising. In 1993 the contractors took 78 per cent of all TV advertising, with Channel 4 taking 17 per cent and cable and satellite taking 5 per cent. A year later ITV had lost 3 per cent of the market, 2 per cent of it to Channel 4 and 1 per cent to cable and satellite.

As well as being affected by all these broadcasters and the two BBC networks, ITV's audience would be hit by a third commercial network, Channel 5, which was to be launched as soon as practicable. What these challenges really demonstrate is that if – given the technology and economics of TV broadcasting – it ever made sense to operate a regional system in a country as small as Britain, it is making much less sense in the 1990s. All the contractors' competitors on the other channels operate on a scale which is at least national, and in order to match them mergers and takeovers have occurred within the third channel.

Consolidation began soon after the 1992 franchise round. That year Yorkshire TV and Tyne Tees Television were allowed to unite. In May 1993 LWT paid £14 million for a 14 per cent stake in Yorkshire-Tyne Tees. A month later Granada paid £68 million for a 15 per cent stake in LWT, and at about the same time Carlton took over Central (which already owned 20 per cent of Meridian) as well as having a 20 per cent interest in GMTV. The whole of the third channel may shortly be divided between three groups: United News and Media, Carlton and Granada.

In fact the history of the bidding for the new Channel 5 suggests that in an era of global and multichannel broadcasting even a national franchise is not a particularly tempting prospect. Offers were invited in April 1992. At the closing date for the applications three months later, only one bid had been received – from Channel Five Holdings, which the ITC rejected because dissatisfied with its business plan.

The franchise was re-advertised and in 1995 awarded, on a modest bid of £22 million, to Channel 5 Broadcasting, a consortium of Pearson, United News and Media, and CLT, the Luxembourg based broadcasters. But there were subsequent difficulties and delays. Its transmission area was patchy, covering only 85 per cent of British homes, and even within that area 90 per cent of domestic video recorders would be affected by its signal, committing the company to a costly re-tuning operation. Nor would it be allowed to transmit until 90 per cent of the re-tuning was completed. Channel 5 was eventually launched on Easter Sunday 30 March 1997, offering 'mainstream' programming twenty-four hours a day. An important aim of the 1996 Broadcasting Act was to allow the emergence of British commercial broadcasters big enough to hold their own in the international media market. To this end, companies were no longer restricted to major shareholdings in just two ITV licences but subject to the more flexible limit of a 15 per cent share of the total audience. Moreover as well as being allowed to hold stakes in several TV broadcasters (Granada and Pearson both have major shareholdings in Rupert Murdoch's BSkyB) companies were subject to much less control on cross-media ownership.

At a time of growing media convergence the government's aim was to lump newspapers, TV and radio into a single media market, in which the main restraint was a 'public interest' test that could be fairly flexibly interpreted according to three criteria. If mergers or acquisitions occurred, what economic benefits would result? What would be the effect on competition? And would diversity in information sources be reduced?

Approaching a crossroads: Channel 4

Channel 4 spent its infancy trying, in Sylvia Harvey's words, 'to give a voice to the new pluralism of the 1980s' (1994: 118), and on most counts it succeeded. Programmes like *Out on Tuesday* (1988) and *Sex Talk* (1990) explored sexuality of various kinds; *Union World* (1984–5) served the needs of trade unionists; *Handsworth Songs* (1987) and *Looking for Langston* (1990) were the creations of black British film-makers. From 1987 *The Media Show* was the first real series for those who wished to take an informed and critical look at television itself.

Perhaps the channel's most extraordinary and famous achievement was the series *Film on Four*, a collaboration with the movie industry to produce feature films for both TV screening and cinema exhibition. It supplied 22 per cent of the budget of *Paris, Texas* (1986) and 100 per cent of the budget of *My Beautiful Launderette* in 1987. In that year alone its screenings of new films included *Letter to Brezhnev*, *Caravaggio* and *The Company of Wolves*.

However as a result of the 1990 Broadcasting Act the character of the channel changed somewhat. It ceased to be a subsidiary of the IBA and became an independent trust whose board members were nominated by the ITC, and to further the Act's aim of making broadcasting more competitive it was obliged to sell its own advertising from 1993. Since this had been a likely development ever since the publication of the Peacock Report in 1986, the channel's Chief Executive, Michael Grade, who succeeded Jeremy Isaacs in 1988, gave its schedules a slightly more populist slant. The soap opera *Brookside* swelled the ratings, as did several drama series which were bought in from America: *Cheers*, *The Cosby Show*, *The Golden Girls*, and later, *Friends* and *ER*. Audience share rose from 8.8 per cent in 1988 to around 11 per cent in 1993, surpassing BBC 2's. Whereas even in its early years a heartening 50 per cent of the viewing public watched something on Channel 4 in any one week, nearly 80 per cent were doing so in 1991. Its core audience of youngish, affluent professionals was an attractive prospect for many advertisers in 1993, and in any case the channel retained a connection with the main ITV network through a 'safety net' agreement.

This provided that if Channel 4's revenue fell below 14 per cent of the total advertising income of terrestrial television, the ITV companies would be obliged to intervene and contribute up to 2 per cent of that amount. If, however, Channel 4 acquired more than 14 per cent of total revenue any surplus was to be shared between itself and the ITV companies.

In the event the channel was a victim of its own success. With S4C its share of net advertising revenue grew to over 21 per cent by 1997, committing it to make huge payments to the ITV companies, a deal from which it was released by the 1996 Broadcasting Act only shortly before Grade's departure.

Whether or not the channel continues to prosper, it faces much the same danger. If it is hit hard by the growing competition – in 1996 its share of viewing was overhauled for the first time by satellite and cable, and from 1997 it might be damaged by Channel 5's search for a young audience – it could either be forced further into the mainstream or try for a profitable niche, in either case sacrificing several kinds of minority programming.

But financial success could have much the same consequence. The channel is presently valued at between £2 billion and £3 billion and still in public ownership. A future government of any hue might be strongly tempted to privatize it – and private ownership could threaten investment in programmes and erode the channel's distinctiveness, especially the provision of programmes to unprofitable minorities. It still remains to be seen whether the commercial model of TV broad-casting is genuinely able to support a service which caters to a range of minority interests.

Sky without limit: the rise of satellite television

We noted in the last chapter that satellite TV made slow progress in its early years because viewers were already blessed with an abundance of material from the terrestrial channels, not to mention video rental and retail outlets. Eric Hobsbawm draws our attention to a stupendous fact that we all too easily overlook: by 1990 people were living in 'a world which could bring more information and entertainment than had been available to emperors in 1914, daily, hourly, into every household' (1994: 12). Not only was the provision lavish beyond the most fervid imaginings of anyone living seventy-five years earlier: after the purchase of a receiver it was – and this is what made it universal – virtually *free*.

The achievement of broadcasting, and especially television, was to bring news, sport, drama, comedy, music and so on, to those otherwise too poor to obtain them through separate cash payments. It was an egalitarian process which appealed to the most radical social reformers on the one hand and to old-fashioned patricians like John Reith on the other. As Hobsbawm puts it: 'entertainments hitherto only available as personal services to millionaires were now in the most modest of living rooms' (1994: 307).

This is the profoundest sense in which television broadcasting in particular is a democratic phenomenon, for it is the precondition of those other democratic effects which we discerned earlier in this book. We noted its tendency to impugn expertise, reduce status and demystify authority, and we observed its power to expose the most obscure political misdeeds of individuals and nations. But it is 'democratic' only because it does these things before millions upon millions of viewers of every social background.

In his mention of households and living rooms Hobsbawm draws attention to another 'democratic' fact about broadcasting which we have stressed throughout this book: the privacy and individuality of its reception. To avail themselves of this lavish and 'free' facility audiences are not even obliged to go anywhere: it comes to each consumer's own space. She almost invariably owns the receiver and her consumption of broadcasting does not lessen, neither is it lessened by, that of others, no matter how many they number. In the sense that this consumption is atomistic, sometimes solitary, we could say that there is a sense in which the cultural integration, the almost physical sense of national unity, that Reith sought to instil was working against the grain of the medium itself. The private, idio-syncratic nature of listening and viewing has, if anything, been compounded by the increasing choice of channels.

Nevertheless, what the rise of satellite television has shown is that broadcasting may not be virtually free for much longer since its conditional access technology – the means of allowing or preventing the transmission or reception of its signals – can establish a firm connection between what one watches and what one pays for. As a result we may look back on the primitive age of four-channel terrestrial television as 'the good old days'.

The only way in which BSkyB could prosper was to offer an even better diet than terrestrial television – or, which came to the same thing, to appropriate the most popular bits of it – for audiences were canny enough to realize that more TV channels did not necessarily mean more choice. Like ITV's in the mid-1950s, BSkyB's first years were modest and faltering and prompted rash predictions of failure. But by acquiring exclusive rights to big movies and sporting events and by assiduous marketing, mostly through Murdoch's own newspapers, it made steady progress as the decade wore on. During 1992 no less than twenty-nine satellite and cable services were launched, and 1993 marked the turn of BSkyB's fortunes, when the previous year's loss of £20.4 million was replaced by a profit of £62.2 million.

But it was 1995 which saw one of the most adroit deals in the satellite sector. Though Murdoch himself owned 50 per cent of BSkyB, other major shareholders included Granada, the oldest of the ITV regional contractors, with 13.5 per cent, and the Pearson Group, both of which had held shares in BSB, the ill-fated venture that Sky took over. BSkyB now acquired from Granada the rights to 3,000 vintage episodes of *Coronation Street* as part of a plan to launch several new satellite channels in 1996. The channel which recycled old programmes from both Granada and LWT, a company which Granada now owned, would be called Granada Gold Plus. The deal enabled BSkyB to win many more viewers to pay TV, and for Granada it meant swift and cheap elevation to broadcasting on a higher plane.

By 1996 about 5 million homes boasted satellite dishes and one in five British households was able to receive BSkyB either directly or via cable. The year was also full of dark omens for the traditional broadcasters. Sky won the exclusive right to televise the world title boxing match between Frank Bruno and Mike Tyson, but to general indignation would beam it only to those of its subscribers who were prepared to pay a £10 surcharge. However, given Bruno's propensity to become rapidly intimate with the canvas, it was not surprising that the transmission turned out to be poor value.

The company was well aware that it particularly needed to buy up sporting events because unlike movies, its other staple fare, these did not suffer from the disadvantage of being pre-recorded. A live sporting event is a genuine TV premiere: there is a certainty that viewers will not have seen it before. But thanks to the cinemas and video outlets the same cannot be said for the great majority of movies, although this situation might change in the future. As BSkyB clinches more and more exclusive deals on sport – and on movies, despite the fact that some of its subscribers will already have seen them – the old-fashioned, terrestrial broadcasters will come to resemble its poor relations.

Even the government is growing anxious. It used the 1996 Broadcasting Act to prevent BSkyB or other subscription companies from obtaining the exclusive right to broadcast any of eight major British sporting events, including the FA Cup and the Grand National. Yet it may be trying to stop the unstoppable. A few months later both the BBC and BSkyB won rights to screen premiership soccer until the year 2001. But whereas the BBC could afford to bid only for recorded highlights, Sky bought live transmissions of whole matches.

In global terms Murdoch's organization is only one of three big players. Another is Ted Turner's US entertainment conglomerate which includes the Cable

News Network (CNN), the MGM film library and television interests in Asia; and a third is Sumner Redstone's empire whose main operating subsidiary, Viacom, embraces Paramount, the Hollywood studio, the MTV networks and Blockbuster Video. But aside from his press interests Murdoch owns Fox, a US television network, and a Hollywood movie studio, holds stakes in Australian broadcasting, and has a majority share in Star TV, the Asian satellite network whose potential for growth is massive.

This is a global picture rather than a British one, but the distinction is, as we have seen, growing porous. For the international operator the prizes are incalculably great because the rules which individual countries have framed so as to limit foreign programming will be unworkable. Indeed it is presently hard to imagine any form of state media regulation which will be better than impotent.

However the most immediate challenge which British broadcasting faces from BSkyB is its launch of 200 digital TV channels planned for the end of 1997. All British broadcasters will offer digital services in the near future, but in order to decode them viewers will need a set-top box – and presently only BSkyB has in place the conditional access technology. It could thus control access even to the standard digital channels which would be operated by the five terrestrial broadcasters, something which could precipitate an era of exclusive or near exclusive pay TV either by subscription or pay per view. And in that case, as we noted above, we may look back on the first sixty-five years of television as a golden age which ended at the same time as the twentieth century – an age when, despite the paucity of channels, content was in many ways as rich as, or even richer than, that of the global and digital era, yet which cost the consumer almost nothing.

Wiring up: the progress of cable TV

We have seen that the singular strength of cable was media *convergence*: because it could carry an enormous quantity of data and offer two-way communication it could simultaneously act as a channel for broadcasting, telecommunications, computing and closed circuit television systems. In the last chapter we also suggested that a single piece of apparatus might come to be used for all these functions. Yet as we shall see in Part III, cable's potential is even greater than this.

It is not merely the case that these different media could exist, as it were, side by side within a single box: cable could bring about a process of media *integration*, a merging of broadcasting, telecoms and informatics in which the different technologies would be almost indistinguishable from one another. In the case of broadcasting, the main concern of our book, the audience would be able not only to *respond* to broadcasts within the same medium rather than via a separate telecoms network, for instance in voting for a 'man of the match'; but *modify* the broadcasts as they happen by choosing camera angles, frame freezes, re-runs and so on; and even to *initiate* broadcasts – that is, to choose what programmes to receive, not from published schedules as at present, but from a vast library of material of every imaginable kind.

From the 1980s it was possible to run videos and computer programmes on domestic TV screens, but that was a dedication of the television set to uses other than broadcasting. The possibility that we are now contemplating is *interactive broadcasting*, something we shall look at more closely in the final section.

We noted that after an indifferent start cable was given a boost by the 1990 Broadcasting Act because it allowed the operators to offer telecoms services to their customers. In 1992 the number of cable franchises providing such services jumped from ten to twenty-four, and by 1994 the cable had passed more than a million homes.

Two years later 40 per cent of the networks had been built, yet the cable companies had captured only one in five of their potential customers. The problem quite simply was that it was hard for them to compete against DBS for the entertainment-led, broadcasting side of their business, while the more unique telecoms and informatic services they offered were either not yet available or not yet tempting to the wider public. Most of the cable TV channels were also available on satellite, and the terms on which they were supplied by BSkyB, an organization that was to a large extent in competition with the cable operators, were stringent.

One channel which was exclusive to cable was SelecTV. Another was L!ve TV, which was supplied by the Mirror Group, and whose contribution to broad-casting history was the introduction of topless darts and of someone called News Bunny. Despite these frantic attempts at notoriety the channels did not win large audiences, and it was clear that cable needed to secure a larger supply of its own programming.

But towards the middle of the decade the industry faced a challenge even in those interactive services that are its particular strength. British Telecom had been prohibited until 1997 from using its network to wire broadcast television to its customers, since this would be an unfair use of its position as a near monopoly. But BT was developing the facility to transmit video films on near demand, claiming that this would not count as broadcasting because the transmissions would be piecemeal – offered individually and only to those customers who had ordered them. However it seems possible that even the broadcasting prohibition might shortly be lifted from BT.

In autumn 1996 the cable industry at last moved to meet some of the forces that threaten it. Cable and Wireless merged its telecoms subsidiary, Mercury, with three of the main cable operators, Bell Cablemedia, Nynex and Videotron, to form Cable and Wireless Communications, which would be able to give the industry a more unified brand image and compete more effectively with BT on the one hand and BSkyB on the other.

Everybody's listing: a postscript

At the beginning of the decade the deregulation of broadcasting was mirrored by developments in the press: the *Radio Times*'s monopoly of the BBC's programme listings and the *TV Times*'s monopoly of ITV's were ended in 1991.

The first challenge to these giants had been mounted in 1983 by a pygmy, the London magazine *Time Out*; but after a legal battle which cost it some £300,000 their copyrights were upheld. However in 1989 the government, acknowledging the need for increased consumer choice in all aspects of broadcasting, announced an end to the duopoly. Even so, the battle for deregulation was not quite won, for both the BBC and ITP, the publishers of the *TV Times*, attempted to force rival publications to pay huge fees for the right to reproduce the listings, something it took another copyright tribunal to overturn in 1992.

Since then both the *Radio Times* and the *TV Times* list the programmes of all the television channels, not merely those of their parent broadcasters, but so do innumerable other publications and the circulation of these quondam giants has dropped.

Sources/further reading

For much of its data and the chronology of the main events of the first half of the decade, this chapter draws on *Media Week* (1995). The boom in commercial radio is described in Horsman (1996b) and there is a discussion of Classic FM's pop format in Crisell (1994). However the decline in radio's popularity among the young is remarked in Brown (1995).

As a background to the issues of public service broadcasting and the BBC, MacCabe and Stewart (1986) is still relevant, and Smith (1990) discusses them in the context of the 1990s. Tusa (1994) offers a conservative view of the BBC's future role as the provider of a 'sense of social cohesion'. For an account of the launch of the Corporation's digital radio service see Williams (1995b). There is a penetrating analysis of broadcasting economics in Garnham (1994), which also explores the case for the retention of the BBC's licence fee. On the BBC's partnership with Flextech, see Horsman (1996e) and on its plans to launch a service of digital television, see Horsman (1996d).

O'Sullivan, Dutton and Rayner (1994) contains the details of the ITV franchising auctions which followed the 1990 Broadcasting Act, and is also useful on the globalizing tendency of modern media and the company takeovers and channel formatting it entails. Negrine (1994) is equally helpful on these matters, on the problems and implications of new media technology, and on the future issues and difficulties confronting the BBC.

For the challenges facing ITV 1 in the 1990s see Horsman (1995b). MacDonald (1995b) explains the government's aim to allow British broadcasting organizations to get bigger in order to compete globally, and Williams (1995a) and Cicutti (1995) predict the growth of cross-media ownership which was allowed by the 1996 Broadcasting Act.

My vignette of Channel 4 is based on the very useful potted history of its first ten years by Harvey (1994), and my speculations about its future owe something to Bell (1997). A personal account of its first five years is in Isaacs (1989).

For his remarks on the miraculous abundance and cheapness of broadcasting in 1990 see Hobsbawm (1994). MacDonald (1995a) outlines the BSkyB/Granada deal involving *Coronation Street*. Horsman (1995a) describes the main competitors in global satellite broadcasting, discusses BSkyB's plans to launch digital services (1996c) and surveys the present problems and future prospects of cable (1996a).

Part III

From broadcasting
to multimedia

We began this historical study by noting that from its inception broadcasting was a live medium which was *private* in the sense that it was *domestically* received. From about the 1960s it was becoming even more private because increasing numbers of people could afford their own *individual* radio and television sets – sets whose use was no longer confined to the home.

In Part II we noted that this development was broadly contemporary with another: a growth in audience *activity* which was made possible in the case of radio by the audio-cassette recorder and in the case of television by such new devices as the remote controller, teletext and above all the VCR. What the more important of these technologies allowed the viewer and listener to do was to opt out of live broadcasting, to use their receivers for messages other than those devised for them by the broadcasters.

In the present decade another kind of audience activity is developing which has been presaged by the arrival of cable television: the viewer will be able not only to opt out of broadcast messages but to modify, respond to, even initiate them *within the same medium*. In other words, broadcasting will become a two-way or *interactive* medium which means, as we have seen, a *merging* of TV with such other media as the telephone and the computer. It also means a considerable modification of what we have traditionally understood by the term 'broadcasting' and thus makes the 1990s a neat point at which to bring this history to a close.

In the present section we shall consider what seem to be the most significant technological developments that have occurred, or will occur, during this decade – digitization and media integration – and explore their implications. Sometimes we shall make firm predictions, but at least as often we shall content ourselves with a judicious, or perhaps merely cowardly, balancing of possibilities. There will be important implications of a social, political and institutional nature which we shall be careful to point out, but as befits a book of this nature we shall concentrate on the medium of broadcasting itself, and especially television – the implications for its content, the way in which it will be presented and structured, and thus for the experience of the viewers.

The technology we must consider first is that of *digital* broadcasting, whose arrival in Britain is imminent. Hitherto, television has been based on *analogue* technology: frequencies were allocated to individual broadcasters, with one frequency needed for each channel. Digital technology, which can be used by satellite, cable or traditional broadcasters, reduces transmissions to a stream of data expressed as a series of ones and zeros and results in a much more efficient use of scarce spectrum space: a single frequency will be able to accommodate several channels, each offering high quality sound and vision.

Presently it seems as if the free-to-air BBC and ITV terrestrial channels will be guaranteed access to the digital system, but many of the other channels will be funded either by subscription or pay per view. Since the satellite and cable broadcasters are especially eager to digitize (we noted in the last chapter that BSkyB aims to launch 200 digital channels in late 1997), there could be anything from 400 to 1,000 TV channels in a few years' time, with a similar expansion occurring in radio. To receive digital transmissions the viewer will need either to buy a set-top converter, which will probably cost about £200 at today's prices, or a new television set.

Digitization raises a number of large issues, but we will begin by considering its impact on audience behaviour. It will surely increase the global tendency of broadcasting, both that which is aimed at an international audience and that which may be aimed only at a national audience but will be receivable elsewhere. Apart from programming whose appeal transcends linguistic differences, such as sport and rock music, the world domination of the English language means that the French, Russians, etc. are more likely to watch our broadcasts than we theirs. However there will probably be considerable cross-national viewing between Britain, Canada and the United States, with the bulk of the output originating, as at present, from the latter. Yet the position of English as the world language of broadcasting will last only as long as the economic and political pre-eminence of the United States, and in the distant future Chinese may replace it.

Digitization is also likely to lead to an increased use of the remote controller, for in order to avoid missing out on something good many viewers will go 'surfing' – sample the output of each channel. This potential restlessness may even mean that fewer viewers will be willing to watch whole programmes and could lead to their partial replacement by 'sequences', a tendency we shall explore later.

If there are scores of channels through which the viewer may browse with ease, a number of them offering content that is duplicated or triplicated elsewhere, their individual significance is bound to be diminished. Many viewers who are not immediately transfixed by what one channel has to offer will hop to another. Digitization may also mean an increase in the use of television as a secondary medium, for it is not inconceivable that certain channels will offer nothing but 'moving wallpaper' – landscapes or underwater scenes rather like the interludes which punctuated programmes in the early days of BBC television, and whose aim will be to occupy the idle eyes of customers in bars, shopping centres and airport lounges. (In passing, we might note how even in today's world the visual media are bursting their traditional bounds: in post offices and doctors' waiting rooms our attention is solicited by video monitors and TV sets, presumably in the belief that wherever we go we must have something to gaze at.)

Hence digitization, following upon our ability to put receivers to uses other than live television or radio, means that broadcasting will have to take itself less seriously in the future and will become in certain respects less influential. We will no doubt continue to watch a great deal of TV and listen to a fair amount of radio, but their effects will be diffuse and attenuated. In such circumstances talk of 'public service obligations' seems at best quixotic and at worst pompous.

As is clear from what has already been said, and *pace* the cynics who feel that this point was reached in 1955, digitization will probably mark the first time in broadcasting that there will be more channels available than content to fill them. It will certainly create a huge demand for the latter, one which has already been growing over the last twenty-five years.

Presently the cable operators seem to be more interested in carriage than content, despite needing to find programme sources other than BSkyB; and BT, though keen to provide wired television and video on demand, is equally keen to remain a mere carrier and find others to provide its programming. But the likeliest consequence of digitization will be a scramble among broadcasting *carriers* – whether satellite, cable or the traditional operators – to secure distribution rights to the best sources of *content*: indeed they will probably seek to own them outright. The reason Rupert Murdoch acquired Twentieth Century Fox was to feed the growing needs of his satellite channels, and in the near future film and TV production companies like Disney could well become targets for one or other of the big carriers.

But because broadcasting will be delivered by cable and phone lines as well as in the traditional atmospheric way; and because, as we shall see, the first two systems will permit an interactive element, *new* carriers are likely to emerge – telecoms operators, TV rental companies, computer manufacturers – and, conceivably, new producers of broadcastable *content* such as book publishers.

But whether or not carriers and distributors become integrated with producers, the key issue in broadcasting will be who owns or controls access to the digital channels. Perhaps the least worst gatekeeper would be the government, but we have seen how the development of global broadcasting is even now eroding the power of individual states. How successfully would it be able to regulate content much of which emanates from overseas, enforce balance and objectivity in the coverage of the news, prevent a monopoly ownership of certain kinds of programmes, impose limits on company holdings or market share? It is likelier that *de facto* control will be in the hands of the big commercial operators such as BSkyB, which already holds the lead in conditional access technology. The major broadcasters can thus be expected to share the most popular and lucrative channels among themselves.

Yet because of its dawning abundance one can still take a sanguine view of broadcasting's future. Channels will be so numerous that as in press and magazine publishing, where one or two large companies monopolize the most popular titles, there could still be room for a shoal of independent operators at the margins. Moreover, the proliferation of channels may trigger further developments in access technology which make gatekeeping virtually impossible: the power of the state or of the big commercial operators to determine what we watch would then be reduced.

Yet we need to consider this technology in terms of production as well as consumption, for it may even bring about an easier access to broadcasting in the way that easy access to information and data has been brought about by the internet. If broadcasting and informatics remain distinguishable (an assumption we can make with less and less confidence), we could see the redress of an imbalance in the former which has existed for some time.

For the last twenty years or so video camcorders have enabled 'ordinary people' to make their own TV programmes, yet with virtually no prospect of transmitting them. Henceforth the vast increase in channels could offset the otherwise global tendency of broadcasting by allowing some of those people to gain access to a mass, if modestly sized, audience – yet another instance of the democratizing effects of broadcasting. In other words, thanks to digitization, the technology of cheap distribution could at last catch up with the technology of cheap production, and we can be sure that from this naive 'do it yourself' broadcasting occasional programme ideas will bubble up which will be swiftly appropriated by the major operators.

However there is little doubt that the 'DIY' channels will command tiny audiences – that even in a system offering such a range of variety and choice the traditional networks and powerful satellite operators will continue to attract the majority, as they still do in the multichannelled United States. This is because viewers crave 'big production values': blockbuster movies, top sporting events, lavish music and comedy shows, all evincing high technical and artistic standards.

We can make two other firm predictions, both of them relating to broadcasting content. The first is that whatever the efforts of the big organizations to acquire the best new content that money can buy and viewers will pay for, one inevitable consequence of digitization will be an increase in the vast amount of *recycling* which already takes place.

For many viewers certain broadcasts have a value which transcends the ephemeral way in which they are experienced. Historically it was easy to prize sculptures, paintings, musical scores and works of literature because they existed in space. It was less easy to prize theatrical, musical or balletic *performances* in the same way because these things, which were the lifeblood of broadcasting, existed in time: but the problem was solved by the arrival of recording technology. (Indeed it is most probably recording technology which has underpinned the recent growth of academic interest in 'cultural studies', for broadcasting provides much of the material for such studies, and it is surely no coincidence that academic research into British television began just one year after the arrival of Ampex videotape.)

Not all recorded output is deemed valuable, of course, and as channels have increased both in number and in transmission hours much recycling has been the result of sheer pragmatism: but with the arrival of digitization the appetite for material will be unprecedented, and given the limits to human originality we can expect a huge growth in recycling.

It is worth reviewing the forms that recycling can take. First, broadcasting makes extensive use of *borrowings* and *adaptations*, which could be seen as recyclings from other media with which many of its audiences are also likely to be familiar. The most obvious examples of borrowing are television's screenings of cinema films and (more rarely nowadays) of theatrical plays. Adaptations involve some alteration of the original, as for example, in BBC television's celebrated dramatizations of Jane Austen's novels.

Rather more obvious examples of recycling are those innumerable *programme repeats* – second, third, etc. showings of what has originated within broadcasting itself. Sky Gold and Granada Sky are reminders that whole channels are now being dedicated to repeats, a trend which is bound to intensify. In fact Granada Sky's screening of old episodes of *Coronation Street* vividly illustrates the effrontery which distinguishes so much clever marketing, for viewers must be prepared to pay for material which is not merely old but which was first seen free of charge.

Remakes, updated versions of old broadcasting artefacts, constitute a third form of recycling. Recently viewers were able to watch the comedian Paul Merton's not very successful attempt to revive some Galton and Simpson scripts which had first been performed by Tony Hancock. Earlier in the decade viewers were also offered remakes of the 1960s classic series, *Maigret* and *Dr Finlay's Casebook*, themselves adaptations of the literary endeavours of Georges Simenon and A. J. Cronin respectively.

But a big increase in recycling is not the only prediction we can confidently make about broadcasting. The audiences which the traditional networks and major satellite channels will manage to retain will be large in relation to those captured by their numerous and smaller rivals; but as channels increase in number they will spread more and more thinly. Hence digitization will further weaken, probably destroy altogether, the old Reithian case for public service broadcasting which, we will recall, rested largely on the scarcity of the medium. I suggested in the last chapter that with the prospect of digital TV even the 30 per cent audience share which Nicholas Garnham (1994) felt would be enough to justify the BBC's licence fee now begins to seem highly optimistic.

Consequently, even if the traditional networks continue to offer some mixture of programming it will not be of public service dimensions but more like 'narrowcast populist': varied only within the limits of popular taste. TV will have to become consumer- instead of producer-driven: viewers must be given what *they* want rather than what broadcasters choose to give them. However, that newer notion of public service which consists in meeting the needs of minorities should thrive because there will be so many channels that the most highbrow or recherché tastes could be catered for – if not by the BBC or Channel 4 then by others.

Hence digitization and the growth of demand-led broadcasting mean that the second thing we can predict is an increase in the 'theming' or *formatting* of channels – something which, we noted, began with satellite and cable TV in the 1980s. Formats give you what you want at any time you want it. An important part of their aim is to preclude the viewer's use of both the remote controller and the VCR by declaring in effect: 'No need to switch channels in search of your favourite kind of programme; no need to pre-record it or to get a cassette of your favourite movie: it, or its type, is always on air – twenty-four hours a day'.

Formats have a certain flexibility: while some are dedicated to a single kind of output, such as MTV, others may offer a variety of programmes, but one which is unified within a single theme. 'Gold' channels, for example, may provide comedies, dramas, quiz games and so on, but within some such implicit theme as 'nostalgia' or 'classic TV'. The names of satellite and cable channels like Sky Movies, Screensport, MTV, the Comedy Channel, the Arts Channel, the Learning Channel and the Parliamentary Channel evoke the range of interests that format television has already catered for; but digitization will hugely extend it, with several hundred channels offering everything from sailing to soft porn and thus rendering broadcasting very similar to a large store like W. H. Smith, where the consumer can find a galaxy of publications ranging from daily newspapers and popular journals to special interest magazines.

Much depends on the content carried by the various TV formats, but since it will be substantially unvarying within a particular channel we can expect to see some replacement of self-contained programmes with the more indeterminate 'sequences' that already typify format radio. In any case, the *segment* or 'bite' of which so much broadcasting content is composed – the interview, rock video, commercial break, comic sketch, brief report, feature or whatever – will become the salient or significant feature.

Nevertheless, segmentation on television has a slightly different rationale from that of radio. Radio is a secondary or background medium, and segments allow the listener to 'enter' or 'leave' its content without feeling that she has missed or will miss anything of importance. Segmentation has a similar function on those television channels which can also be treated in a secondary or inter-mittent way, such as MTV.

But whereas *intermittence* is the key to segmentation on the radio, the main aim of the latter on television is not only to attract viewers at all times but – because TV is mostly a primary medium – to *hold* them, whether they have just switched on for the first time, or have changed channels, or are merely browsing. In effect, however, there is little difference, for on television as on radio segmentation affords continuous accessibility while also seeking to retain its existing audience by providing a constant change of stimulus. We might sum up its function by saying that it seeks to preclude the 'horizontal' desultoriness of the viewer – her inclination to keep browsing among all the channels available to her – by offering 'vertical' desultoriness: a constant change of stimulus within a single channel. But in so doing it strengthens that tendency to treat complex matters in a fitful, superficial way which, we argued in an earlier chapter, seems already inherent in the television medium.

We must not exaggerate this aspect of viewing behaviour or the measures which TV channels take to counter it. Not all viewers are compulsive channel switchers, nor is all format television obviously segmented: movies, for instance, and some sport, require sustained attention. But since the television set, with its myriad broadcasting channels and accompanying video facility, is the main if not the only cultural and intellectual source for so many, the often fragmentary nature of the experiences it offers is a matter for some concern. In one characteristically laden sentence the historian Eric Hobsbawm reviews some of the remarkable advantages that the modern media have brought, yet sounds a cautionary note:

> It is barely possible for someone who has been brought up in the age when electronic and mechanically generated music is the standard sound heard on live and recorded pop music, when any child can freeze frames, and repeat a sound or visual passage as once only textual passages could be re-read, when theatrical illusion is as nothing to what technology can do in television commercials, including telling a dramatic narrative in thirty seconds, to recapture simple linearity or sequentiality of perception in the days before modern high-tech made it possible to move within seconds through the full range of available television channels.
>
> (1994: 502)

What does television do for patience, concentration, the ability to construct meaning through sustained narrative or argument? With the help of the remote controller, interactivity can simply mean hyperactivity and suggests that old-fashioned passive viewing may have its virtues after all.

Because multichannel format broadcasting as well as video will soon provide us with what we want whenever we want it, we can see a further weakening of the link between entertainment and cultural consumption on the one hand and what we might term 'the sense of occasion' on the other: a weakening which has been taking place over several centuries. Historically, the business of being entertained or culturally edified has been more or less separate from the banalities of existence.

From the brief glance at the evolution of the media which we allowed ourselves in Part I we can see how the loss of occasion began with print, because print enabled the consumer to replace attendance at a poetic recitation or dramatic performance in a public space and at a certain time with the activity of reading in her own space and time. But, especially important in the case of drama, the temporal elements – sound and moving vision – were lost in the substitution.

With broadcasting the sense of occasion was further eroded because many more of the original elements of the event could be transposed to the consumer's own space: first sound could be conveyed on the radio, then both sound and moving vision on television. Finally, since the 1980s television has, thanks to formatting, emulated video in enabling the consumer to view what she wants *in her own time* – an important effect of which is to 'banalize' entertainment, to assimilate it more closely than ever before to the daily routines of the individual.

In a previous chapter we hinted that from the early 1970s, when the restriction on broadcasting hours was lifted, television moved nearer to the rhythms of ordinary life: cookery, hobbies and education were covered during the day, children's programmes were broadcast at teatime, general entertainment was provided in the evening. What TV was doing, of course, was reflecting the fact that the consumption of certain cultural artefacts, or the attendance at certain cultural events, has traditionally been associated with particular times of the day: we speak of a film or theatre 'matinée', for instance.

However format TV takes this assimilation even further by affording much greater autonomy to the individual viewer; for she might now, if she prefers, watch a Humphrey Bogart film on Sky Movies or a cycle race on Eurosport not in the afternoon or evening but over breakfast. Nor need this preference be merely eccentric: the lifestyle of the modern individual may diverge from the traditional pattern either because she has more free time through being un-employed or because the recent revolution in the nature of employment (now often home-based and occurring at flexible and irregular hours) has resulted in unusual and irregular periods of leisure.

What has made the continuous and specialized nature of modern television so much easier to provide is, of course, the increasingly global conduct of broadcasting: we can watch live cycle racing over breakfast because it is being transmitted in the early evening from Australia. Yet the experience can be disorientating. Before broadcasting became global we were used to pre-recorded elements within it which were of such high quality that we could not tell them from live transmissions. Now, because we might be sitting in broad daylight watching an event which is evidently taking place in darkness, or vice versa, live transmissions often look as if they are recordings. Hence as O'Sullivan, Dutton and Rayner acutely point out:

> In the 'global village' differences of time and space are eroded as the result of the 'instantaneous' nature of modern communications. We are all synchronised into a randomised 'world time' and to a 'cocktail' of programme content – places, events, personalities, narratives, aesthetic values. We have been dislocated and resynchronised into a new kind of simulated and 'hyperspace' world.
>
> (1994: 283)

In one respect, then, we can make television subserve our individual needs and whims: in another it lures us into a free-floating world of its own, untrammelled by the normal laws of time and space.

The increasing subjugation of broadcasting to the individual lifestyles of its audience in one sense devalues the culture and entertainment that it offers. We often speak of television not so much as a source of entertainment in itself but as a poor alternative to 'real' entertainment ('I think I'll just stay in and watch the telly tonight'), and this despite the fact that what it offers us – its scripted and unscripted discourse, its aesthetic experiences, its visual wonders, its technical and production standards, the calibre of its performers, its ability to reproduce artefacts which originated in other media, including the entire oeuvre of the cinema – is of a magnitude, range and quality unimaginable to previous generations.

Perversely, what we consider as 'real' entertainment is often bound up with a sense of occasion, something we have to make an effort to *get to* rather than that which we can consume in our own space at any time. This casual, almost contemptuous attitude to broadcasting content again makes talk of 'public service obligations' seem a trifle antiquated and self-important.

But if digitization means that the cultural content of television will be treated even more 'functionally' than before – as a casual and basic resource rather like the gas or water supply – this may encourage development of the medium's more *obviously* functional possibilities. Traffic, travel and weather formats already exist on satellite and cable, as well as the home shopping channel, QVC, which stands for Quality, Value and Convenience.

What may further encourage conventional TV broadcasting to develop its more functional or utilitarian side is a possibility, which we shall explore shortly, that its entertainment role may be cut back by the introduction of interactive channels which will allow viewers to select their own videos from a vast and varied programme library.

Mention of video and interactivity is an important reminder that not everything we can see on our TV screens, or hear on our radio sets, is broadcasting in the conventional sense – and this is a history of broadcasting. Several people watching a home video of a wedding or an off-air or commercial recording of a feature film would not be a *mass* audience, nor are they watching in 'real' time. They are not part of that live context of broadcasting which means that the audience receive messages, whether live or pre-recorded in themselves, at the moment they are sent.

Yet broadcasting's boundaries are growing ever hazier. Let us restate our definition of it. It is the live or instantaneous transmission, over distances, of messages in the form of moving pictures and sound, or of sound alone, to a multitude (albeit atomized) of receivers. These messages may, however, be in pre-recorded form, as in television broadcasts of Hollywood movies or of 'canned' programmes. Live sound and moving pictures, as distinct from text and fixed images, rule out instantaneous communications from a sender to a multitude of receivers on the internet, but probably only for a short time. As a corollary of our definition we might say that broadcasting has inevitably been an activity initiated by the broadcaster or sender, who usually gives notice in some such listings magazine as the *Radio Times* of the messages that will be broadcast.

However, whereas until now the audience was interactive only in the sense that by using the remote controller or channel change button it could discriminate among them, or by using the VCR opt out of them altogether in order to watch something else, we have already noted that cable will soon allow us to *respond* to broadcast messages by sending a signal back to the broadcaster; to *modify* them by choosing our own camera angles; and even to *initiate* them by ordering our own programmes.

One kind of interactivity which is almost with us is a digital distribution and display system (DDDS) based on computer technology. DDDS enables the viewer to select from and manipulate broadcast output by sending messages back to the source. In a live transmission of a soccer match, for instance, the viewer may not wish to take the sequence of pictures chosen for her by the producer. Instead she can select her own camera angles from a range offered to her in windows at the foot of the screen, and make use of her own freeze, slow-motion and replay facilities.

Videotron has already provided a modified version of this service involving instant replays and time-lag transmissions, but it is not quite as sophisticated as it seems because it makes use of extra channels. But interactive TV will shortly allow viewers not only to modify output but to register their responses to it, most pertinently in the home shopping channels.

We noted that the first of these, QVC, is already in business. Since October 1993 it has been offering on both satellite and cable what it describes as '24-hour shopping from a product showcase', but whereas its viewers presently place their orders over the telephone, cable viewers will soon be able to use the cable itself by means of a keypad. It is quite likely, too, that QVC or some similar channel will offer virtual shopping. The viewer will be able to use the keypad to browse at leisure among the images of a shopping mall, look at the shelves, order goods, and have them home delivered – the domestication of yet another activity, shopping, which has hitherto been public and communal.

Finally viewers via cable and perhaps even ordinary phone lines may soon be able to order programmes from broadcasters by a process called near video-on-demand (NVOD) which has recently undergone trials in Cambridge, Colchester and Ipswich. The time lapse between ordering and screening would be no more than a few minutes, and so NVOD could well mean a reduction in the number of video rental shops, or even their extinction, especially as the catalogue from which viewers could select would extend beyond conventional cinema feature films to TV programmes of every kind. (We might recall at this point that the question of who owns the rights to all this material – movies, documentaries, TV golden oldies, rock videos, and so on – will be a huge one, involving millions of pounds.)

Of the 200 digital channels that BSkyB will launch in Autumn 1997 it is expected that between sixty and a hundred will be used to launch films on near demand, involving a waiting time of no longer than fifteen minutes. It remains to be seen whether cable subscribers will be able to use the same medium to place their orders: DBS subscribers will presumably order by telephone. There is little doubt that many of the terrestrial digital channels will also be dedicated to NVOD, a phenomenon which will result in an even further empowerment of the broadcasting audience.

As we have seen, these forms of interactivity mean a merging of 'television' in its traditional sense with other media, computers and telephones, which have always been interactive: it thus marks the beginning of the transformation of broadcasting pure and simple into 'multimedia'. NVOD would be broadcasting in the traditional sense that it involves a live transmission to a multitude of receivers, yet not in the sense that it transmits different if simultaneous messages to different receivers, many of which have been initiated by the latter. Such transmissions will thus resemble printed texts in being consumed at any time the receiver chooses. They are an opt-out from conventional broadcasts and also, in a sense, two-way.

What, then, will broadcasting be like in the future? Two main possibilities suggest themselves. The first is that the merging of certain media, which at the institutional level could lead to the BBC delivering programmes down telephone lines or BT becoming a conventional broadcaster, might culminate in a single piece of consumer hardware which would act as TV set, radio, computer and telephone (and probably also as a fax machine, CD player, VCR and several other things besides).

Since this multimedia apparatus would serve the purposes of work as well as leisure, it is conceivable, as we hinted above, that the functional or utilitarian role of broadcasting could increase relative to its entertainment role. We have already seen how multichannel and formatted television, as well as video and other forms of interactive technology, have somewhat banalized culture and entertainment. From this, it seems but a small step to television as an instrument of the world's work: weather, traffic and travel channels, educational channels, home shopping channels, business channels, all operating with low budgets and relatively small audiences.

But another possibility is that social and professional pressures could counter technological ones and that the media remain separated into those which mainly serve the sphere of entertainment, and those, such as computers, phones and fax machines, that have important roles in the world of work. Radio and TV would fall into the first category because they are instruments of broadcasting, which despite having informative, educational and utilitarian roles – roles we suggested the 'banalizing' effects of these media may help to extend – is still overwhelmingly associated with leisure and recreation, and likely to remain so in the future. Moreover, even though, as we noted, radio and TV sets can serve uses other than broadcasting in its traditional sense, most of these are also in the sphere of entertainment.

Though most broadcasting will continue to be devoted to culture and entertainment and radio and TV sets perhaps remain physically separate from computers and telephones, the interactive facility they have borrowed from informatics and telecoms will become even more important. We will go on using our television for home shopping and to browse through teletext, though we are just as likely to do these things on our computer. But we will also use it to select our camera angles in a soccer match or to re-run a spectacular goal; we will use it to vote for the comedian we thought was funniest in the talent show; and eventually we will use it to order the programme of our choice.

Whether radio and television sets remain separate pieces of equipment or become part of a single multimedia entity, this latter function may well mark broadcasting's most momentous development; for NVOD, whether or not we define it as broadcasting, could take over a substantial part of what has been broadcasting's traditional domain. The films, sitcoms, soaps, variety shows, travelogues, documentaries, features, quiz games and so on, which television now provides within its daily pre-published schedules might simply be stored in a vast library where they will wait to be summoned by the individual viewer. If that is so, what would television broadcasting in its traditional one-way sense be left to provide?

It would most likely specialize in *new* material. This would include first screenings of programmes that are not yet available through NVOD and/or trailers for programmes which can be accessed *only* through NVOD. But even more important would be *topical* content, the kind of material which is broadcast in 'real time' or which quickly loses its value if recorded: news, current affairs and sport. Thus television would revert to its earliest days when hardly any of its content was pre-recorded, and usefully remind us that whatever its other possibilities, as a medium of broadcasting it is essentially *live*.

The possibility is an interesting one, but who can really tell? Yet in harking back to the medium's infancy it creates a pleasing circularity which does, at least, bring our history to a neat conclusion.

Sources/further reading

Many of the speculations and predictions in this section are merely my own and will doubtless embarrass me in the years to come. However some of them are influenced by the bracing and audacious prophecies of McRae (1996).

On the forthcoming launch of digital television and some of its implications see Lister (1995), and on digital satellite broadcasting Horsman (1996c) is useful.

My discussion of sequences and segmentation owes a large debt to Williams (1974) and Ellis (1982), even though the three of us discuss these phenomena in slightly differing ways.

A discussion of the effect of modern television on human perceptions is in Hobsbawm (1994), while the hyperspace world created by modern global broadcasting is neatly evoked in O'Sullivan, Dutton and Rayner (1994).

The digital distribution and display system which can be built into modern interactive television is described in Kipper (1989) and Videotron's modified use of it is outlined in Blackall (1995).

For details of the near video-on-demand trials and some of their implications, see Blackall and Wheelwright (1995).

Bibliography

Alvarado, M., Gutch, R. and Wollen, T. (1987) *Learning the Media*, London: Macmillan Education.

Ang, I. (1985) *Watching Dallas: Soap Opera and the Melodramatic Imagination*, London: Methuen.

Annan Committee, The (1977) *Report of the Committee on the Future of Broadcasting, 1977*, Cmnd 6753.

Appleyard, B. (1995a) 'An unjustified death on the box', *Independent*, 15 March.

—— (1995b) 'Virtual reality of TV justice', *Independent*, 4 October.

Armes, R. (1988) *On Video*, London: Routledge.

Bakewell, J. and Garnham, N. (1970) *The New Priesthood: British Television Today*, Harmondsworth: Allen Lane/The Penguin Press.

Barnard, S. (1989) *On the Radio: Music Radio in Britain*, Milton Keynes: Open University Press.

Barnouw, E. (1966) *A Tower in Babel: A History of Broadcasting in the United States to 1933*, New York: Oxford University Press.

—— (1977) *Tube of Plenty: The Evolution of American Television*, New York: Oxford University Press.

Baron, M. (1975) *Independent Radio*, Lavenham: Dalton.

Bates, A. (1984) *Broadcasting in Education: An Evaluation*, London: Constable.

BBC (1967) *Handbook 1968*, London: British Broadcasting Corporation.

—— (1969a) *Broadcasting in the Seventies*, London: British Broadcasting Corporation.

—— (1969b) *Handbook 1970*, London: British Broadcasting Corporation.

Bell, E. (1997) 'Panic station as Channel 4 faces an ungraded future', *Observer*, 2 February.

Beveridge Committee, The (1951) *Report of the Broadcasting Committee, 1949*, Cmd 8116.

Black, P. (1972a) *The Biggest Aspidistra in the World*, London: British Broadcasting Corporation.

—— (1972b) *The Mirror in the Corner*, London: Hutchinson.

Blackall, L. (1995) 'Testing time for cable's visionaries', *Independent*, 8 May.

Blackall, L. and Wheelwright, G. (1995) 'The shopping mall in your sitting room . . . with a video library thrown in', *Independent*, 30 January.

Booker, C. (1970) *The Neophiliacs*, London: Fontana Books.

Bowen, D. (1994) 'After the media earthquake', *Independent*, 6 March.

Boyle, A. (1972) *Only the Wind Will Listen*, London: Hutchinson.

Bridson, D. (1971) *Prospero and Ariel*, London: Gollancz.

Briggs, A. (1961) *The History of Broadcasting in the United Kingdom: Volume I – The Birth of Broadcasting*, London: Oxford University Press.

—— (1965) *The History of Broadcasting in the United Kingdom: Volume II – The Golden Age of Wireless*, London: Oxford University Press.

—— (1970) *The History of Broadcasting in the United Kingdom: Volume III – The War of Words*, London: Oxford University Press.

—— (1979) *The History of Broadcasting in the United Kingdom: Volume IV – Sound and Vision*, Oxford: Oxford University Press.

—— (1985) *The BBC: The First Fifty Years*, Oxford: Oxford University Press.

—— (1995) *The History of Broadcasting in the United Kingdom: Volume V – Competition*, Oxford: Oxford University Press.

Briggs, S. (1981) *Those Radio Times*, London: Weidenfeld and Nicolson.

Brown, M. (1995) 'Warning: your wireless is exploding', *Independent*, 19 January.

Brunsdon, C. and Morley, D. (1978) *Everyday Television: 'Nationwide'*, London: BFI Television Monograph, 10.

Buckingham, D. (1996) '*EastEnders*: creating the audience' in Marris, P. and Thornham, S. (eds) *Media Studies: a Reader*, Edinburgh: Edinburgh University Press.

Bulkley, K. (1992) 'Telephone support for infant cable', *Independent*, 30 June.

Burns, T. (1977) *The BBC: Public Institution and Private World*, London: Macmillan.

Buscombe, E. (1991) 'All bark and no bite: the film industry's response to television' in Corner, J. (ed.) *Popular Television in Britain*, London: BFI Publishing.

Cardiff, D. (1980) 'The serious and the popular: aspects of the evolution of style in the radio talk, 1928–39', *Media, Culture and Society*, 2.

—— (1988) 'Mass middlebrow laughter: the origins of BBC comedy', *Media, Culture and Society*, 10.

Cardiff, D. and Scannell, P. (1981) 'Radio in World War II', *Open University*, U203 Popular Culture, Block 3, Unit 8.

Carpenter, H. (1996) *The Envy of the World: Fifty Years of the BBC Third Programme and Radio 3*, London: Weidenfeld and Nicolson.

Caughie, J. (1991) 'Before the golden age: early television drama' in Corner, J. (ed.) *Popular Television in Britain*, London: BFI Publishing.

Chapman, R. (1992) *Selling the Sixties: The Pirates and Pop Music Radio*, London: Routledge.

Cicutti, N. (1995) 'Market frenzy after TV Bill', *Independent*, 16 December.

Corner, J. (1991) 'General Introduction: television and British society in the 1950s' in Corner, J. (ed.) *Popular Television in Britain*, London: BFI Publishing.

—— (1995) *Television Form and Public Address*, London: Edward Arnold.

Corner, J., Harvey, S. and Lury, K. (1994) 'Culture, quality and choice: the re-regulation of TV 1989–91' in Hood, S. (ed.) *Behind the Screens: The Structure of British Television in the Nineties*, London: Lawrence and Wishart.

Crawford Committee, The (1926) *Report of the Broadcasting Committee, 1925*, Cmd 2599.

Crisell, A. (1986) *Understanding Radio*, London: Methuen.

—— (1991) 'Filth, sedition and blasphemy: the rise and fall of television satire' in Corner, J. (ed.) *Popular Television in Britain*, London: BFI Publishing.

—— (1994) *Understanding Radio*, London: Routledge, 2nd edn.

Cumberbatch, G. and Howitt, D. (1989) *A Measure of Uncertainty: The Effects of the Mass Media*, London: John Libbey.

Curran, J., Smith, A. and Wingate, P. (eds) (1987) *Impacts and Influences: Essays on Media Power in the Twentieth Century*, London: Methuen.

Curran, J. and Seaton, J. (1991) *Power Without Responsibility*, London: Routledge, 4th edn.

Davis, A. (1976) *Television: Here is the News*, London: Independent Television Books.

Day-Lewis, S. (1992) *TV Heaven: A Review of British Television from the 1930s to the 1990s*, London: Channel Four Television.

Donovan, P. (1992) *The Radio Companion*, London: Grafton.

Drakakis, J. (ed.) (1981) *British Radio Drama*, Cambridge: Cambridge University Press.

Dyer, R. (1973) *Light Entertainment*, London: BFI Monograph, 2.

Ellis, J. (1982) *Visible Fictions*, London: Routledge and Kegan Paul.

Fink, H. (1981) 'The sponsor's v. the nation's choice: North American radio drama' in Lewis, P. (ed.) *Radio Drama*, London: Longman.

Fiske, J. (1987) *Television Culture*, London: Methuen.

Fornatale, P. and Mills, J. (1980) *Radio in the Television Age*, Woodstock, NY: The Overlook Press.

Frith, S. (1983) 'The pleasures of the hearth: the making of BBC light entertainment' in Donald, J. (ed.) *Formations of Pleasure*, London: Routledge and Kegan Paul.

Frye, N. (1971) *Anatomy of Criticism*, Princeton: Princeton University Press.

Gable, J. (1980) *The Tuppenny Punch and Judy Show*, Harmondsworth: Michael Joseph.

Garnham, N. (1994) 'The broadcasting market and the future of the BBC', *Political Quarterly*, 65.

Geraghty, C. (1996) 'The continuous serial: a definition' in Marris, P. and Thornham, S. (eds) *Media Studies: A Reader*, Edinburgh: Edinburgh University Press.

Gielgud, V. (1957) *British Radio Drama, 1922–1956*, London: Harrap.

Gifford, D. (1985) *The Golden Age of Radio*, London: Batsford.

Gillard, F. (1964) *Sound Radio in the Television Age*, BBC Lunch-time Lectures, 2nd series, no. 6.

Goddard, P. (1991) '"Hancock's Half Hour": a watershed in British television comedy' in Corner, J. (ed.) *Popular Television in Britain*, London: BFI Publishing.

Goldhamer, H. (1971) 'The social effects of communication technology' in Schramm, W. and Roberts, D. (eds) *The Process and Effects of Mass Communication*, Urbana, Ill: University of Illinois Press, revised edn.

Goldie, G. (1977) *Facing the Nation: Television and Politics, 1936–1976*, London: The Bodley Head.

Golding, P. (1974) *The Mass Media*, London: Longman.

Golding, P., Murdock, G. and Schlesinger, P. (1986) *Communicating Politics: Mass Communications and the Political Process*, Leicester: Leicester University Press.

Goodfriend, A. (1988) 'Satellite broadcasting in the UK' in Negrine, R. (ed.) *Satellite Broadcasting: The Politics and Implications of the New Media*, London: Routledge.

Gorham, M. (1952) *Broadcasting and Television since 1900*, London: Andrew Dakers Ltd.

Harris, P. (1970) *When Pirates Ruled the Waves*, London and Aberdeen: Impulse Books, 4th edn.

Harvey, S. (1994) 'Channel 4 television: from Annan to Grade' in Hood, S. (ed.) *Behind the Screens: The Structure of British Television in the Nineties*, London: Lawrence and Wishart.

Harvey, S. and Robins, K. (1994) 'Voices and places: the BBC and regional policy', *Political Quarterly*, 65.

Hill, J. (1991) 'Television and pop: the case of the 1950s' in Corner, J. (ed.) *Popular Television in Britain*, London: BFI Publishing.

Hilton, J. (1938) *This and That*, London: George Allen and Unwin.

Hobsbawm, E. (1994) *Age of Extremes: The Short Twentieth Century*, Harmondsworth: Michael Joseph.

Hobson, D. (1982) *Crossroads: The Drama of a Soap Opera*, London: Methuen.

Hood, S. (1975) *Radio and Television*, Newton Abbot: David and Charles.

—— (1980) *On Television*, London: Pluto Press, 2nd edn.

Hood, S. and O'Leary, G. (1990) *Questions of Broadcasting*, London: Methuen.

Horsman, M. (1995a) 'Three lock horns in battle of the TV titans', *Independent*, 8 May.

—— (1995b) 'The battle of Britain's favourite TV channel', *Independent*, 4 July.

—— (1996a) 'On the media', *Independent*, 6 February.

—— (1996b) 'On radio advertising's boom', *Independent*, 16 April.

—— (1996c) 'Sky plans 200 digital channels', *Independent*, 8 May.

—— (1996d) 'BBC plugs into new age for television', *Independent*, 10 May.

—— (1996e) 'BBC plans eight pay channels', *Independent*, 28 September.

Hughes, P. (1990) 'Today's television, tomorrow's world' in Goodwin, A. and Whannel, G. (eds) *Understanding Television*, London: Routledge.

Hughes, R. (1995) 'Who wants to watch it anyway?', *Television*, 32.

Isaacs, J. (1989) *Storm Over Four: A Personal Account*, London: Weidenfeld and Nicolson.

Kermode, F. (1967) *The Sense of an Ending*, New York: Oxford University Press.

Kerr, P. (1990) 'F for Fake? Friction over faction' in Goodwin, A. and Whannel, G. (eds) *Understanding Television*, London: Routledge.

Kipper, P. (1989) 'Television's future is interactive', *Feedback*, 30.

Laing, S. (1991) 'Banging in some reality: the original "*Z Cars*"' in Corner, J. (ed.) *Popular Television in Britain*, London: BFI Publishing.

Lambert, S. (1982) *Channel Four: Television with a Difference?*, London: BFI Publishing.

Levin, B. (1972) *The Pendulum Years: Britain and the Sixties*, London: Pan Books.

Lewis, J. (1990) 'Are you receiving me?' in Goodwin, A. and Whannel, G. (eds) *Understanding Television*, London: Routledge.

Lewis, P. (1981) 'Radio drama and English literature' in Lewis, P. (ed.) *Radio Drama*, London: Longman.

Lewis, P. M. and Booth, J. (1989) *The Invisible Medium: Public, Commercial and Community Radio*, London: Macmillan.

Lister, D. (1995) 'Digital launch heralds TV explosion', *Independent*, 11 August.

Livingstone, S. and Lunt, P. (1994) *Talk on Television: Audience Participation and Public Debate*, London: Routledge.

MacCabe, C. and Stewart, O. (eds) (1986) *The BBC and Public Service Broadcasting*, Manchester: Manchester University Press.

MacDonald, M. (1995a) 'Sky's deal with Granada for the Rover's golden days', *Independent*, 14 December.

—— (1995b) 'Ministers plan to scrap ties on media control', *Independent*, 16 December.

McDonnell, J. (1991) *Public Service Broadcasting: A Reader*, London: Routledge.

MacKenzie, J. (1987) 'Propaganda and the BBC Empire Service, 1932–42' in Hawthorn, J. (ed.) *Propaganda, Persuasion and Polemic*, London: Edward Arnold.

McLuhan, M. (1962) *The Gutenberg Galaxy*, London: Routledge and Kegan Paul.

McNair, B. (1994) *News and Journalism in the UK*, London: Routledge.

McQuail, D. (1987) *Mass Communication Theory*, London: Sage Publications, 2nd edn.

McRae, H. (1996) 'Normal service will end shortly. (For good . . .)', *Independent*, 10 May.

Mansell, G. (1982) *Let Truth Be Told: 50 Years of BBC External Broadcasting*, London: Weidenfeld and Nicolson.

Media Week, 1985–1995 (1995), London: EMAP Media Limited.

Mepham, J. (1990) 'The ethics of quality in television' in Mulgan, G. (ed.) *The Question of Quality*, London: BFI Publishing.

Mercer, D. (ed.) (1988) *Chronicle of the Twentieth Century*, London: Longman.

Moores, S. (1988) '"The box on the dresser": memories of early radio and everyday life', *Media, Culture and Society*, 10.

Morley, D. (1992) *Television, Audiences and Cultural Studies*, London: Routledge.

Mulgan, G. (1990) 'Television's holy grail: seven types of quality' in Mulgan, G. (ed.) *The Question of Quality*, London: BFI Publishing.

Nathan, D. (1971) *The Laughtermakers*, London: Peter Owen.

Negrine, R. (1985) 'Cable television in Britain' in Negrine, R. (ed.) *Cable Television and the Future of Broadcasting*, London and Sydney: Croom Helm.

—— (1988) 'Satellite broadcasting: an overview of the main issues' in Negrine, R. (ed.) *Satellite Broadcasting: The Politics and Implications of the New Media*, London: Routledge.

—— (1994) *Politics and the Mass Media in Britain*, London: Routledge, 2nd edn.

Ong, W. (1982) *Orality and Literacy*, London: Methuen.

O'Sullivan, T., Dutton, B. and Rayner, P. (1994) *Studying the Media: An Introduction*, London: Edward Arnold.

Parker, D. (1977) *Radio: The Great Years*, Newton Abbot: David and Charles.

Paulu, B. (1956) *British Broadcasting: Radio and Television in the United Kingdom*, Minneapolis: University of Minnesota Press.

—— (1961) *British Broadcasting in Transition*, Minneapolis: University of Minnesota Press.

—— (1981) *Television and Radio in the United Kingdom*, London: Macmillan.

Peacock Committee, The (1986) *Report of the Committee on Financing the BBC, 1986*, Cmnd 9824.

Pegg, M. (1983) *Broadcasting and Society, 1918–1939*, London: Croom Helm.

Philo, G. (1990) *Seeing and Believing: The Influence of Television*, London: Routledge.

Pickering, M. (1994) 'Race, gender and broadcast comedy: the case of the BBC's *Kentucky Minstrels*', *European Journal of Communication*, 9.

—— (1996) 'The BBC's *Kentucky Minstrels*, 1933–1950: blackface entertainment on British radio', *Historical Journal of Film, Radio and Television*, 16.

Pilkington Committee, The (1962), *Report of the Committee on Broadcasting, 1960*, Cmnd 1753.

Plomley, R. (1980) *Days Seemed Longer*, London: Eyre Methuen.

Postman, N. (1986) *Amusing Ourselves to Death*, London: Heinemann.

Potter, J. (1989) *Independent Television in Britain: Volume III – Politics and Control, 1968–80*, London: Macmillan.

—— (1990) *Independent Television in Britain: Volume IV – Companies and Programmes, 1968–80*, London: Macmillan.

Reith, J. (1924) *Broadcast Over Britain*, London: Hodder & Stoughton.

—— (1949) *Into the Wind*, London: Hodder & Stoughton.

Rowland, R. (1982) 'Video education' in Wenham, B. (ed.) *The Third Age of Broadcasting*, London: Faber and Faber.

Scannell, P. (1979) 'The social eye of television, 1946–1955', *Media, Culture and Society*, 1.

—— (1980) 'Broadcasting and the politics of unemployment, 1930–1935', *Media, Culture and Society*, 2.

—— (1981) 'Music for the multitude? The dilemmas of the BBC's music policy, 1923–1946', *Media, Culture and Society*, 3.

—— (1986) '"The stuff of radio": developments in radio features and documentaries before the war' in Corner, J. (ed.) *Documentary and the Mass Media*, London: Edward Arnold.

—— (1990) 'Public service broadcasting: the history of a concept' in Goodwin, A. and Whannel, G. (eds) *Understanding Television*, London: Routledge.

Scannell, P. and Cardiff, D. (1982) 'Serving the nation: public service broadcasting before the war' in Waites, B., Bennett, T. and Martin, G. (eds) *Popular Culture: Past and Present*, London: Croom Helm.

—— (1991) *A Social History of British Broadcasting: Volume I, 1922–1939: Serving the Nation*, Oxford: Basil Blackwell.

Schlesinger, P. (1978) *Putting 'Reality' Together*, London: Constable.

Scott, R. (1967) *Radio 1 and Radio 2*, BBC Lunch-time Lectures, 6th series, no. 1.

Selsdon Committee, The (1935) *Report of the Television Committee, 1935*, Cmd 4793.

Sendall, B. (1982) *Independent Television in Britain: Volume I – Origin and Foundation, 1946–1962*, London: Macmillan.

—— (1983) *Independent Television in Britain: Volume II – Expansion and Change, 1958–1968*, London: Macmillan.

Seymour-Ure, C. (1991) *The British Press and Broadcasting since 1945*, Oxford: Basil Blackwell.

—— (1996) *The British Press and Broadcasting since 1945*, Oxford: Basil Blackwell, 2nd edn.

Sherrin, N. (1983) *A Small Thing – Like an Earthquake*, London: Weidenfeld and Nicolson.

Sieveking, L. (1934) *The Stuff of Radio*, London: Cassell.

Silverstone, R. (1994) *Television and Everyday Life*, London: Routledge.

Silvey, R. (1974) *Who's Listening?*, London: George Allen and Unwin.

Smith, A. (ed.) (1974) *British Broadcasting*, Newton Abbot: David and Charles.

—— (1976) *The Shadow in the Cave*, London: Quartet Books, revised edn.

—— (1990) *Broadcasting and Society in 1990s Britain*, London: W. H. Smith Contemporary Papers, no. 4.

Snagge, J. and Barsley, M. (1972) *Those Vintage Years of Radio*, London: Pitman.

Sparks, C. (1994) 'Independent production: unions and casualization' in Hood, S. (ed.) *Behind the Screens: The Structure of British Television in the Nineties*, London: Lawrence and Wishart.

Stuart, C. (ed.) (1975) *The Reith Diaries*, London: Collins.

Sykes Committee, The (1923) *Broadcasting Committee Report*, 1923, Cmd 1951.

Took, B. (1976) *Laughter in the Air*, London: Robson Books/BBC.

Tracey, M. (1983) *A Variety of Lives: A Biography of Sir Hugh Greene*, London: The Bodley Head.

Trethowan, I. (1970) *Radio in the Seventies*, BBC Lunch-time Lectures, 8th series, no. 4.

Tunstall, J. (1983) *The Media in Britain*, London: Constable.

—— (1993) *Television Producers*, London: Routledge.

Tusa, J. (1994) 'Implications of recent changes at the BBC', *Political Quarterly*, 65.

Ullswater Committee, The (1936) *Report of the Broadcasting Committee, 1935*, Cmd 5091.

Walker, A. (1992) *A Skyful of Freedom: 60 Years of the BBC World Service*, London: Broadside Books.

Ward, K. (1989) *Mass Communications and the Modern World*, London: Macmillan.

Watt, I. (1963) *The Rise of the Novel*, Harmondsworth: Penguin Books.

Wenham, B. (1982) 'Into the interior' in Wenham, B. (ed.) *The Third Age of Broadcasting*, London: Faber and Faber.

Whale, J. (1969) *The Half-Shut Eye*, London: Macmillan.

Whannel, G. (1990) 'Winner takes all: competition' in Goodwin, A. and Whannel, G. (eds) *Understanding Television*, London: Routledge.

—— (1991) '"*Grandstand*", the sports fan and the family audience' in Corner, J. (ed.) *Popular Television in Britain*, London: BFI Publishing.

Williams, R. (1974) *Television: Technology and Cultural Form*, Glasgow: Fontana.

Williams, Rhys (1995a) 'A new set of rules for the media game', *Independent*, 24 May.

—— (1995b) 'BBC switches on CD-quality radio', *Independent*, 28 September.

Wilmut, R. (1980) *From Fringe to Flying Circus*, London: Book Club Associates.

Worsley, F. (1948) *ITMA*, London: Vox Mundi.

Index

Index